COMPUTER
BOOK SERIES
FROM IDG

Tcl/Tk For Dun

Grouping and Substitution

Grouping/substitution	Syntax	What does it do?
variable	$variable-name	replace $ plus the variable's name with the content of the variable
backslash	\t	replace \ plus a second character with a new, single character. For instance, \t is replaced with the tab character. A \ at the end of a line is replaced with a single space.
curly-braces	{cost: $1.00}	make the enclosed material into a single Tcl word and protect it from substitution; no variable or backslash substitution will be performed between the braces
double-quotes	"cost: $cost"	make the enclosed material into a single Tcl word; variable and backslash substitution s will be performed (if the quoted material contains the $ or | symbols.)

Common Options for the grid Command

Option	Function
-padx	horizontal space between a widget and its left and right neighbors
-pady	vertical space between a widget and its upper and lower neigbors
-ipadx	horizontal padding inside a widget
-ipady	vertical padding inside a widget
-column	column coordinate of the widget
-row	row coordinate of the widget
-columnspan	number of columns the widget is allowed to occupy
-rowspan	number of rows that the widget can occupy
-sticky	edges of the widget that touch the adjacent column or row

...For Dummies: #1 Computer Book Series for Beginners

Tcl/Tk For Dummies®

Cheat Sheet

Common Widget Properties

Property	Controls	Example usage
-foreground	color of text (or image)	button .b -foreground red
-background	background color of widget	label .l -background white
-font	font used for display	text .t -font {Courier 12}
-relief	kind of 3-D graphics used to render the widget	button .b -relief raised
-text	text message that the widget displays	.message -text "Hello, World"
-cursor	shape of the cursor when it's over the widget	scale .s -cursor gumby
-textvariable	name of the variable associated with the widget	entry .e -textvariable myValue

Basic Events

Syntax	Description
<1>	User left-clicks with the mouse (or clicks with a Mac mouse)
<2>	User right-clicks with the mouse
<Key>	User presses a keyboard key
<Enter>	mouse cursor moves into the widget's area
<Leave>	cursor moves out of the widget's on-screen real estate
<Motion>	cursor moves around inside the widget's territory

Common Options for the Pack Command

Option	Function
-padx	horizontal space between a widget and its left and right neighbors
-pady	vertical space between a widget and it upper and lower neigbors
-ipadx	horizontal padding to be added inside a widget
-ipady	vertical padding to be added inside a widget
-anchor	which corner of the available space the widget is to be added to
-fill	controls whether or not the widget is to be stretched to fill the available space

...For Dummies: #1 Computer Book Series for Beginners

TCL/TK

FOR

DUMMIES®

TCL/TK FOR DUMMIES®

by Tim Webster
with Alex Francis

IDG Books Worldwide, Inc.
An International Data Group Company

Foster City, CA ♦ Chicago, IL ♦ Indianapolis, IN ♦ Southlake, TX

Tcl/Tk For Dummies®

Published by
IDG Books Worldwide, Inc.
An International Data Group Company
919 E. Hillsdale Blvd.
Suite 400
Foster City, CA 94404
www.idgbooks.com (IDG Books Worldwide Web site)
www.dummies.com (Dummies Press Web site)

Library of Congress Catalog Card No.: 97-70743

ISBN: 0-7645-0152-6

Printed in the United States of America

10 9 8 7 6 5 4 3 2 1

1E/SS/QZ/ZX/IN

Distributed in the United States by IDG Books Worldwide, Inc.

Distributed by Macmillan Canada for Canada; by Transworld Publishers Limited in the United Kingdom; by IDG Norge Books for Norway; by IDG Sweden Books for Sweden; by Woodslane Pty. Ltd. for Australia; by Woodslane Enterprises Ltd. for New Zealand; by Longman Singapore Publishers Ltd. for Singapore, Malaysia, Thailand, and Indonesia; by Simron Pty. Ltd. for South Africa; by Toppan Company Ltd. for Japan; by Distribuidora Cuspide for Argentina; by Livraria Cultura for Brazil; by Ediciencia S.A. for Ecuador; by Addison-Wesley Publishing Company for Korea; by Ediciones ZETA S.C.R. Ltda. for Peru; by WS Computer Publishing Corporation, Inc., for the Philippines; by Unalis Corporation for Taiwan; by Contemporanea de Ediciones for Venezuela; by Computer Book & Magazine Store for Puerto Rico; by Express Computer Distributors for the Caribbean and West Indies. Authorized Sales Agent: Anthony Rudkin Associates for the Middle East and North Africa.

For general information on IDG Books Worldwide's books in the U.S., please call our Consumer Customer Service department at 800-762-2974. For reseller information, including discounts and premium sales, please call our Reseller Customer Service department at 800-434-3422.

For information on where to purchase IDG Books Worldwide's books outside the U.S., please contact our International Sales department at 415-655-3200 or fax 415-655-3295.

For information on foreign language translations, please contact our Foreign & Subsidiary Rights department at 415-655-3021 or fax 415-655-3281.

For sales inquiries and special prices for bulk quantities, please contact our Sales department at 415-655-3200 or write to the address above.

For information on using IDG Books Worldwide's books in the classroom or for ordering examination copies, please contact our Educational Sales department at 800-434-2086 or fax 817-251-8174.

For press review copies, author interviews, or other publicity information, please contact our Public Relations department at 415-655-3000 or fax 415-655-3299.

For authorization to photocopy items for corporate, personal, or educational use, please contact Copyright Clearance Center, 222 Rosewood Drive, Danvers, MA 01923, or fax 508-750-4470.

is a trademark under exclusive license to IDG Books Worldwide, Inc., from International Data Group, Inc.

About the Authors

Tim Webster became a computer weenie long, long ago when he taught himself assembly language on his truly underpowered Timex-Sinclair. Currently, Tim is a freelance writer and consultant. His books include *Web Designer's Guide to NetObjects Fusion 2, Web Designer's Guide to PNG, GIF and JPEG*, and this very book, *Tcl/Tk For Dummies*. Tim lives with his wife, Chris Corcoran, on the south side of Chicago — the baddest part of town. You can find Tim's perpetually unfinished web page at www.orbis-tertius.com.

Alex Francis is a graduate student of linguistics and psychology at the University of Chicago. He uses Tcl/Tk as much as possible, and thinks you should, too. His next book had better be his dissertation.

ABOUT IDG BOOKS WORLDWIDE

Welcome to the world of IDG Books Worldwide.

IDG Books Worldwide, Inc., is a subsidiary of International Data Group, the world's largest publisher of computer-related information and the leading global provider of information services on information technology. IDG was founded more than 25 years ago and now employs more than 8,500 people worldwide. IDG publishes more than 275 computer publications in over 75 countries (see listing below). More than 60 million people read one or more IDG publications each month.

Launched in 1990, IDG Books Worldwide is today the #1 publisher of best-selling computer books in the United States. We are proud to have received eight awards from the Computer Press Association in recognition of editorial excellence and three from *Computer Currents'* First Annual Readers' Choice Awards. Our best-selling *...For Dummies*® series has more than 30 million copies in print with translations in 30 languages. IDG Books Worldwide, through a joint venture with IDG's Hi-Tech Beijing, became the first U.S. publisher to publish a computer book in the People's Republic of China. In record time, IDG Books Worldwide has become the first choice for millions of readers around the world who want to learn how to better manage their businesses.

Our mission is simple: Every one of our books is designed to bring extra value and skill-building instructions to the reader. Our books are written by experts who understand and care about our readers. The knowledge base of our editorial staff comes from years of experience in publishing, education, and journalism — experience we use to produce books for the '90s. In short, we care about books, so we attract the best people. We devote special attention to details such as audience, interior design, use of icons, and illustrations. And because we use an efficient process of authoring, editing, and desktop publishing our books electronically, we can spend more time ensuring superior content and spend less time on the technicalities of making books.

You can count on our commitment to deliver high-quality books at competitive prices on topics you want to read about. At IDG Books Worldwide, we continue in the IDG tradition of delivering quality for more than 25 years. You'll find no better book on a subject than one from IDG Books Worldwide.

John Kilcullen
CEO
IDG Books Worldwide, Inc.

Steven Berkowitz
President and Publisher
IDG Books Worldwide, Inc.

*Eighth Annual
Computer Press
Awards ≥1992*

*Ninth Annual
Computer Press
Awards ≥1993*

*Tenth Annual
Computer Press
Awards ≥1994*

*Eleventh Annual
Computer Press
Awards ≥1995*

IDG Books Worldwide, Inc., is a subsidiary of International Data Group, the world's largest publisher of computer-related information and the leading global provider of information services on information technology. International Data Group publishes over 275 computer publications in over 75 countries. Sixty million people read one or more International Data Group publications each month. International Data Group's publications include: **ARGENTINA:** Buyer's Guide, Computerworld Argentina, PC World Argentina; **AUSTRALIA:** Australian Macworld, Australian PC World, Australian Reseller News, Computerworld, IT Casebook, Network World, Publish, Webmaster; **AUSTRIA:** Computerwelt Osterreich, Networks Austria, PC Tip Austria; **BANGLADESH:** PC World Bangladesh; **BELARUS:** PC World Belarus; **BELGIUM:** Data News; **BRAZIL:** Annuário de Informática, Computerworld, Connections, Macworld, PC Player, PC World, Publish, Reseller News, Supergamepower; **BULGARIA:** Computerworld Bulgaria, Network World Bulgaria, PC & MacWorld Bulgaria; **CANADA:** CIO Canada, Client/Server World, ComputerWorld Canada, InfoWorld Canada, NetworkWorld Canada, WebWorld; **CHILE:** Computerworld Chile, PC World Chile; **COLOMBIA:** Computerworld Colombia, PC World Colombia; **COSTA RICA:** PC World Centro America; **THE CZECH AND SLOVAK REPUBLICS:** Computerworld Czechoslovakia, Macworld Czech Republic, PC World Czechoslovakia; **DENMARK:** Communications World Danmark, Computerworld Danmark, Macworld Danmark, PC World Danmark, Techworld Denmark; **DOMINICAN REPUBLIC:** PC World Republica Dominicana; **ECUADOR:** PC World Ecuador; **EGYPT:** Computerworld Middle East, PC World Middle East; **EL SALVADOR:** PC World Centro America; **FINLAND:** MikroPC, Tietoverkko, Tietoviikko; **FRANCE:** Distributique, Hebdo, Info PC, Le Monde Informatique, Macworld, Reseaux & Telecoms, WebMaster France; **GERMANY:** Computer Partner, Computerwoche, Computerwoche Extra, Computerwoche FOCUS, Global Online, Macwelt, PC Welt; **GREECE:** Amiga Computing, GamePro Greece, Multimedia World; **GUATEMALA:** PC World Centro America; **HONDURAS:** PC World Centro America; **HONG KONG:** Computerworld Hong Kong, PC World Hong Kong, Publish in Asia; **HUNGARY:** ABCD CD-ROM, Computerworld Szamitastechnika, Internetto online Magazine, PC World Hungary, PC-X Magazin Hungary; **ICELAND:** Tolvuheimur PC World Island; **INDIA:** Information Communications World, Information Systems Computerworld, PC World India, Publish in Asia; **INDONESIA:** InfoKomputer PC World, Komputek Computerworld, Publish in Asia; **IRELAND:** ComputerScope, PC Live!; **ISRAEL:** Macworld Israel, People & Computers/Computerworld; **ITALY:** Computerworld Italia, Macworld Italia, Networking Italia, PC World Italia; **JAPAN:** DTP World, Macworld Japan, Nikkei Personal Computing, OS/2 World Japan, SunWorld Japan, Windows NT World, Windows World Japan; **KENYA:** PC World East African; **KOREA:** Hi-Tech Information, Macworld Korea, PC World Korea; **MACEDONIA:** PC World Macedonia; **MALAYSIA:** Computerworld Malaysia, PC World Malaysia, Publish in Asia; **MALTA:** PC World Malta; **MEXICO:** Computerworld Mexico, PC World Mexico; **MYANMAR:** PC World Myanmar; **NETHERLANDS:** Computer! Totaal, LAN Internetworking Magazine, LAN World Buyers Guide, Macworld Netherlands, Net, WebWereld; **NEW ZEALAND:** Absolute Beginners Guide and Plain & Simple Series, Computer Buyer, Computer Industry Directory, Computerworld New Zealand, MTB, Network World, PC World New Zealand; **NICARAGUA:** PC World Centro America; **NORWAY:** Computerworld Norge, CW Rapport, Datamagasinet, Financial Rapport, Kursguide Norge, Macworld Norge, Multimediaworld Norge, PC World Ekspress Norge, PC World Nettverk, PC World Norge, PC World ProduktGuide Norge; **PAKISTAN:** Computerworld Pakistan; **PANAMA:** PC World Panama; **PEOPLE'S REPUBLIC OF CHINA:** China Computer Users, China Computerworld, China InfoWorld, China Telecom World Weekly, Computer & Communication, Electronic Design China, Electronics Today, Electronics Weekly, Game Software, PC World China, Popular Computer Week, Software Weekly, Software World, Telecom World; **PERU:** Computerworld Peru, PC World Profesional Peru, PC World SoHo Peru; **PHILIPPINES:** Click!, Computerworld Philippines, PC World Philippines, Publish in Asia; **POLAND:** Computerworld Poland, Computerworld Special Report Poland, Cyber, Macworld Poland, Networld Poland, PC World Komputer; **PORTUGAL:** Cerebro/PC World, Computerworld/Correio Informático, Dealer World Portugal, Mac*In/PC*In Portugal, Multimedia World; **PUERTO RICO:** PC World Puerto Rico; **ROMANIA:** Computerworld Romania, PC World Romania, Telecom Romania; **RUSSIA:** Computerworld Russia, Mir PK, Publish, Seti; **SINGAPORE:** Computerworld Singapore, PC World Singapore, Publish in Asia; **SLOVENIA:** Monitor; **SOUTH AFRICA:** Computing SA, Network World SA, Software World SA; **SPAIN:** Communicaciones World España, Computerworld España, Dealer World España, Macworld España, PC World España; **SRI LANKA:** Infolink PC World; **SWEDEN:** CAP&Design, Computer Sweden, Corporate Computing Sweden, Internetworld Sweden, it.branschen, Macworld Sweden, MaxiData Sweden, MikroDatorn, Nätverk & Kommunikation, PC World Sweden, PCaktiv, Windows World Sweden; **SWITZERLAND:** Computerworld Schweiz, Macworld Schweiz, PCtip; **TAIWAN:** Computerworld Taiwan, Macworld Taiwan, NEW ViSiON/Publish, PC World Taiwan, Windows World Taiwan; **THAILAND:** Publish in Asia, Thai Computerworld; **TURKEY:** Computerworld Turkiye, Macworld Turkiye, Network World Turkiye, PC World Turkiye; **UKRAINE:** Computerworld Kiev, Multimedia World Ukraine, PC World Ukraine; **UNITED KINGDOM:** Acorn User UK, Amiga Action UK, Amiga Computing UK, Apple Talk UK, Computing, Macworld, Parents and Computers UK, PC Advisor, PC Home, PSX Pro, The WEB; **UNITED STATES:** Cable in the Classroom, CIO Magazine, Computerworld, DOS World, Federal Computer Week, GamePro Magazine, InfoWorld, I-Way, Macworld, Network World, PC Games, PC World, Publish, Video Event, THE WEB Magazine, and WebMaster; online webzines: JavaWorld, NetscapeWorld, and SunWorld Online; **URUGUAY:** InfoWorld Uruguay; **VENEZUELA:** Computerworld Venezuela, PC World Venezuela; and **VIETNAM:** PC World Vietnam.

3/24/97

Dedication

Dedicated to my grandfathers,
Pete Webster and Robert Douglas,
who taught me the value of craftsmanship.

tw

Author Acknowledgments

I was first introduced to Tcl/Tk by Howard Nusbaum, who continues to encourage me to write everything in Tcl/Tk. Paul Pomerleau provided inspiration in the form of questions about how to do things in Tcl, followed by better answers than my own. I'm also grateful to Jacob Levy for helping me understand the idiosyncrasies of the plugin.

Obviously, I could not have contributed anything to this book without the advice and encouragement of Tim Webster, and I thank him (and also all the folks at IDG Books Worldwide) for this opportunity. Above all, I am grateful to Elaine Jones for her support and confidence.

Alex Francis

Tim would like to thank

Jim Azim, for the fancy lawyerin';
Don Crabb, for the continuing expert guidance;
Alex Francis, my co-author, who wrote the coolest parts;
Brian Gill, my agent, for his exemplary patience with my raving paranoia;
Sharon Koontz, the U of C's hottest secretary, for many a FedEx favor;
Jacob Levy, architect of the Tcl/Tk plug-in, for his enthusiastic support and assistance;
John Ousterhout, for Tcl/Tk;
Melba Hopper, Pat O'Brien, and Colleen Rainsberger, who provided the silk purse;
the crackerjack editorial and production team at IDG Books Worldwide;
and, as always, my wife Chris Corcoran, who kept my brain from exploding.

Publisher's Acknowledgments

We're proud of this book; please send us your comments about it by using the IDG Books Worldwide Registration Card at the back of the book or by e-mailing us at feedback/dummies@idgbooks.com. Some of the people who helped bring this book to market include the following:

Acquisitions, Development, and Editorial

Project Editor: Pat O'Brien

Acquisitions Editor: Gareth Hancock

Media Development Manager: Joyce Pepple

Associate Permissions Editor:
Heather H. Dismore

Copy Editor: Patricia Pan

Technical Editor: James A. Armstrong

Editorial Managers: Colleen Rainsberger,
Mary C. Corder

Editorial Assistant: Darren Meiss

Production

Project Coordinator: Regina Snyder

Layout and Graphics: Lou Boudreau,
Angela Bush-Sisson, J. Tyler Connor,
Maridee V. Ennis, Angela F. Hunckler,
Drew R. Moore, Heather N. Pearson,
Brent Savage, Deidre Smith, Kate Snell

Proofreaders: Nancy L. Reinhardt,
Michelle Croninger, Joel K. Draper,
Nancy Price, Rebecca Senninger,
Janet M. Withers

Indexer: Liz Cunningham

Special Help

Melba Hopper

General and Administrative

IDG Books Worldwide, Inc.: John Kilcullen, CEO; Steven Berkowitz, President and Publisher

IDG Books Technology Publishing: Brenda McLaughlin, Senior Vice President and
Group Publisher

Dummies Technology Press and Dummies Editorial: Diane Graves Steele, Vice President and
Associate Publisher; Kristin A. Cocks, Editorial Director; Mary Bednarek, Acquisitions and
Product Development Director

Dummies Trade Press: Kathleen A. Welton, Vice President and Publisher

IDG Books Production for Dummies Press: Beth Jenkins, Production Director; Cindy L. Phipps,
Manager of Project Coordination, Production Proofreading, and Indexing;
Kathie S. Schutte, Supervisor of Page Layout; Shelley Lea, Supervisor of Graphics and
Design; Debbie J. Gates, Production Systems Specialist; Robert Springer, Supervisor of
Proofreading; Debbie Stailey, Special Projects Coordinator; Tony Augsburger, Supervisor of
Reprints and Bluelines; Leslie Popplewell, Media Archive Coordinator

Dummies Packaging and Book Design: Patti Sandez, Packaging Specialist; Lance Kayser,
Packaging Assistant; Kavish + Kavish, Cover Design

♦

The publisher would like to give special thanks to Patrick J. McGovern,
without whom this book would not have been possible.

♦

Contents at a Glance

Cartoons at a Glance

By Rich Tennant

page 149

"What is it Lassie? Is it Gramps? Is it his hard disk? Is he stuck somewhere, girl? Is he trying to write CGI programs to a Unix server running VRML? What, girl, what?!"

page 59

"I couldn't get this 'job skills' program to work on my PC, so I replaced the motherboard, upgraded the BIOS, and wrote a program that links it to my personal database. It told me I wasn't technically inclined and should pursue a career in sales."

page 215

"I don't know how it happened, but there's an applet in the toaster and some guy in Norway keeps burning my toast."

page 321

"He's our new Web Bowzer."

page 7

Fax: 508-546-7747 • *E-mail:* the5wave@tiac.net

Table of Contents

• •

Introduction

This is a book about creating Tcl/Tk programs that run inside Web pages. Why would you ever want to do such a thing?

- ✔ Programming in Tcl/Tk is much easier than programming in other languages. All of the hard stuff, like memory management and graphics commands hide behind the virtual curtains.

- ✔ Tcl/Tk is free. All of the tools that you need to create working Tcl/Tk programs are freely available on the Internet. You can download the basic Tcl development tool, called Wish, in about half an hour.

  Wish is on the *Tcl/Tk For Dummies* CD-ROM, too. (You're welcome.)

- ✔ It's portable. Almost all of the scripts that you write when you're in Windows 95 will run just fine on any platform that supports Tcl/Tk, including Windows 3.*x*, the Mac operating system, all of the basic varieties of Unix, and even obscure little platforms like the BeOS.

- ✔ It's Web-friendly. Special Tcl/Tk programs called tclets can run as part of a Web page, just like Java applets and ActiveX controls do now.

- ✔ It's cool. Telling people that you program in a language that they haven't heard of instantly elevates you to the lofty company of rocket scientists and brain surgeons. People will accept your advice about *everything.* (Be sure to use this power only for good!)

- ✔ It's educational. The best way to understand how computer programs work is to write a few. You will gain new insights into programs you use every day, like word processors and spreadsheets, and your video-game scores will rise dramatically.

- ✔ It's hip. Your web page will sport cutting-edge technology that Sun Microsystems estimates will be on a million desktops within a year.

What Is Tcl/Tk, and What's the Tcl/Tk Plug-in?

The scripting language Tcl/Tk has been around for a few years now, quietly gaining a following for its ease of use and handy graphics tools. Many of the tasks that are difficult in languages like Java and C++ are simple to do in Tcl/Tk, and so it's widely used for little programs that do simple things.

By happy coincidence, Web pages are the ideal place for little programs that do simple things. It was inevitable that Tcl/Tk and the Web came together. In the summer of 1996, Jacob Levy of Sun Microsystems released a plug-in for Navigator and Internet Explorer that allowed Web page creators to embed Tcl/Tk-based applications, or tclets, right inside Web pages.

Almost all of the basic Java applets that you may have seen can be coded in Tcl/Tk, and it's much, much easier. I don't mean to knock Java — it's a great tool for building big programs, but Tcl/Tk is a much better language for little applets and interactive elements for the readers of your Web pages.

Who Are You?

If you've read this far already, I suspect you're a Web master or Web site designer who wants to jazz up a site with a little bit of interactive content. Maybe you've even tried a little Java programming, and decided that it was just too complicated for the simple projects you had in mind.

✔ You *don't* need to know how to program in Java, JavaScript, C++, or Visual Basic.

✔ You *do* need to have some experience with HTML — at least enough to go into an HTML document and do a little editing. I'll show you the special tags you need to put tclets into your Web page. (If you create most of your pages with a WYSIWYG editor like Claris HomePage or NetObjects Fusion, that's okay . . . so do I.)

✔ You *do* need to know how to operate a basic Web browser like Netscape Navigator or Microsoft Internet Explorer. You don't need to know how to do anything fancy, but you should be able to load pages and look up URLs.

If you *have* done a little programming before — great! The syntax of Tcl/Tk commands may be new to you, but basic concepts, like variables and control structures, will probably seem pretty familiar.

Also, you don't *need* to create tclets with Tcl/Tk. Tcl/Tk is a general purpose scripting language, and you can use it to create all sorts of utilities. I won't focus on creating custom utilities for your own use, but you can certainly apply the techniques in this book to whatever projects you like.

What You Need

✔ *A computer.* You can use a Macintosh, a Windows machine, or anything else that runs Netscape Navigator or Microsoft Internet Explorer.

- ✔ *A Web browser.* Both Netscape and Explorer support the Tcl/Tk plug-in. If a hot new browser that supports the Netscape plug-in architecture suddenly appears on the market, you can use that, too.

- ✔ *A Tcl/Tk interpreter.* You'll need a development tool that allows you to create Tcl/Tk programs. Fortunately, there are plenty of free tools available. I've included the most recent versions of the Wish development environment on the CD-ROM that comes with this book, and I'll point you to places on the net where you can download future updates.

- ✔ *The Tcl/Tk plug-in.* You'll need the Tcl/Tk plug-in to run tclets inside a browser. There's information about where to find updates at Sun's Tcl site on the internet.

What's on the CD?

In addition to the basic necessities mentioned above, I've put some extra goodies on the CD, including all of the example code from the book. I strongly suggest that you enter the code by hand. The easiest way to learn the syntax of a programming language is to type in code. However, as a backup, all of the code is on the disk for you to play with as you like.

How to Use this Book

This is a book about programming. If you've never programmed before, you'll need to master some basic concepts before you get into the fancy stuff. We'll start by looking at where you can find the things that you need to start creating tclets, and then work through a basic introduction to programming and the Tcl/Tk language. I suggest you work through the first two sections of the book from start to finish.

Afterwards, we'll look at specific Tcl/Tk interface components, or widgets, and how you can build tclets with each kind of widget. This section of the book is organized like a cookbook, and you can read it like a cookbook, skipping around from recipe to recipe according to your taste. You don't need to read it in any particular order, although the first few chapters of Part III provide a basic overview that it may be helpful to read first.

A hands-on approach is the best way to learn a language. Almost every chapter of this book will contain tclets for you to write and problems for you to solve. Furthermore, I'll make suggestions about projects that you can pursue on your own. As long as you're using the Tcl/Tk plug-in as interpreter, you can't do anything *too* crazy or dangerous with a tclet.

Typographic Conventions

There's a lot of code in this book. To differentiate the Tcl/Tk from my prose, the code embedded in text is set in a different typeface, like this:

regular text `snippet of Tcl/Tk code` regular text

The variable `bozo_count` stores the number of clowns employed by the circus.

Very often, big chunks of several lines of code will be set off in their own paragraphs. These blocks of code will use the same special font as the source code that's embedded in the middle of regular text:

```
label .l1 -text "hello world"
pack .l1
label .l2 -text "hello again"
pack .l2
```

Usually the code will contain comments — lines that are not strictly part of the program, but are included in the source code to help other programmers figure out how the program works. I'll explain what's going on in the body text, but I'll also add comments to the source code. A comment line always starts with a pound sign (#) character, like this:

```
# create a message to be displayed
.l1 -text "hello world"
```

Whenever I need to use a placeholder for specific information, I'll use italic type. For instance, let's say that the URL of your home page is `http://www.myserver.com/home.html`. If I ask you to type a line of code like this:

```
set url your-homepage-url
```

You should type:

```
set url http://www.myserver.com/home.html
```

How this book is organized

This book is divided into a few basic sections. I've split up each section into little bite-sized chapters. To keep things simple, I'll try to introduce just one new idea or technique in each chapter. (The language reference section is a tiny bit denser, because I'll introduce most of the major Tcl commands.)

The first sections of the book cover some basic territory: what Tcl's all about, how to find and use the basic tools, and the basic language syntax. These sections are arranged in a fairly linear fashion, and you can read them straight through, skipping over anything that's familiar to you.

The subsequent sections of the book are samples of the kinds of tclets you can build. Each chapter is meant to be a both a reference on a particular species of Tk widget, and a demonstration of how you might use the widget in a tclet in the so-called real world.

Part I: What's Tcl/Tk?

Part I is as philosophical as it's going to get. I'll explain a little bit more about the history of Tcl/Tk , and of the Web, and why the two are meant for each other. As a precaution, I'll discuss the security issues that arise any time you deliver a program via a Web page, Finally, you'll take a tour of the Web and see some of the exciting things that people are doing with the Tcl/Tk plug-in, and take a look at some of the exciting things that *you'll* be doing once you've got a grip on writing tclets.

Part II: Language Reference

The basic building blocks of the language: how to create basic Tcl statements, and how to construct a valid program out of basic statements. You'll learn how to control the flow of a program with conditionals and loops, how to build your own commands with procedures and functions, and how to handle the most common kinds of data — strings and lists.

Part III: Widget Science

Tk stands for "toolkit", and the Tk toolkit is full of basic graphic user interface components, or *widgets.* In this section, you'll learn about the kinds of things that widgets have in common: things like widgets' size and color, the way that widgets respond to user input and activity, and how widgets are displayed in on screen.

Part IV: Tclet Cookbook

Each chapter will look at a new widget, and you'll see each widget in the context of a working (and groovy) tclet that does something that you might actually want a tclet to do on your web page. In later chapters of the section, you'll orchestrate groups of different kinds of widgets into more complex (and even groovier) tclets.

Part V: The Part of Tens

The infamous and mysterious Part of Tens, hallmark of Dummies Press.

Icons used in this book

You can safely skip right over material marked with the Technical Stuff icon. It's there to explain nuances that aren't really important to a basic understanding of Tcl/Tk, or to provide little technotidbits that you can lob out when you're meeting with supervisors and clients.

Every once in a while, doing the wrong thing can get you into trouble. You won't melt your CPU or erase your hard drive doing anything in this book, but you might accidentally do something that causes your tclet to act in a bizarre and undesirable way. I'll mark such pitfalls with the Warning icon.

Sometimes, there's an easy way and a hard way to accomplish a particular goal, or a clever way to work around a problem. If I can save you some trouble, or if I'm particularly proud of a hack that I've worked out, I will flag my tips and tricks with the Tip icon.

I've marked the most important things with the Remember icon.

Whenever the text refers to a goody that I've put on the book's CD-ROM, I'll add the On the CD icon to remind you to take a look at the CD.

The Tcl plug-in is very nearly completely cross-platform — a tclet runs in the same way, no matter what computer platform or "browser platform" that hosts the tclet. However, there are a few special cases where platform is important. When I cover such issues, I will mark the text with the Platforms icon.

Now What?

It's time to get started. Grab a hot/cold, steaming/frosty, mug/bottle of your favorite knowledge-enhancing beverage and turn the page!

Part I
What's Tcl/Tk?

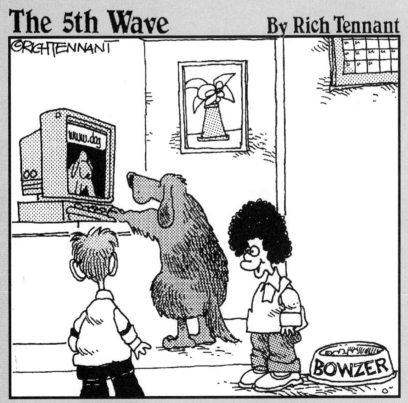

"He's our new Web Bowzer."

In this part . . .

This first part starts with the basics: What Tcl/Tk is;
where you can find and download the tools that you
need; how to create Tcl/Tk programs, or *tclets;* how to put
tclets in your Web page; and, most importantly, how to
pronounce Tcl/Tk.

Chapter 1

Getting Started

● ●

In This Chapter

▶ What is Tcl/Tk?

▶ Where is Tcl/Tk and the Tcl/Tk plug-in?

▶ How do you get them going?

● ●

*B*egin by making sure that you have all of the software that you need to start coding your tclets. (Otherwise, the rest of the book will be pretty tough sledding.)

You can find essential Tcl/Tk tools — Wish — on the CD-ROM that comes with *Tcl/Tk For Dummies*. You find upgrades and plenty of Tcl/Tk information at many sites on the Web.

Identifying the Development Applications

Throughout *Tcl/Tk For Dummies*, I refer to Tcl/Tk as if it's one, single language. (It's usually pronounced *Tickle-tee-kay.*) In fact, Tcl and Tk are separate languages, but languages that have a special relationship with each other.

Tcl

The core language that came before anything else is Tcl, which stands for *Tool command language.* Tcl is the part of Tcl/Tk that concerns itself with basic programming stuff, such as keeping track of the values of variables and controlling the flow of the program with loops and conditional statements.

Tk

Tk is really an extension to Tcl — it's not really part of the core Tcl language. Tk stands for *Tool kit,* and the tools that Tk provide are basic user interface elements such as the buttons, checkboxes, and scrollbars shown in Figure 1-1. Tk isn't the only extension to Tcl, but it's the most widely used extension, and it's incredibly handy for giving programs the familiar Mac and Windows graphical look and feel.

Figure 1-1:
Tk provides
a set of
basic
graphic
user
interface
components,
such as
buttons,
checkboxes
and
scrollbars.

The *tools* in the name Tool command language are software tools, not exotic hardware like robotic arms or computer-controlled drill presses. Software tools are just programs that do practical things, such as database queries or scientific calculations. Tcl was designed so that programmers could concentrate on writing the tools, rather than writing the routines that managed the tools.

There are software development packages available, such as tclsh, that handle Tcl exclusively, and don't recognize commands that are part of the Tk extension. These tools aren't very helpful for building tclets for plug-ins, so you won't work with other software development packages in *Tcl/Tk For Dummies.* Also, there are extensions to Tcl other than Tk. For example, extensions make it easy for Tcl to access particular databases, and extensions allow Tcl to generate 3-D graphics. Such extensions sound very cool, but they're not very useful for cooking up tclets.

So what you need is a development application that recognizes both Tcl and Tk. That application is Wish, which stands for *Windowing shell.* Wish executes Tcl commands as soon as they are entered, and displays Tk widgets in its own window. For the sake of consistency, I'll use the term "Tcl/Tk" throughout the book, even if what I'm talking about is technically strictly a Tcl command or a Tk command.

Figure 1-2 shows the Wish application at work. At the left is the console, where you enter Tcl/Tk commands, and at the right is the program built with the script entered in the console.

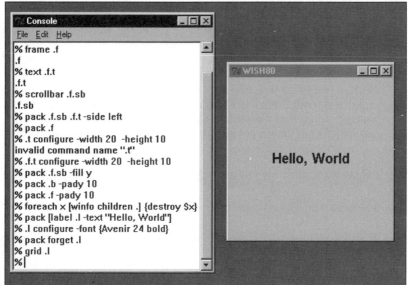

Figure 1-2:
The Wish
Application

Wish is an *interpreter.* As soon as you type in a line of source code, Wish executes the instructions in the code. Some languages (such as C, C++, and Java) are compiled — an entire program is converted to machine readable code (an .exe, or *executable,* file), and isn't processed on a line-by-line basis. A Tcl/Tk compiler *is* under development, but you won't be able to build tclets with it.

Mini-applications

Practical little applications are easy to write in Tcl/Tk. The ready-made *application parts* that are built into Wish make it easy to create user-friendly applications that you can build into your Web page.

What do I mean by application parts? Tcl/Tk provides basic interface components, such as buttons, scrollbars, and text boxes, which your tclets' user can interact with. It's very simple to create little buttons that do things with Tcl/Tk.

Writing and drawing

Some of the Tcl/Tk interface components are practically applications in themselves. For example, if you've already installed the Wish application, you can give it a spin right now to see the sophistication that's built into Tcl/Tk's text widgets.

Launch Wish (by double-clicking on it). In the window labeled Console, type

```
pack [text .t]
```

and hit the Enter key. (Be sure to type exactly what appears in the preceding line of code!) Wish creates a text box widget. Try typing in the text widget: you'll find its behavior is like a simple text editor. You can type, select text, and even cut and paste (if you have Insert and Delete keys on your keyboard). After playing with the text widget, just type

```
destroy .t
```

(in the Wish console, not the text widget) to destroy the widget.

It's just as simple to draw with simple Tcl/Tk commands. For a tiny taste right now, go back to the Wish console and type

```
pack [canvas .c]
.c create rectangle 50 50 150 150 -fill black
```

to create a little rectangle. As you'll see in Chapter 17, you can draw just about anything you can imagine on a canvas widget. You can delete the rectangle just as easily as you created it:

```
.c delete 1
```

and delete the whole drawing surface with the simple command

```
destroy .c
```

Make sure that you destroyed the old canvas if you created one in the last section, then type the following code into a text file, *exactly* as it appears:

```
canvas .c -background white
foreach x [split $embed_args(words)] {
    .c create text [expr [clock clicks] % \
    $embed_args(width)] [expr [clock clicks] % \
    $embed_args(height)] -text $x
}
.c bind current <B1-Motion> {.c coords current %x %y}
pack .c -fill both
```

Save your text file with the name `poetry.tcl` anywhere on your hard disk. (Just in case you really hate typing, or in case you can't seem to get it to work, I've put a copy of this file on the CD-ROM that comes with this book under the name `poetry.tcl`.) That's it for the tclet. Now, you just need an HTML page to hold the tclet. In a separate text document, enter:

```
<html>
<head>
<title>The magnetic poetry page</title>
</head>
<body>
<embed src ="poetry.tcl" width = 450 height = 200
words = "the only emperor is the emporer of ice cream
this tears are shaken from the wrath bearing tree
this honey is sweet but it burn the throat">
</body>
</html>
```

The words that are included as the *words* parameter of the <embed> tag,

```
words = "the only emperor is the emporer of ice cream
this tears are shaken from the wrath bearing tree
this honey is sweet but it burn the throat">
```

are the words that the tclet will display. (I just picked three lines from three of my favorite poems.) You can change them to anything you like, as long as you make sure that the list of words begins and ends with a double quote, with no double-quotes in between. (Single quotes are fine.) Save the HTML file as `poetry.html` (or whatever you want to call it) and make sure that it's in the same folder as the `poetry.tcl` file. Now, open the HTML file with your Web browser — use the File⇨Open command, or just drag the HTML file onto the browser's icon.

I promised you that programming with Tcl/Tk is easy. You don't need to spend all of your time messing around with Tcl code to put genuinely interesting applications on your Web pages. (***Warning:*** you may find yourself spending all of your time messing around with Tcl/Tk code, whether you need to or not.) Very soon, you'll be able to crank out groovy little tclets with just an hour or two of work.

Finding Wish

The easiest way to find a copy of Wish is to stick the CD-ROM that comes with this book into your CD-ROM drive. That's simple enough, isn't it? Inside the Wish folder, you'll find separate folders for Windows and MacOS versions of Wish.

Naturally, one of the best places to look for Tcl is at the official source — Sun's ftp site. To access the site, point your Web browser at the URL `http://www.sunlabs.com/research/tcl/download.html`

The source distribution

The source distribution of Tcl/Tk is the "raw" form of the Wish and Tclsh applications. It's not something that you can run as a program immediately, it's source code written in the C language. If you've got a C compiler and a lot of patience, you can create a working program for the source code, but it's really not worth the trouble for first-time programmers. The source code is there for the expert programmers who have experience compiling their own applications. Unless you have this kind of experience, skip the source code distribution.

Packages (pre-compiled binaries)

Here's the good stuff. Sun provides a complete set of compiled, ready-to-install applications for most platforms, including all of the variations on Windows and MacOS. "Binaries" just means "applications" — this is the way that Unix folks talk when they think we're not looking.

Be sure to double-check the version number of the package that's on the Sun Web site against the version of Tcl/Tk that's on the CD-ROM. You only need to download a new version of Wish if there's a newer release than the one that came with *Tcl/Tk For Dummies*. Even if there's a new version, you don't necessarily need to grab a copy right away: you should be able to run every single snippet of code in *Tcl/Tk For Dummies* with Tcl 8.0 and Tk 4.5. The download page will explain new features of new versions of Tcl/Tk; read these notes to decide whether you want to upgrade right away.

The Windows package is a self-running .exe file — all you need to do is download the file, and when it's done, double-click on it. Wish will install itself by magic.

The Mac version of Tcl/Tk is encoded in binhex form; the easiest way to decode it is to use Aladdin's StuffIt Expander program. (You need the Expander Enhancer package, too, which is part of the DropStuff distribution. You can find both StuffIt Expander and DropStuff at Aladdin's Web site at `http://www.aladdinsys.com`, and at the usual Mac shareware Web sites.) After you decode the binhex file, it's a regular Mac installer: double-click on it to install Wish.

The Tcl/Tk plug-in

Sun's download page also contains a link to the Tcl/Tk plug-in. You can download a new version of the plug-in via this link, but it's probably better to take a look at http://www.sunlabs.com/tcl/plugin. Jacob's page has the most complete, up-to-date information about the latest version of the plug-in and the cool things that people are doing with it.

You only need to download the plug-in if there's a new version that's significantly different from the one that you already have. You should be able to run every bit of code in *Tcl/Tk For Dummies* using the version of the plug-in on the CD-ROM.

Other cool stuff

There's more cool stuff to investigate on Sun's Tcl download page: most of this stuff is Web-related, and it's all pretty cutting-edge. If you want to explore, you'll find:

- ✔ **SpecTcl/SpecJava:** SpecTcl and SpecJava are applications written in Tcl that allow you to create Tk and Java interfaces for applications — essentially, they write quite a bit of code automatically. It's quite a bit like using Visual Basic or a product like Sun's Java Programmer's Workshop.

- ✔ **WebTk:** WebTk is a WYSIWYG HTML editor that lets you design HTML pages by simply cutting and pasting Web page elements into your own page.

- ✔ **Tcl HTTPd:** Tcl HTTPd is a simple Web server that's written entirely in Tcl/Tk. If you're serving your Web site from a Unix machine, you can use Tcl HTTPd to serve your whole Web site. Naturally, this server is especially tclet-friendly.

Taking Inventory

The Tcl/Tk distribution isn't just the Wish interpreter program; there's a lot of stuff in there. No matter what platform you're using, there are some basic parts that will always be there. Here's a quick tour of the Tcl/Tk folder (or directory, or whatever you prefer to call it) to see what's inside.

Copyrights on Wish and Other Tcl/Tk stuff

Wish and the Tcl/Tk plug-in have been copyrighted by Sun. The license agreement for Wish allows you to distribute Wish however you like, *as long as the license document goes along with the software*. There's some other legal stuff in there too, of course — you should read the license agreement before you give the software to someone else, but you can pass along the Wish software from this book's CD-ROM.

Tcl is a flexible, extensible language, and the Tcl copyright allows anyone who writes an extension to Tcl to copyright that extension, even if Tcl itself can not be copyrighted. Similarly, programs written in Tcl/Tk can be copyrighted. For example, the publisher holds the copyright on the tclets that I wrote for *Tcl/Tk For Dummies*. Before you pass along a Tcl/Tk-based software product other than Wish, make sure that that you're not breakin' the law.

Wish

Wish is the most essential part of the Tcl/Tk distribution, at least as far as *Tcl/Tk For Dummies* is concerned: you'll be using Wish to try out your Tcl/Tk code in every chapter of *Tcl/Tk For Dummies*. Chapter 4 looks at the basic care and handling of the Wish application; for now, you can let Wish sit.

Tclsh

Tclsh is a pure Tcl interpreter. Tclsh understands and executes basic Tcl commands, but it doesn't know about Tk or widgets, and it doesn't draw anything on screen — Tclsh just replies to text with text. *Tcl/Tk for Dummies* doesn't cover Tclsh, but you can certainly use Tclsh to try out plain Tcl code if you like.

Why use Tclsh, if it doesn't do as much as Wish does?

- ✔ Tclsh is a hair faster than Wish, because Tclsh doesn't need to worry about managing graphics and such.

- ✔ Tclsh doesn't require as much memory as Wish, so Tclsh may be handy if RAM is in short supply.

Tclsh is more useful later in your Tcl-programming career, when you want to write little scripts (such as CGIs for your Web sever) that don't need a user interface.

Libraries

The `Library` folder contains a collection of Tcl and Tk scripts that extends each language with new commands. The commands defined in libraries are like the basic commands built into the language, but it's easier to add new scripts to a folder than to rewrite Wish or Tcl to recognize a few new commands. As I'll say many times in *Tcl/Tk For Dummies,* Tcl/Tk is really, really easy to customize.

If you're using a Macintosh, the Library folder isn't in the Tcl/Tk folder — it's in the System Folder's Extensions folder, in a folder called `Tool Command Language`. If you're ever in doubt about where your libraries reside, just type

```
info lib
```

at the Wish prompt. The Wish interpreter will reply with the location of your library files.

Documentation

The most critical part of any software package is the documentation. You'll learn the most important Tcl/Tk commands in *Tcl/Tk For Dummies,* but I don't cover everything (the bare-bones Tcl/Tk documentation that comes with Wish doesn't fit in a book twice this size). From time to time, you'll need to look at the documentation to figure out how a particular command works.

Different platforms handle help files differently, but the help is there, no matter which platform you're using. (In fact, the help file format is probably the biggest difference between the implementations of Wish on different platforms.) Here's where to find help:

- **Windows:** The Tcl/Tk documentation is in standard Windows Help format (those little purple book icons that open a table-of-contents window when you click on them). The Wish Help file is stored in the Tcl directory.

- **MacOS:** The Mac version of Wish offers documentation in HTML format; every command is listed on its own Web page. You can find the HTML files in the `HTML Documentation` folder in the `Tcl/TK` folder. Open the file `index.html` for a frame-based index to all of the Tcl/Tk basics.

- **Unix:** The Unix documentation for Tcl/Tk is in "man page" format — if you're a Unix user, man pages are probably one of the first things that you learned about. Just type `man tcl` at the shell prompt.

The HTML version of the Tcl/Tk documentation is also available on the Web at `http://www.tcltk.com/TclTkMan/TclTkManPages.html`. This is a really handy way to check the latest version of the documentation.

Playing It Safe

After you've got a copy of the Tcl/Tk plug-in, you're nearly ready to start experimenting with the Tcl/Tk language and making tclets for your pages. First, though, take a minute to look at the security issues.

Security risks on the Internet

Let me warn you before I start talking about security and danger. I am a complete and utter coward. In fact, I'm a little worried that a meteorite will come through the wall and strike me down as I type.

When I talk about security risks, I'm usually describing the worst possible scenarios. These things probably won't happen to you, even if you're sometimes lax about security. However, if you've ever lost a file to a computer virus or been the victim of credit card fraud, you know too well that there are some bad people out there, and it's possible for you to get hurt.

I should also point out that the kinds of security problems that I discuss here aren't unique to Tcl/Tk. Security issues arise every time that you download files from an unknown source. Tcl/Tk programs are dangerous only because they're programs, and it's dangerous to run a program when you don't know what the program does.

Programs that are embedded in Web pages, such as tclets, Java applets, and ActiveX controls, are especially problematic. When you download a program or script to your disk, you are consciously choosing to download the file and run it. If you want to be certain, check out the program by researching it on the Web or run a virus check.

However, an application embedded in a Web page can launch itself as soon as the Web page is loaded in the browser. Users often don't have a choice about running the program.

Invisible applications and scripts that copy themselves from system to system wreaking havoc as they go are called *viruses.* Programs that pretend to be useful applications but actually do nasty things are called *Trojan Horses.* There isn't an official name for dangerous programs embedded in Web pages, but I like the term (which I can't take credit for myself) *hostile applets.*

In general, you don't have to worry about documents, such as word processor files, sound files, images, and Web pages. Such things aren't programs, and they don't do anything by themselves. Rather, they sit there with smug looks on their faces until a program comes along and does something with them. Only files that run by themselves, such as executable applications or scripts, can do damage.

In some cases, documents can have programs embedded inside them: for example, a Microsoft Word file can contain an embedded macro script, and that script may be a variation on the infamous Word macro virus.

Vandalism: protecting hard disks

Perhaps the most annoying and destructive thing that malicious programs such as viruses and Trojan horses can do is to simply damage and destroy files. Sometimes viruses will delete files; sometimes they rename important files with random names; sometimes, they trash the whole hard disk.

An ordinary, trusted application, such as the ones that you buy from a software vendor, uses the disk as an essential tool when it works for you.

A malicious program does its damage with these same basic reading and writing capabilities. To limit the damage that a hostile tclet can do, the plug-in limits the tclet's ability to use the hard disk.

- ✔ **Write to specified directories.** This prevents the tclet from replacing important security files, or trashing important documents.

- ✔ **Limit file sizes.** Suppose that someone decides to write a malicious virus that fills up your hard disk with giant files of random characters. Why would someone do want to do this? I'm not really sure, but I suspect it's the same crew that enjoys writing in library books and melting toy soldiers with magnifying glasses. Anyway, the plug-in protects you from this kind of goofball attack by limiting the size of the file that the tclet can create on your disk.

Crank calls: arbitrary connections

Your connection to the Internet and your unique e-mail address are valuable resources. They're not quite as personal as your underwear, but they're surely not resources you want strangers to use.

In other words, giving a program free reign to make connections over the Internet is something like loaning out your long-distance credit card. If you lend the card to a trusted friend, you're probably safe. If you lend your card to a bored teenager, you may wind up with some explaining to do.

To protect you and your good name from arbitrary connections by hostile applets, the Tcl/Tk plug-in "screens" the connections made by the tclet, and only allows the tclet to connect to certain Internet addresses. In fact, by default, the plug-in does not allow *any* kind of connections at all.

Tcl Sources on the Internet

There are plenty of resources on the Internet, including real, live programmers, that can help you work through the thorniest of problems,

Usenet News Groups

Usenet is the Internet's meeting ground for many different kinds of people: mostly veteran Internet users, new users, cranky old curmudgeons, and people who are avoiding work at their day jobs. Usenet offers thousands of forums, called *newsgroups,* for the discussion of every topic imaginable, and then some. There are two newsgroups for the discussion of Tcl/Tk:

- ✔ Comp.lang.tcl is a discussion of everything that's going on in the Tcl/Tk language. Posters to `comp.lang.tcl` ask beginning to advanced questions about the language, report possible bugs in Tcl/Tk software, announce new Tcl/Tk-based releases, and just plain hang out. As Usenet newsgroups go, it's a pretty friendly place. If you post questions to `comp.lang.tcl`, you'll usually get a very prompt reply — often from some of the most important developers of Tcl/Tk.

- ✔ Comp.lang.tcl.announce is reserved for announcements of new Tcl/Tk based software products, such as new versions of Wish or new extension packages for Tcl. Reading `comp.lang.tcl.announce` is the best way to keep up to date about the latest developments.

To read or participate in either of these groups, load the URLs `news:comp.lang.tcl` or `news:comp.lang.tcl.announce` with your Web browser. (Your browser may not be configured to read newsgroups — if so, ask your Internet service provider for help.)

Web Pages

There are quite a few Web pages that provide information about Tcl/Tk. You can find tutorials, information about new extensions to the language, and other technical reference material. Here are a few important index pages:

- ✔ `http://www.sunlabs/research/tcl`
- ✔ `http://www.tcltk.com`
- ✔ `http://www.tcltk.com/tclets/index.html`
- ✔ `http://www.sco.com/Technology/tcl/Tcl.html`

Chapter 2

Your Wish Is My Command

· ·

In This Chapter

▶ What is Wish, and why should I care?

▶ Starting a Wish session

▶ Sourcing files in Wish

▶ Saving stuff from Wish

▶ Quitting Wish

· ·

Chances are, if you are new to programming in Tcl/Tk, or like me, just
prefer not to pay attention to picky syntactic details, you probably
can't just sit down and write a Tcl/Tk script (a "tclet") that works perfectly
the first time you try. That's absolutely normal. One of the first things
anyone discovers about working with computers is that almost nothing ever
works right the first time. That's why the space shuttle has three backup
computers. In this chapter, you'll learn how to use Wish, the software that
you'll use to test and develop your tclets.

Fortunately, you have a magical Tcl/Tk development tool, called *Wish*, that
lets you work out Tcl/Tk code step-by-step in the comfort of your own home
(or corner coffee shop, or wherever your computer happens to be at the
moment). Wish executes any Tcl/Tk command as soon as it's typed into the
Wish console. Trust me, this kind of instant feedback makes programming
much, much easier. Even experienced programmers like to be able to try out
little snippets of code to make sure they work before they put them all
together in a huge program that may take days to debug. When you use
Wish, you don't need to write your whole program at once and hope that
it works.

Wish allows you to try out lots of different variations on a single line of code
until you get it just right. For those of you who just like to cut loose and
start writing code even before you have a clear idea of what the tclet is
supposed to do, Wish is wonderful. While I don't recommend this strategy
for everyone, it does make coding more fun for me.

Getting Your Wish

Strictly speaking, Wish is not part of the Tcl/Tk plug-in. Wish is an independent program that happens to do exactly what the plug-in does (lets you use Tcl/Tk), but in a manner that makes it easier to write tclets, as well as view them.

What Wish and the Tcl/Tk plug-in share in common is a Tcl/Tk *interpreter*. An interpreter is that part of the software that reads in a Tcl/Tk command, processes it, and executes the instruction. (I like to think of the interpreter as a genie; officially, Wish stands for <u>Wi</u>ndowing <u>Sh</u>ell, but the Wish interpreter does seem to grant wishes instantly.) Wish and the Tcl/Tk plug-in both use exactly the same interpreter to handle Tcl/Tk code, but Wish is geared for developing tclets and other Tcl/Tl-based software, and the plug-in is designed to display the resulting tclets in a browser window.

Chapter 1 has information about finding the most recent copy of Wish. After you have a copy in hand, installing Wish is as easy as installing the Tcl/Tk plug-in.

For Windows 95 and the Mac, Wish comes as a self-extracting archive. Wish simply installs itself! (I know you were skeptical about the genie part. Do you believe me now?) Simply double-click on the installer icon, and your computer will do the rest for you. Here's where the installer will put the Wish software:

- ✔ **On Windows 95, Wish is installed automatically as a group called Tcl/Tk in the Start menu.** For the record, the Tcl/Tk directory, which contains the Wish application and documentation, is installed by default in the `Programs` directory.

- ✔ **On Mac OS, Wish is installed within a folder called, for obvious reasons,** `Tcl/Tk`. During the installation you are asked where you want put this folder. It doesn't really matter where you put it, but I suggest you put it near the folder in which you will be storing your tclet files.

- ✔ **If you use Linux or other Unix-like operating system, there is good news and bad news about installing Wish.** The bad news: Installation is not as simple as for Windows or the Mac. You will probably have to talk to your systems administrator to find out how and where Wish can be installed. The good news: Most Linux distributions already come with Tcl/Tk (including Wish) installed (usually in `/usr/bin`), so you won't have to do anything.

Starting Wish

After you install Wish, you can start it just like any other application on your computer. Simply double-click on the Wish icon, or using Windows 95, select Tcl⇨Wish from the Start menu. If you're using a Mac, just double-click on the Wish icon. If you're using Linux (or other Unix-like OS) just type `wish` at the X-Windows prompt.

When you start Wish, your monitor should look something like Figure 2-1. Wish uses two main windows:

- ✓ **The first window, called the Console, will have a % symbol followed by a blinking cursor.** The Console window is where you type commands for the Wish genie.

- ✓ **The second window, called the Display, will be blank when you first launch Wish.** This window is where your tclets appear, in exactly the same form as they appear when you put your tclet on a Web page.

Using Wish

The best way to get a feel for how Wish works is just to dive right in and give it a shot. (That's exactly what Wish was designed for.) You'll start off with a version of the classic "Hello, world" program which is traditionally the first

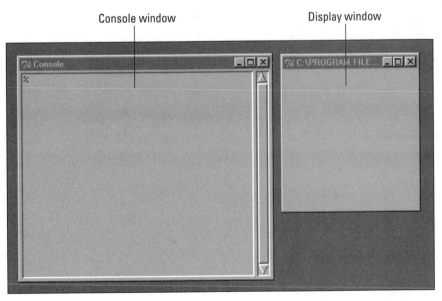

Console window   Display window

Figure 2-1:
You will use the Console window to enter Tcl/Tk commands into Wish, and you'll see the results in the Display window.

program that anyone ever writes when they learn a new programming language. This little tclet simply puts the words "Hello, world" into the Display window.

After you start Wish, and you see both the Console and Display windows, enter the following command in at the prompt in the Console window (after the % sign) and press the Enter key:

```
message .msg -text "Hello, world!"
```

Don't worry too much about how this command works. You're trying to get a feel for Wish here — you don't have to write any tclets on your own just yet.

Wish always responds to what you type with a message telling you the results of what you typed. This response may seem a little redundant at first, but it is a good way of double-checking that your command had the effect that you wanted it to have. In this case, Wish responded with

```
.msg
```

to indicate that the widget .msg has been successfully created.

You may be surprised that nothing appeared in the Display window. As I said, the message returned by the interpreter, .msg, indicates that the widget .msg is the result of your command. That is, your command has created .msg. Getting Wish to *display* the widget is a whole different problem (but, luckily, one that's easily solved). Just type

```
pack .msg
```

This command is simply an instruction to Wish to pack the widget .msg into the Display window. Wish responds to this command by displaying the widget .msg in the Display window. Now your screen should look something like the display in Figure 2-2, with the message *Hello, World* cheerily displayed in the Display window.

Figure 2-2:
The Display window shows the widget that you create with the `message` command.

Improvising your own widgets

For the record, the message command tells Wish to create a message widget with the name .msg. The widget .msg contains the text Hello, world!. Instead of .msg, you can call this widget .Fred, or .My_very_first_widget_that_greets_strangers, or whatever, and you can use any text message you like, as long as it's in quotes.

Names of widgets must be a single string. You cannot name your widget Super Widget or William the Conqueror. If you like multiple-word names (and I do, because they allow me to make my code a bit more readable), I recommend that you connect the words with an underscore (_) or a dash (-), though you can use just about any character you want, except a period (.).

The . in front of the name of the widget actually means something in this case, and connecting parts of a widget name with a period may have results very different from what you intend. For the moment, the rules for governing where you should or should not put a period are more complicated than useful, and they're not really relevant to doing fun things with Wish. (You can read more about them more in the part of the book called "Widget Science".) For now just name all your widgets whatever you like (as long as it's a single string of characters), and then put a dot in front of the name.

Note: Wish collapses the Display window to the size of your widget. You can always resize the window by grabbing the bottom-left corner and dragging. The widget stays the same size, even when you resize the window.

Now, look at a couple different ways to use Wish. I won't go into too much detail about how the commands work — you'll find out how to build your own commands in later chapters. At the moment, you should just use these exercises to become familiar with Wish as a programming tool. As you work through the rest of the book, you might find it best to have Wish running so that you can type the example commands and get a feel for how they work on your computer.

Clearing the board

Before you start making new widgets, there is one detail to take care of. Every widget in the Display window must have a unique name. If you created the "Hello, world" message in the previous example, you must get rid of it so that you can use the .msg widget again. Specifically, you must destroy the old widget, so that it can be created again with new content. (Don't worry, this action doesn't require a hard hat, or a crowbar, or any other implements of destruction.) To destroy the widget called .msg, just type

```
destroy .msg
```

at the Wish prompt (%) to clear the Display window and set .msg free to be re-created. It's a good idea to destroy any widgets you've created as soon as you finish using them so that you can reuse the names if you like, especially if you use descriptive but nonspecific names like .msg.

If you *don't* destroy the widget and try to make another widget with the same name, the interpreter will not obey you. Instead, the genie will report the following error:

```
window name ".msg" already exists in parent
```

The moral: Either give all the widgets in a particular Wish session a different name (see the sidebar "Improvising your own widgets" for more details on widget naming) or destroy the .msg widget each time before you re-create it with a new command.

If you decide not to destroy .msg but to make a new message with a different name (always an option — Tcl/Tk is nothing if not versatile!), you will get some interesting results when you pack the second widget. Go ahead and try — nothing bad will happen. Wish simply puts the new message directly below the first one. Take a look at Figure 2-3.

Figure 2-3:
The Display
window
shows the
message
"Hello,
Moon"
displayed
under the
message
"Hello,
World."

You can always destroy any of the widgets you create just by typing the following command, where *widget_name* stands for whatever the name of the widget is that you want to destroy.

```
destroy widget-name
```

The CD-ROM that comes with this book includes a very simple tclet called destructo.tcl. You can load it into Wish (using the instructions on sourcing tclets a little later in this chapter), and you will have a convenient widget-vanquishing utility at your disposal.

After you load the destructo program, if you type

```
clean widget-name
```

the designated widget is destroyed, just as though the destroy command had been used. However, if you type

```
clean all
```

every widget in the window disappears. The command clean all is very useful if you are trying to debug a tclet that creates a large number of widgets or if you just like blowing stuff up. Every time you want to reload a tclet into Wish, you must destroy all the existing widgets that were created the last time you loaded the program. The clean all procedure makes removing several widgets much easier to do.

Your $2,000 desk calculator

Here's a simple arithmetic example to demonstrate just how easy it is to execute commands in Wish.

To multiply two numbers, type the following line on the command line (after the %) in the Console window:

```
expr 13 * 17
```

Wish returns the result of the command in the following line of the console:

```
% expr 13 * 17
221
```

In fact, you can enter expressions that are as complicated as you can dream up:

```
% expr (2 * ((18/3) + 4) * sin (6.28))
-0.063706
```

I'm not suggesting that you throw away your calculator just yet. It's not very practical to fire up a $2,000 (or more) computer, start Wish, and write Tcl/Tk code just to multiply two numbers, but it's a good place to demonstrate one of the most fundamental characteristics of Tcl/Tk — instant gratification. As soon as you type a command, Wish provides the result.

Strings and things

You'll probably do a lot of string processing when you start writing real-word tclets, and Wish is a great tool for checking out how string commands work. Say that you want to sort out a list of stuff that the user enters, and you're not quite sure you remember how the sort command is supposed to work. To try out the string command, you might set up a string as a test case. You can set up a variable that holds the string by typing a command at the wish prompt:

```
set my_string "mercury venus earth mars"
```

Wish returns the value of the variable, to let you know that it's paying attention:

```
% set my_string "mercury venus earth mars"
mercury venus earth mars
```

Now you can try different variations of the lsort command, to see what kind of results you get. Don't worry about the particulars of how I set up these commands — just say "oooh!" when Wish sorts the list for you and prints the result as soon as you hit the return key.

```
% lsort $my_string
earth mars mercury venus
% lsort -increasing $my_string
earth mars mercury venus
% lsort -decreasing $my_string
venus mercury mars earth
```

Doing these kinds of little tests in Wish is a real time-saver. If you try each possibility using your final tclet code that runs in the browser, your routine will be something like the following:

1. **Create the tclet code in a source file.**

2. **Create an HTML file that contains the tclet.**

3. **Load the HTML in the browser.**

4. **Edit the tclet code in the source file, substituting in the new command.**

5. **Reload the HTML in the browser.**

6. **Repeat Steps 4–6 for each line of code to be tested.**

Fine-tuning widgets

When you create an object in the Display window, you can make a lot of choices about the object's appearance. Depending on the kind of object, you can choose different colors, sizes, typefaces, and textures.

Making decisions about the appearance of widgets isn't a technical process — it's a question of taste. No programming secrets exist that make pink type look good on a green background! The only way to make the appearance of a widget just right is to fuss with it. Wish can change the appearance of a widgets as quickly as it can evaluate an expression or process a text string.

Now, create a hum-drum looking button with wish:

```
button .b -text "click me."
pack .b
```

Figure 2-4 shows this drab little guy: The background is the same color of the window, the type is tiny, and the label is apologetic. Very often, you want buttons to be unobtrusive, and this button is fine for such occasions, but see if you can dress it up a little.

Figure 2-4:
You can use
Wish to
dress up
this drab
little button.

First, make the message a little stronger:

```
.b configure -text "Click me or else!"
```

When you enter this command at the Wish prompt, the interpreter instantly reconfigures the text of the button widget. You can see the new type in Figure 2-5.

Figure 2-5:
Wish
automatically
updates the
button
when you
type in
a new
command.

I know this is a book about programming, but I am actually a designer by trade. Allow me let you in on the first secret of graphic design: *When in doubt, make it big.* Here's how you can pump up the text in Wish:

```
.b configure -font "*-avenir-bold-*—*-100-*-*-*-*-*-*-*"
```

Oops! The new text is a little big. (As you'll see if you try.) Showing this in a figure would require a fold-out page. Try again, tweaking the size value:

```
.b configure -font "*-avenir-bold-*—*-24-*-*-*-*-*-*-*"
```

You can put in any font in place of Avenir and any size in place of 24, if you like. (You'll look at this command in more detail later, of course.) Figure 2-6 shows the big-type version of the widget.

Figure 2-6:
You can
configure
the type
with new
sizes, until
it's just
right.

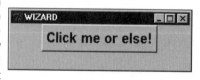

When you press the keyboard's up arrow, Wish retypes the last command for you. To back up and change the 100 to 24 in the preceding example, rather than type the whole line again, just press the up arrow and fix the size.

Because you've been very good, I'll tell you the second rule of graphic design: *When really in doubt, make it big and red.* Again, it's easy to do with Wish:

```
.b configure -foreground white -background red
```

Figure 2-7 shows the final big, red button (in vibrant black-and-white):

Figure 2-7:
Try these
commands
at home to
verify that
the button
is actually
red!

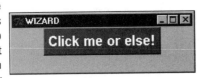

Now that I know the options I want for the button, when it's time to write my program, I can set all of the appearance values in one fell swoop:

```
.b2 button -text "Click me, or else!" \
-font "*-avenir-bold-*-*-24-*-*-*-*-*-*-*" \
-foreground white -background red
```

When a command is too long for one line, you use the \ character to tell Wish that you want to continue the command, as I have above. Wish gives you some feedback in return: When Wish is expecting the second line of a multiline command, the prompt changes from % to >.

A real program

You can write your own Tcl/Tk commands. Programmer-defined commands are called *procedures,* and they behave in the same way as ordinary Tcl/Tk commands. You discover the finer points of procedure writing in Chapter 10, but take a second now to see how you can define your own commands and then use them in Wish.

If you want to make a procedure (and believe me, eventually you will), the first things you must do are to name and define it. Here's a handy little procedure that takes a string like

```
Franklin, Benjamin
```

and returns a new string, like

```
Benjamin Franklin
```

This procedure's pretty complicated — don't worry about the details of it's internal workings. Just type it into Wish. Notice that the open left curly brace at the end of the first line behaves something like the \ character: Wish will give you the > prompt at the beginning of each line until you close the left curly with the right curly brace on the last line.

```
proc reverse_name name {
    set name_list [split $name ,]
    set first_name [lindex $name_list 1]
    set last_name [lindex $name_list 0]
    set output [concat $firstname " " $lastname]
    return $output
}
```

After you create this procedure, congratulate yourself. You just (temporarily) changed the Tcl/Tk language so that it has a new command called `reverse_name`. `reverse_name` takes a string input, splits it up on the comma, reverses the two halves, and writes the result. To make this command work, you just need to run the procedure on a string, such as `Washington, George`, as you did before. The easiest way to do this is to create a message widget that contains a call to `reverse_name` — just as though this procedure were one of the original Tcl/Tk commands. For example,

```
message .abe -text [reverse_name "Lincoln, Abraham"]
pack .abe
```

will do the trick nicely.

A little history

When trying out Tcl/Tk commands in Wish, you often end up having to retype the same long line again and again while making only minor changes. For example, you may not be sure exactly how wide a message window you need, so you may want to try the same command again and again with different values until it looks just right. With the line

```
message .msg -width 240p \
-text "Howdy there, and welcome to my web site"
```

you'd have to type the same thing over and over just to try out different widths, which gets really boring, really fast. However, Wish has a handy device, called the `history` command, to save you some trouble. Wish remembers what you've typed, and you can use `history` to call back a previous line in one of two ways.

Easy messages in Wish

There are many different ways to display a text message in Wish. The quickest method is the `puts` command. For example, if you enter

```
puts "Hello, World!"
```

at the Wish prompt, nothing new appears in the Display window. Instead, output from the command appears on the next line of the Console window, like so:

```
% puts "Hello, World!"
Hello, World!
```

Another common way to display the message is to put it in a message widget:

```
message .msg -text "Hello,
   World!"
pack .msg
```

If you just want to display a message, using `puts` is a lot simpler than using a message widget. If what you are testing involves the graphic appearance of widgets or text output, you must use commands that display output in the Display window.

I don't recommend that you get in the habit of using the `puts` command. In early versions of the Tcl/Tk plug-in, `puts` does different things on different platforms, and on the Mac platform, it does nothing at all. Your better choice is to use message and textbox widgets to display information because those are guaranteed to show up, not just in Wish, but in real tclets as well.

First, you can use the up arrow to scroll up the lines you have typed. Press the up arrow once, and your current input line shows the last command you typed. Press it again, and you see the command you typed before that, and so on. After you have the line you want, you can use the mouse to select only those characters you want to change. Press the enter key (which is called "return" on a Mac keyboard) when you're done, and the edited line will be treated just as if you had typed the whole thing in from scratch.

Alternatively, if you don't want to edit the line but just want Wish reexecute the same command, you can use the exclamation point followed by the first letter of the command, and Wish will repeat the last command that started with that letter. For example, you might want to repeatedly destroy all the widgets that you've created and then re-source a particular tclet each time you make changes in the tclet. The commands you're likely to be using most are

```
source my-tclet.tcl
```

to load in the tclet and see what it looks like and

```
clean all
```

(assuming you've sourced the `destructo.tcl` tclet from the CD) to destroy all the widgets.

Instead of typing

```
source my-tclet.tcl
```

a second time, however, you can just type

```
!s
```

and Wish will repeat the last command that started with s. Then you can type

```
!c
```

to repeat the `clean` command (that started with c) and so on. If you have two commands that start with the same letter, just type as much of the command as necessary to make it clear which command you mean. For example, if you have defined a procedure called `clear` in addition to the `clean` procedure in the `destructo.tcl` tclet, typing

```
!c
```

repeats the one that you used most recently. However, typing

```
!clear
```

makes it clear that you want to repeat the `clear` command, not the `clean` command.

History lasts through only one Wish session. When you quit Wish and start it again, it will not remember any of the commands from the last session.

Sourcing Files into Wish

As you become more proficient using Tcl/Tk, you will probably use Wish less and less, except as a debugging tool. Although Wish is good for trying out every step of a tclet before you actually enter it into a text file, prototyping every single line in Wish first can be very time-consuming. If you already know exactly how to use most or all of the commands in your tclet and want to go straight to writing real code, that's what you should do.

More important, you don't want to retype the whole tclet into Wish every time you want to experiment with particular lines. If you've defined procedures or set up variables, you don't want to retype them to play around with the way a widget works. However, the procedure or variable may have to be in place before you create the widget.

In these situations, the source command comes in handy. You can use source to load an existing text file into Wish — with the same result as though you had typed all the text in the file into the Wish Console window. Wish treats this text as a series of Tcl/Tk commands (or tries too — if the text is not well-formed Tcl/Tk code, you will get exactly the same errors as though you had typed the illegal commands directly into Wish). To use the source command, just type

```
source file_name
```

where file_name is the name of the file to load, including all necessary path instructions if the file to be loaded is not in the directory from which you are running Wish.

PLATFORMS

Telling Wish where to look for a source file

You use slightly different techniques to tell Wish where to look for a source file.

If you're running Windows, Wish starts looking for the file in the top-level directory of the disk on which it is located. If you're running Mac OS, Wish starts looking in the Tcl/Tk folder.

For example, if Wish is located in the directory C:\Netscape\Tclplug\Wish, your Wish session looks for the source file in the C:\ directory. To access tclets saved in any other directory, you need to specify the absolute pathname. For example, if you have a tclet called tcl_test.tcl in the directory C:\Netscape\Tclplug\Wish\New, you have to type:

```
source
    "c:\Netscape\Tclplug\Wish\New\
    tcl_test.tcl"
```

at the prompt in the Wish.

If you're using a Mac, you don't need to use the source command. Just choose Source from the File menu, and use the resulting Mac dialog box to navigate to the source file. (Even writing Tcl/Tk code is easier on a Mac!) You can use the source command on the Mac, if you like, but remember the way to specify folders and subfolders is with colons, like so: Hard Drive:Big Folder:Another Folder:Tcl/Tk:tcl_test.tcl.

Try opening the `rn-proc.tcl` file on the CD using a text editor and saving it as a text file on your hard drive. Remember to save your file as plain text and give it an easy to remember name like `rn-proc.tcl`. (I have an uncle named *rn-proc.tcl,* so it's especially easy for me to remember.)

To load the procedure, use the `source` command, or the Mac's File⇨Source menu item. Wish will act just as it would if you had typed the whole procedure. Try making a message in the Display window using the same commands as in the preceding example by typing just these lines:

```
reverse_name "Lincoln, Abraham"
```

The command works just as though you had typed the whole `reverse_name` procedure into Wish. The real advantage to sourcing a file into Wish is that you can change the text in one window using your text editor, save it, and re-source the file into Wish to get the results of the new version immediately without having to quit either your text editor or Wish (assuming you have enough memory to run both at the same time).

For example, try reopening the file `rn-proc.tcl` in your text editor without quitting Wish. In the editor, change the line

```
set output [concat $first_name " " $last_name]
```

to

```
set output [concat $first_name "::" $last_name]
```

That is, just replace the middle space with two colons, and then save the text file. Then re-source the file into Wish by typing

```
source rn-proc.tcl
```

on the Wish command line. Next, either destroy and re-create the `.msg` widget using

```
destroy .msg
```

and

```
message .msg -text [reverse_name "Filmore, Millard"]
```

or create a new message widget (for example, with the name `.msg2`) like this:

```
message .msg2 -text [reverse_name "Filmore, Millard"]
```

Finally, pack `.msg` or `.msg2`, depending on which you created. The result should be a line of text like

```
Millard::Filmore
```

either alone in the Wish Display window (if you destroyed and re-created `.msg`) or following the already existing line

```
Abraham Lincoln
```

if you created a new message widget, `.msg2`, and packed it without first destroying `.msg`.

Quitting Wish

Tcl/Tk is a very easy-to-use language, but the easiest thing in the world is quitting Wish. Simply type `exit` at the command line, and Wish quits.

Chapter 3

Creating a Tclet Source File

· ·

In This Chapter

▶ Choosing a basic text editor

▶ Using a specialized source code editor

▶ Following basic formatting conventions

· ·

After you develop a working program in Wish, it's time to create a Tcl/Tk source code file to store the program. (Otherwise, distributing your tclet would be a little tricky — you'd need to travel around the world typing code into other people's Wish consoles.) To spare you this inconvenience, I show you in this chapter how to create a properly formatted Tcl/Tk source file, using tools that you probably already have.

Tackling Tclet Source Code with a Text Editor

All you really need to create a tclet source code file is a basic text editor. You don't even need a fancy word processor. Although you can certainly use a word processor to create your tclet file (with excellent results), you can't use any of the program's special features, such as text formatting, outlining, and page layout, when you edit source code.

You will be a very happy programmer if you have enough RAM to run Wish, Netscape Navigator, or Internet Explorer and your text-editing program simultaneously. Because you can't do much about the memory requirements of Wish and Netscape, you should shop around for sleek little text editors if you're feeling the memory pinch. (I suggest a few tools that I like to use in the sidebar, "Selecting a specialized source code editor," later in this chapter.)

Using a preinstalled text editor

I am nearly as stingy as I am lazy, and whenever possible, I use free software. Fortunately, plenty of free text editors are available. As I hinted earlier, you almost certainly have some kind of text editor already installed on your machine. Check out the text editors commonly preinstalled on basic platforms:

Platforms	*Text-Editing Applications*
Windows	Wordpad, Notepad
Mac OS	TeachText, SimpleText
UNIX(es)	vi, emacs

The applications in the preceding table offer the following basic enhancements:

- ✔ Can have more than one file open at a time
- ✔ Can paste text that you copy from other applications
- ✔ Can save files in different platform formats — that is, with or without line breaks
- ✔ Can adjust tab stops — or at least big ready-made tabs that are easy to see

If your favorite text editor doesn't offer all these features, don't worry. You should use the application that you know the best and are most comfortable using.

Using Automatic Formatting Features

For the most part, *automatic formatting* means that the text editor has special tools for indenting and otherwise wrangling whole blocks of text. Suppose that you have a block of text like the convert_to_celsius procedure, shown in the following code. Don't worry about what the code means just yet — just notice that the lines are all piled up one after another.

```
proc convert_to_celsius  {temperature} {
set new_temperature [expr ($temperature - 32) * 5 / 9]
return  $new_temperature
}
```

PLATFORMS

Selecting a specialized source code editor

At some point in your coding career, you may want to invest in a specialized source code editor. Source code editors offer a few conveniences that you'll really appreciate when you're coding, without all the RAM-hogging extras that are included in a word processor.

Mac OS users should check out BBEdit Lite (which is free), BBEdit 4.0 (the full-featured version), and Alpha, which is a very, very Tcl-friendly text editor. Windows users should take a look at WindEdit.

Different applications offer different features, but almost every source code editor provides many of the following basic tools:

- ✔ Automatic indentation features
- ✔ Color coding
- ✔ Parenthesis balancing
- ✔ Searching with regular expressions

Adding the correct indentation makes reading the code a lot easier because the indentation organizes the code into logical units — you can *see* how the code fits together. You read more about common formatting conventions later in this chapter. For now, just note that the middle two lines should be indented as follows, so that it's easier for humans to read:

```
proc convert_to_celsius  {temperature} {
    set new_temperature [expr ($temperature - 32) * 5 / 9]
    return  $new_temperature
}
```

How do you indent this code in a word processor? Most likely, you can add a tab at the beginning of each indented line. In some programs, you need to peck furiously at the space bar to add several spaces at the beginning of each appropriate line. Enter the source code editor's *indentation feature* — most source code editors allow you to select a block of text or group of lines and indent the whole thing with one menu command or keyboard shortcut.

Most source code editors also automatically retain indentation as you type. In other words, when you enter an indented line, the next line starts with the same indentation, rather than at the left margin. This feature would probably be a nuisance in a word processor, but it helps to create good-looking, legible code when you're programming.

Understanding color codes

Many source code editors help you out by *colorizing* the code to your program. The basic idea is to tag special words and characters with color type. Color coding is subliminal feedback about the correctness of your code — after a while, the different colors help you to see typos right away because the colors are wrong.

Coloring reserved words

Most source code editors look for reserved words in a programming language and mark them with color, or bolding, or both. Suppose that you enter the following code into a source code editor configured for Tcl/Tk:

```
expr 2 + 2
```

As soon as you type the r in expr, expr changes to blue or green or some other color, indicating that it's a word that has a special meaning in the Tcl/Tk language (it's not just sick). If you had accidentally typed wxpr instead of expr, wxpr would stay black, because wxpr doesn't mean anything in Tcl. When you notice that words you expect to change *don't* change, you can spot the typo almost immediately.

Many source code editor applications won't be set up to deal with the reserved words in Tcl/Tk, but you can usually define your own list somewhere in the source code editor's preferences. The Alpha Editor for Mac OS does know the Tcl/Tk reserved words and marks them with blue type. (You can change the color if you want.)

Using color to find problems with quote marks

Many source code editors take special notice of the double-quote character and mark characters after a double quote with a special color. Usually, when you close a string with a second double quote, the whole string changes color *again* to indicate that the string is closed.

For example, the line of code below is wrong. There's only one double quote; the Tcl/Tk plug-in expects double quotes in pairs.

```
message .m -text "Hello, Goober!
```

If your source code editor is set up to find *open strings* (or whatever the editor program calls strings without a closing quote), "Hello, Goober!" appears in colored type. If you close the string with another double quote, like this:

```
message .m -text "Hello, Goober!"
```

"Hello Goober!" changes color again.

Using this feature, you can set up your text editor to color those bug-generating open strings with whatever color you find most eye-catchingly obnoxious. Often, you can catch your typos as soon as you create them.

Balancing parentheses

All too soon, you will find yourself typing code like the following:

```
set x [expr 102.5 + sin([expr ($total + ($value / 2)) \
* 6.28 / 360]) * -55]
```

As my grandmother used to say, "Good night!" In order for this statement to be exactly right, every left parenthesis must be chaperoned by a matching right parenthesis.

Of course, you can simply look at each parenthesis or bracket and find its mate. This approach is a lot like hitting yourself over the head with a big stick, and causes the same numbness and slurring of speech. To solve this problem, most source code editors offer parenthesis-balancing features. Most of the time, this means that the editor gives you feedback about parenthesis matching as you type and provides an easy way to test code to see where the pairs are.

Here's how the feedback-as-you type routine usually works: When you type a right parenthesis or bracket, the editor looks for a matching left parenthesis. If it finds one, the matching parenthesis flashes briefly, as though to say "Hey, I'm the mate for that parenthesis!" If the editor can't find a matching parenthesis or bracket, the editor beeps to draw your attention to the lonely punctuation. These little reminder features can help you avoid making typographical errors and, hence, save you debugging time later on.

The more active form of parenthesis balancing finds the innermost pair of parentheses or brackets that contains the insertion point. Take another look at the parenthesis-choked line of code that I showed you in the preceding code example:

```
set x [expr 102.5 + sin([expr ($total + ($value / 2)) \
* 6.28 / 360]) * -55]
```

insertion
point here

When you pick your source code editor's *balancing command,* the editor highlights all the text that's between the *innermost* pair that contains the insertion point. If the insertion point is positioned as it is in the preceding example, the editor will highlight the text like this:

```
set x [expr 102.5 + sin([expr ($total + ($value / 2)) \
* 6.28 / 360]) * -55]
```

insertion
point here

Then move the insertion point out of the selected paragraph, like so:

```
set x [expr 102.5 + sin([expr ($total + ($value / 2)) \
 * 6.28 / 360]) * -55]
```

Here's what the editor highlights when you use the balancing command:

```
set x [expr 102.5 + sin([expr ($total + ($value / 2)) \
* 6.28 / 360]) * -55]
```

Ginchy, isn't it? Paragraph-balancing helps you to make sure that your code is split into logical units in the way that you *think* that you've split it into units.

Following Formatting Conventions

You should follow a few programming conventions when you're entering code. A few conventions, like the rule about breaking a single command across more than one line, are important to ensure that your tclet runs properly. Most of the other conventions are used to make figuring out exactly what's going on in the program easier for you or other programmers.

Using one command per line

The rule of thumb for creating tclet source code is easy to remember:

```
one line of text = one Tcl/Tk command.
```

Your best bet is to try to follow the one-command-to-a-line rule, unless you have a good reason to do otherwise.

The Tcl/Tk plug-in and Wish both use invisible end of line characters to tell where one Wish command ends and another begins. It's good coding style to make each line of your text file a separate command, if possible.

Breaking long code into several lines

Sometimes, you may need to break a single command across more than one line. Other times, you may want to squeeze more than one Tcl/Tk command onto a single line of your text file. It gracefully allows these variants to the basic rules.

Those pesky end of line characters

When you enter text in a text editor program, the program inserts a special, invisible character whenever you press the Enter key. You can't see it, but it's there — a sign that the text editor should break the current line and start a new paragraph.

These *end of line* characters are important when you're coding, because the Tcl/Tk plug-in uses the end of line character to recognize where one Tcl/Tk command ends and another begins. If the plug-in can't find an end of line character, it assumes that the whole tclet is one big command. If the tclet isn't really a one-line program, it won't run properly.

So here's the pesky part: Text editors on different platforms use different characters to mark the ends of lines. Macs use the ASCII character called "carriage return" (aka <cr>), UNIX uses the ASCII character called "line feed" (aka <lf>), and Windows and DOS, not to be outdone, use both.

If you do all your coding on one machine or on one platform, you may not have any problems with end of line characters. However, if you

download other people's tclets from the Web or move your tclet files from one platform to another, you may experience difficulties. Fortunately, some text editors handle this problem transparently; they simply figure out what kind of text file is being opened and display the file appropriately. Most of the source code editors mentioned in Tcl/Tk For Dummies are pretty smart about handling end of line snafus.

Some very early versions of the Tcl/Tk plug-in, however, are not so open-minded. The DR3 version, in particular, gets very confused by tclets that are saved in Mac OS text file format.

Be aware that any member of your audience who uses the DR3 version of the plug-in will have trouble loading applets that you save in Mac OS format. You have two easy solutions:

- Save your files in UNIX text format.

- Provide your audience with a link to http://www.sunscript.com, where they can find a newer, friendlier version of the Tcl/Tk plug-in.

Sometimes, a command may be too long to fit on a single line because a particular command takes several arguments, or your variables have really long names that you can't avoid. In these cases, you can use the \ character to continue the current line, just as you do with Wish in Chapter 2 for example:

```
set variable long_name_that_you'd_never_use_in_a_tclet \1
```

Other times, you may want to break a single code across several lines in order to make the code easier to read. For example, the basic code to draw a rectangle looks like this:

```
.c create rectangle x1 y1 x2 y2
```

where *x1, y1, x2,* and *y2* represent the coordinates of corners of the rectangle. (You don't need to worry about the particulars at this point.) Now, suppose that you want to calculate each of the coordinates in some way — maybe x1 = a + b, y1 = c + d, and so on. As you discover in Chapter 6, you can put this kind of calculation right into the command, like this:

```
.c create rectangle [expr $a + $b] [expr $c + $d]
            [expr $e + $f] [expr $g + $h]
```

It's a little hard to see what's being substituted for what in the line of code above. If you break the code so that each substitution is on its own line, it's a little easier to decipher, as shown in the following code example:

```
.c create rectangle [expr $a + $b] \
[expr $c + $d] \
[expr $e + $f] \
[expr $g + $h]
```

As with the line that was just plain too long, you can use the \ character to indicate that the unfinished lines continue on the subsequent lines.

Putting multiple Tcl/Tk commands on a single line

Besides recognizing end of line characters, the Tcl/Tk plug-in also recognizes another separator between commands — the semicolon character. You can use a semicolon to pack more than one Tcl/Tk command on the same line of code.

You can use this technique to enter two short, related lines on a single line. For example, take a look at the following miniprogram:

```
message .m -text "Hello, Persephone"
pack .m
```

The first line creates a message widget and the second line displays it. These lines are so closely related that it can make sense to condense them onto one line, like so:

```
message .m -text "Hello, Persephone"; pack .m
```

Again, this kind of decision depends more on your personal aesthetics and habits more than anything else. Both the two-line version and the one-line version of the tclet are perfectly legal.

Adding comments to your code

One of the most important steps that you can take to make your code easier to understand is to add comments. *Comments* are simply notes to yourself or to others. Comments describe what's going on in the tclet, or what you think or hope is going on. When you create comments by using the standard tclet notation, the Tcl/Tk plug-in (and Wish) ignore the comments, so you can say whatever you like. ("Hello, Mom" and "Kilroy was here" are not particularly useful, however.)

To add comments to your code, start lines with the # character, like this:

```
# The following line creates a message widget "Hello, Io"
```

As long as the first character in the line is the # sign, you can put as many spaces or tabs in front of it as you want, as in the following example:

```
                    # still a comment
```

As with ordinary statements, you can extend a comment onto a second line with your old friend the backslash:

```
# Here's an especially long-winded comment\
  that just can't seem to contain itself to a single line
```

Sometimes when you're reading other people's Tcl/Tk code — and you *should* snoop around in other people's code as often as you can — you may see very elaborate dividers and banners inside comments, like this:

```
# ─────────────────────────────────
#
#
#               Fermat's Last Theorem Prover
#               by Tim Webster
#
#               Developed April 1, 1997
#
#
# ─────────────────────────────── ─
```

Because each line in this little banner starts with the # character, Tcl/Tk ignores the whole thing.

Finally, you can sneak a comment onto the end of another line of code. As you may have guessed, the secret is the semicolon. Here's how it works:

```
message .m -text "Hello, Uranus"; #create a message widget
pack .m ; display the Uranus widget
```

Indentation and grouping

No unbreakable rules exist regarding the way that you indent your code and add space between sections. As long as you are careful to make sure that your multiline commands are properly broken across lines, the rest is up to you.

However, you may find that you want to organize your code with the kind of indentation and grouping used by most programmers. Not only does this convention make your code easier to read, it can teach you to scan through other people's code more quickly.

Managing brackets

As suggested earlier in this chapter, one of the most important parts of writing a working tclet is to make sure that every parenthesis or bracket has a partner. The Tcl/Tk plug-in hates solitary brackets and returns an error if a command contains "unbalanced" brackets or parentheses.

Even if you have a source code editor that helps you balance punctuation, a few steps make things clearer. As you discover in Chapter 10, all the instructions that make up a procedure appear between brackets, like this:

```
proc my_little_procedure {} {
expr 1 + 1
expr 2 + 2
return 3
}
```

Although it may seem better to move that little right bracket hanging at the bottom of the procedure to the end of the previous line (like this),

```
proc my_little_procedure {} {
expr 1 + 1
expr 2 + 2
return 3}
```

it's actually better to leave the bracket hanging. When the bracket is out in the open and easy to see, it's clear that you avoided making the common mistake of forgetting to close the procedure with a right bracket. As far as the Tcl/Tk police are concerned, where the right bracket appears doesn't matter, as long as the brackets are matched. However, Tcl/Tk civilians who may expect to see the bracket dangling from the bottom of the procedure. (If brackets or parentheses are already on the final line of the procedure, the procedure-closing bracket can be even harder to pick out of the crowd.)

A few Tcl/Tk constructs use brackets like this decision, mostly the commands (such as the `if` command) and loops (such as the `while` command). The same rule applies: Put the closing bracket on its own line, so that it's easy to see.

You can't be quite so free-wheelin' with the left bracket of a procedure. At some deep technical level, a *procedure* is a single command that breaks across more than one line, and the left bracket functions like the \ character — it lets the plug-in know that there's more to the procedure below. As a result, you can't use the left bracket in the following way:

```
proc my_little_procedure {}
{
```

The interpreter thinks that the left bracket on the second line is a new command. The left bracket that opens a block of code *must always* appear at the end of the first line.

Indenting your Tcl/Tk code

You can use indentation to make the pairing in `my_little_procedure` even more explicit. Sometimes, a left bracket can get pretty far away from the closing right bracket. If the opening and closing sections of a block of code are vertically aligned, it's easy to see which line contains the opening left bracket. Here's the standard way to structure `my_little_procedure`:

```
proc my_little_procedure {} {
    expr 1 + 1
    expr 2 + 2
    return 3
}
```

When a block of code contains another block of code, using indentation is especially important for highlighting pairs. Check out how this works in a procedure that contains an `if` statement:

```
proc another_little procedure {} {
    expr 1 + 1
    expr 2 + 2
    if { [expr 1 + 1] == 2} {
        return "Math still hasn't changed. Phewww!"
    }
}
```

As you can see, `another_little procedure` ends with two lines in a row, which contain only brackets. Because I've been careful about indentation, however, you can see at a glance that the closing bracket on the last line goes with

```
proc another_little procedure {} {
```

and the closing bracket on the second-to-last line goes with

```
if { [expr 1 + 1] == 2} {
```

Adding horizontal space

Always add blank lines between the different parts that make up your tclet. The Tcl/Tk plug-in and Wish just ignore blank lines, so you can add them as needed to break your code into little bite-sized chunks.

Chapter 4

Putting Tclets into Web Pages

• •

• •

*W*hen you get good at creating a tclet source file, you can put your tclet onto a Web page. You don't do too much fancy Tcl/Tk stuff in this chapter; rather, you focus on the HTML commands that you can use to put your tclets online.

Using the `<EMBED>` Tag

The `<EMBED>` tag is widely used for adding all sorts of things to Web pages — it's really the Superglue of HTML. If you snoop through other people's HTML source code — and who doesn't? — you can see the `<EMBED>` tag used to add things like bitmaps, ActiveX controls, and even stranger critters to Web pages. No wonder, then, that you use `<EMBED>` to put tclets into your Web pages.

The `<EMBED>` tag's basic syntax is very much like that of the widely-used `<IMG>` tag `<EMBED>` always uses the `SRC` attribute; SRC, which stands for *source,* is the filename of the thing that you want to embed. For example, to embed a tclet called `ratso.tcl` in your Web page, you use the following code:

```
<embed src = "ratso.tcl">
```

As is always the case with HTML code, the spaces between words don't count; so code that looks like

```
<       embed       src       =       "ratso.tcl"       >
```

or

```
<embed src =
"ratso.tcl">
```

(though slightly peculiar) is okay, too (if you feel like making your code particularly difficult to read). The quotes around the filename (which should be straight double quotes) are mandatory when the filename contains spaces. (The quotes aren't strictly necessary when the filename is one word, but it doesn't hurt to stick 'em on, either, so most folks do.)

Specifying file paths

When you use a simple tclet filename like `ratso.tcl` in the `<EMBED>` tag, the code implies that the file `ratso.tcl` exists in the same folder that contains the current Web page. That's where the browser looks for it, anyway. If the tclet file is not in the same folder as the Web page, the browser politely pretends that it never saw the `<EMBED>` tag in the first place.

In fact, a tclet can reside anywhere you want (as far as the Web page and the tclet are concerned). As long as the tclet is in a folder that the Web server recognizes and the tclet's file path is properly specified in the page's HTML code, everything is hunky-dory.

For example, suppose that your Web page is in a folder called `HTML`. The `ratso` tclet exists in a folder called `tclets`, which is a subfolder of the `HTML` folder. You can specify this tclet's file path location like this:

```
<embed src = "/tclets/ratso.tcl">
```

This code should be straightforward to those of you who have used this kind of *relative URL* to specify the locations of images or HTML files. (A relative URL, as the name suggests, specifies the location of the source file with respect to the HTML file that contains the link to the source file.) The `<EMBED>` tag uses exactly the same conventions as an `<IMG>` or `<A HREF>` tag for specifying the location of a file. (Take a look at *HTML For Dummies Quick Reference* by Deborah and Eric Ray and published by IDG Books Worldwide, Inc. for the low-down on using relative URLs.)

Setting the tclet's size

The attributes most commonly added to the `<EMBED>` tag are `HEIGHT` and `WIDTH`. Any guesses what these attributes control? Yes! The tclet's spin and mass! (Oops . . . no . . . those are black holes. . . .) Actually, the `HEIGHT` and `WIDTH` attributes determine the size of the tclet's area in the Web page layout, as measured in screen pixels. Pixels may vary slightly in size from monitor to monitor, but basically you have 72 pixels to an inch.

The official word on <EMBED>

If you've paid your HTML dues, you know that at least *three* versions of HTML really exist:

✔ The official HTML specification, overseen by the powerful and mysterious figures at the W3 Consortium

✔ The two unofficial versions, which the R&D folks at Netscape and Microsoft have cooked up to make Web pages more interesting

For example, things like background color and font size aren't really part of the HTML specification; they're extensions to HTML that Netscape has built into the Navigator browser. Because almost everyone uses Netscape Navigator or Microsoft Internet Explorer (which both understand the Netscape tags), hardly anyone makes a fuss over unofficial HTML.

Just for the record, the basic tag that you use to add tclets to your Web pages, the <EMBED> tag, is not official HTML. The <EMBED> tag is officially a Netscape extension to HTML and is recognized only by Netscape-compatible browsers.

You don't *need* to specify the tclet's size in the HTML code. However, if you don't specify the tclet's size, the browser allocates a cute little 25-x-25-pixel square (about the size of a postage stamp) for your tclet. If your tclet happens to be about the size of a postage stamp, you're all set. Otherwise, figure out how large you want the tclet to appear, and then add the HEIGHT and WIDTH attributes to size your tclet appropriately.

Setting the Tclet's MIME Type

Sometimes, it's a good idea to specify the MIME *(Multipurpose Internet Mail Extensions)* type of the tclet in the HTML code. The *MIME type* specification tells the browser that the embedded tclet *is* a tclet, and not some other type of file, such as a video clip or a Java applet. The tclet's MIME type has nothing to do with Marcel Marceau.

In theory, your Web server software recognizes that the tclet is a tclet by the tell-tale .tcl filename extension and passes this information along to the Web browser. Also in theory, the browser recognizes the .tcl extension in the filename (just in case the server isn't on the ball). The browser then knows to load the Tcl/Tk plug-in when it recognizes an incoming tclet. In the real world, sometimes neither the server nor the browser seems to recognize a tclet as a tclet, and then it's up to you, the intrepid Web page creator, to set things straight.

You can specify the MIME type of the tclet by adding the `TYPE` parameter to the `<EMBED>` tag, like this:

```
<embed src = "ratso.tcl" type = "application/x-tcl"
height = 100 width = 100>
```

Not surprisingly, `application/x-tcl` is a unique MIME type used only for tclets. You should add this parameter to your tag if your tclets just don't seem to load properly when you test your Web pages.

The very early versions of the Tcl/Tk plug-in for Mac OS configured Netscape Navigator to look for `tcl`, not `.tcl` at the end of tclet files. As a result, you may have trouble loading tclets stored as local files on a Mac — unless you add the `TYPE` parameter to the `<EMBED>` tag.

Passing Parameters to the Tclet

Sometimes, you may want to pass information between the Web page and the tclet. For example:

- ✔ You want to use the same tclet on several different pages on your Web site (or even on several different sites), but you want to add some customization to each individual tclet without creating several different versions of the code.

- ✔ You want to update parts of the tclet regularly, but you don't want to rewrite the tclet's source code every time that you update the part that changes.

- ✔ You want to distribute your tclet to team members who understand HTML but not Tcl/Tk, and you still want to give such users a way to control the tclet's behavior.

- ✔ The tclet may be on a page that contains some reader-specific information, and you want the tclet to use this information in its routines.

Parameter-passing syntax

The Tcl/Tk plug-in is very flexible about what you pass to a tclet as a parameter. In fact, you can send any message (or any number of messages) to the tclet using the `<EMBED>` tag, like so:

```
<embed "first name" = Tim>

<embed name = "Alex Francis" rank = "graduate student">

<embed x = 100 y = -100 z = 25>
```

As you can see, the general syntax is simply `name = value`. Both the parameter's name and value may consist of more than one word. Names or values that consist of a string of words (like `first name` and `graduate student` in the preceding examples) must be grouped together with double quotes.

The Tcl/Tk plug-in passes these parameters to the tclet in a special array called `embed_args`. (You find out more about arrays and how to handle them in Chapter 5.) Each parameter name is stored as an index of the `embed_args` array, and the corresponding parameter value is stored as the corresponding array value. The parameters passed to the tclet in the first two examples in the preceding code will show up in the `embed_args` array like this:

```
embed_args(first name) == Tim

embed_args(name) == Alex Francis

embed_args(rank) == Graduate Student
```

Note: All the parameters in the `<EMBED>` tag are put into the `embed_args` array, including the `SRC`, `HEIGHT`, `WIDTH`, and MIME type parameters that you read about in earlier sections of this chapter.

Customizing a tclet with parameter information

After the parameter has been passed to the tclet, you can do anything you want with the tclet by grabbing the parameter from the `embed_args` array.

Suppose that you're designing a tclet for a large Web site, with customized pages for each of the site's subscribers. You want to put a message with the user's name (like "Hello, Ratso" for a user named "Ratso") at the top of the tclet's frame, and perhaps elsewhere in the tclet. You also want to write the tclet just once and then have your assistant customize the tclet for each page (via the `<EMBED>` tag) while you sip martinis and listen to old Miles Davis records.

Here's how it works in the HTML code:

```
<embed src = "custom.tcl" height = 100 width = 200 name =
          Ratso>
```

(Assuming, of course, that this is Ratso's page. In general, you put the name of the page's owner in the page parameter.) In the tclet, you can get at the stuff in the `<EMBED>` tag by accessing the ready-made variable `embed_args`. Simply reference the `embed_args` array with standard array handling, like so:

```
label .l -text "Hello, $embed_args(name) "
pack .l
```

The tclet substitutes the name parameter's value in the label, as shown in Figure 4-1. (Don't worry too much about what's going on here — it all becomes clear in a chapter or two.) If you (or your assistant) change the NAME parameter's value in the HTML's <EMBED> tag, the tclet displays a new message, even though the tclet itself remains untouched. Passing this kind of information to your tclet via the <EMBED> tag, rather than hard-coding it into your tclet, makes the tclet more flexible and makes your job easier.

Figure 4-1:
This tclet displays the contents of the <EMBED> tag.

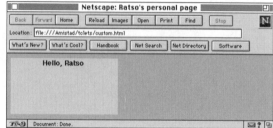

Store the vodka in the freezer before you make the martinis. I prefer *Miles Smiles,* but *Nefertiti* and *ESP* are good, too.

Making an inventory of the tclet's parameters

Figuring out how parameters work is pretty easy. But sometimes things just get weird, and the tag doesn't pass the name or value that you thought you entered. For these special occasions, write a little diagnostic tclet, called feedback.tcl, which simply displays all the parameters passed to the tclet in a little list box in the browser window. You can use feedback.tcl to *debug* (find and remove the problems in) the <EMBED> tag and make sure that you wrote the HTML for the <EMBED> tag correctly.

You don't need to worry about how this tclet works — after all, you haven't started your basic instruction in theTcl/Tk language yet! You can just enter the following HTML code into your source code editor and put it on your Web page. Alternatively, you can just grab the following code off this book's CD-ROM. You will find this code in the Projects/Chapter 5/feedback.tcl folder (although it's always good to practice typing Tcl/Tk code).

```
# loop through array and find values of embedded args
foreach this_arg [array names embed_args] {
    set my_list [lappend my_list "$this_arg =
            $embed_args($this_arg)"]
}

#sort my_list
set my_list [lsort -ascii $my_list]

#create the listbox widget
listbox .lb -width 100

#copy the list into the listbox widget
foreach ctr $my_list {
    .lb insert end $ctr
}

#pack  the listbox
pack .lb
```

Figure 4-2 shows how `feedback.tcl` displays the parameters for the tag used in the HTML file that contains the code.

Figure 4-2:
feedback.tcl
is a tclet that
double-
checks the
contents of
the HTML
`<EMBED>`
tag.

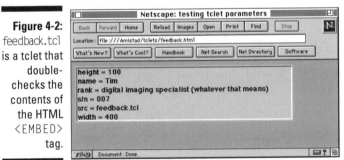

```
<embed src ="feedback.tcl" width = 400 height = 100 name =
            "Tim" rank = "digital imaging specialist (what-
            ever that means)" s/n = "007">
```

The `feedback.tcl` tclet builds a simple table that shows the names and values of the attributes of the `<EMBED>` tag that puts the tclet on the page. If you set up the `<EMBED>` tag properly, you'll see each tag attribute, followed by the value that you gave it in, like so:

```
rank = digital imaging specialist
```

If you see only part of an entry, like this

```
rank = digital
```

or one of the entries is missing completely, go back and double-check the `<EMBED>` tag, paying special attention to the quote marks.

Variations on `feedback.tcl`

The little `feedback.tcl` tclet spends most of its energy making sure that each parameter has its own line in the display and that the parameters are in alphabetical order. If you're feeling lazy and you don't especially care how the parameters appear on-screen, you can simply dump the whole `embed_args` array into a message box, like this:

```
message .m -text [array get
        embed_args]
pack .m
```

It's not pretty, but it does the job.

Part II
Language Reference

The 5th Wave   By Rich Tennant

©RICHTENNANT

"What is it Lassie? Is it Gramps? Is it his hard disk? Is he stuck somewhere, girl? Is he trying to write CGI programs to a Unix server running VRML? What, girl, what?!"

In this part . . .

Tcl/Tk is a programming language, and, like all languages, Tcl/Tk has grammar. In this part, you look at the most important and most useful parts of Tcl/Tk syntax. You figure out how to put Tcl/Tk words together into sentences called *commands*. You even pick up a thing or two about joining small commands into larger commands, just as you join phrases to form compound sentences in English.

You start with Tcl/Tk "nouns" and "verbs" — variables and commands — and go from there to a discussion of the heart of Tcl/Tk, the topic known as *substitution and grouping*. You also learn a bit about basic programming constructs and tools such as loops, conditionals, strings, lists, and procedures.

Chapter 5

Basic Building Blocks: Commands and Variables

● ●

In This Chapter

▶ Understanding commands

▶ Adding arguments to commands

▶ Deciphering online documentation

▶ Finding out about scalar variables

▶ Understanding array variables

● ●

*T*he basic building blocks of tclets (and computer programs in general) are *commands.* Commands are easy to construct in Tcl. *Commands* are lists of "words" that include the command name, and they may also include options and arguments for the command. You store the information used in a program in *variables.* Tcl/Tk supports two variable types: *scalars,* which contain a single value, and *associative arrays,* which can contain many indexed values.

As it turns out, Tcl/Tk is a pretty relaxed language. It contains only a few dozen basic built-in commands, a simple system for specifying variables, and one rule for building a line of correct Tcl/Tk code. In this chapter, you'll learn how to construct commands, and store information in variables using data-handling commands. You will use Wish as a laboratory, typing commands at the Wish prompt, so that you can see just what each command does.

A line of Tcl/Tk code is something like an English sentence. An English sentence can contain nouns, adjectives, and other parts of speech, but it must contain a verb (which describes the action or state of being that the sentence describes) and most contain nouns (which indicate the things or ideas the the sentence describes). A line of Tcl code can contain many different kinds of things but it much contain a command (which describes the action that the line of code requests) and most lines of code contain variables, which are names for data and other "things."

What Are Commands?

The basic building blocks of any application in any language — from a terse little one-line tclet to an industrial-strength commercial application like Adobe Photoshop — are the instructions that you give the language. Different languages have different instruction sets, but the idea is always the same: Your instructions tell the computer what to do.

In Tcl, the basic unit of instruction is the *command*. A command is just a line of Tcl/Tk code that tells the Tcl/Tk interpreter — whether that interpreter is part of the Tcl/Tk plug-in or part of Wish — to do something. The commands that you use in this chapter are built into the Tcl/Tk language. Later, you find out how to create your own commands by writing them in Tcl/Tk code.

So . . . start out your survey of Tcl/Tk with an introduction to the syntax of commands. You've breezed through a few basic commands in the introductory chapters without really taking a look at how commands are assembled or how they work. Now, friends, it's time for the nitty gritty.

Rather than entering the commands in a text file and then running them through the Tcl/Tk plug-in, I suggest using Wish to try the commands in this chapter, but you can use either approach. When you type the command into Wish, you get instant feedback (but if you use the plug-in, you need to take several extra steps before you see the results of your experiments).

The anatomy of a command

The basic unit of the Tcl/Tk language is the *word*. What's a word? Either a bunch of alphanumeric characters run together without spaces, like

```
asaphoetida
```

or like

```
a1sdf23ff999
```

or a word is a bunch of characters *including* spaces that are grouped together with quotes or other characters, like this:

```
"asaphoetida 123"
```

Things to remember when designing a new programming language

✔ A set of built-in commands, which compilers and interpreters understand and translate into machine instructions

✔ A system for the programmers to define variables — that is, a way to name information so that you have a way to talk about it in the program

✔ A set of rules for stringing words together into commands

✔ A system for programmers to define new commands, using the commands that are already in the language

Not every command uses each of the following components, but Tcl/Tk commands are created from these essential parts. Take a look at each of these parts in turn; then after a brief explanation of what the term *word* means in Tcl/Tk, you can see how to put parts together into commands.

Three basic parts can go into a Tcl/Tk command:

✔ command names

✔ command options

✔ command arguments

These parts are ordered as in the following code:

```
command-name option argument#1 argument#2 ... last-argument
```

Italicized words in example code are *placeholders,* which you replace with something else. For example, you do not enter command-name as an actual command; rather, you substitute a command name, such as set, for the word command-name in the sample code. When you see a hyphenated, italicized word (for example, command-name), you can "swap in" a single word. (You don't need to swap in a word with a hyphen.)

Here's one more important part of the command that you do not type when you write the command: the *result* of the command. When the interpreter executes a command, it *returns* a *value* as a result. Sometimes, the result is nothing more than a string with no characters, which is for all practical purposes, nothing. However, it's more correct to say "the result was nothing" than to say "there was no result." (This difference can be compared to the difference between having a bank account with a zero balance and not having a bank account at all.)

Interpreting the command synopsis

The most mysterious-looking part of Tcl/Tk's standard documentation is the command *synopsis*. Don't be intimidated — the synopsis is just a standard way to formally specify the elements required to properly construct a line of correct Tcl/Tk code from a particular Tcl/Tk command. This specification format is used in the HTML documentation that's distributed with Tcl/Tk, in the Tcl/Tk *man pages* (manual pages that are distributed with Tcl/Tk on UNIX platforms) and in other forms of online documentation.

The synopsis wraps up all optional parts of the command in a pair of question marks. For example, the synopsis of the `history` command is

```
history ?option? ?arg arg ...?
```

As you can see, the word `option` is enclosed within a pair of question marks, so it's possible, but not necessary, to add an option to the `history` command. The phrase `arg arg ...` indicates that the command can take more than one argument, and the fact that this part is enclosed with another set of question marks indicates that the arguments, too, are optional. Thus, you can use the `history` command as a single word, like this:

```
history
```

You can also write the `history` command with an option, but with no arguments. The following option causes the command to return the number that will be used to label the next command entered into the Wish session:

```
history nextid
```

Or you can add both an option and arguments to the `history` command. In the following example, `history` reexecutes the command that is numbered with the value in the argument, that is, `commandnumber 1`:

```
history redo 1
```

This system for specifying the structure of Tcl/Tk commands is also used by the Tcl/Tk interpreters in Wish and the Tcl/Tk plug-in when it reports a problem figuring out a line of code. Just remember the basic idea — optional parts of the command are wrapped up in question marks — and you'll find it fairly easy to figure out what the interpreter is trying to tell you if you receive the infamous `wrong # args` error message.

Command names

The name of the command is the most important part of the command. Without the name, the Tcl/Tk interpreter will not know what you want it to do. A command's name is always one word and always the first word in the sequence of words that makes up the total command.

Note: I'm going to cover just the basic, need-to-know command names in this book. Some commands aren't necessary for building Web-based tclets, and some commands are just too esoteric for beginning programmers.

The following Tcl/Tk commands are perfectly valid, even though they consist of nothing more than the command's name. You can try typing these commands into Wish to see what happens when you enter them:

```
beep
history
pwd
```

Yes, beep simply makes the computer beep, or chime, or say "Warning, Will Robinson!" (depending on how you have your system's sounds set up). The history command prints every line that you type into the current Wish session. If you've used UNIX, you may recognize the pwd command, which stands for *print working directory*. The pwd command returns the name of the directory that Wish was last asked to display.

For security reasons, the Tcl/Tk plug-in doesn't support the beep command, even though Wish does. Ringing your system's bell won't hurt your machine (or even wear out your speakers), but it's well known that a few dozen beeps in quick succession can drive you completely nuts. The plug-in's security policies are set up to protect you from this kind of annoyance. If you put beep into a tclet, the command won't work, Likewise, the history command, which gives information about a Wish session, doesn't work in the plug-in environment.

Command options

As you may suspect, single-word commands aren't very flexible, and most built-in Tcl/Tk commands can't stand on their own as a naked command name. You can, however, customize many commands with *options* that give the interpreter more detailed instructions about what you want the command to do.

For example, take a look at the clock command, which returns the current time. Of course, you can list the current time many different ways. Using ordinary English (rather than a programming language), I can describe the time that I'm writing this chapter in one of the following ways:

- ✔ Saturday, July 2, 1997 at 3:00 p.m.

- ✔ Three o'clock on 7/2/97

- ✔ 1500 hours, 2 July '97

- ✔ The hour of the weasel, day of the jackal, hunter's moon, year of the wombat. (Actually, I'm not so sure about this last one.)

To deliver the time in a way that's consistent and easy to process, clock commands in many computer languages return the time as one big number — specifically, the time that has elapsed since midnight on January 1, 1904. Though a little awkward on a wristwatch, when you're programming, it's much easier to manipulate one big number than to process a collection of letters, numbers, and other characters that are all mixed together.

Now if you simply enter the command clock into Wish, Wish returns an error message, like this:

```
% clock
% wrong # args: should be "clock option ?arg ...?"
```

This error message is the interpreter's way of telling you that it can't read your mind and it's not sure exactly what you want the clock command to do. To get a return from clock, you must specify an option that tells the interpreter how you want the results formatted.

For example, let's get the current time, reckoned in the number of seconds since the 1904 zero hour. When you enter clock seconds at the Wish prompt, Wish returns something like:

```
% clock seconds
2930397915
```

Unless you travel back in time to the exact moment I'm writing this, you *won't* get the same number. If you *can* travel back in time, you probably don't need to master Tcl/Tk to impress your friends.

Alternatively, you can ask Wish for the number of *clicks* since the zero hour. Clicks are a time unit based on the computer's processor speed — the faster the machine, the more clicks are contained in a minute. To get the current time in clicks, you can enter clock clicks. I love this command, just for the goofy sound of it, and I use it as often as possible. When you enter this command into Wish, you get something like the following:

```
% clock clicks
4277753567
```

Options are part of the built-in command: You can specify *only* options that the command recognizes, no matter how sensible other options may seem. Available options are built into each command. For example, if you enter clock minutes, the interpreter returns an error message because minutes is not built onto the clock command as a valid option.

Command arguments

Using options to fine-tune commands offers a little more flexibility than using single-word commands, but doing so still doesn't allow you to customize the command to handle your particular data. Command arguments, on the other hand, allow you to feed a command any data you like, and the command processes whatever data you give it. Take a look at the expr command, which evaluates mathematical expressions like 1 + 1 or sin (3.14/2). The expr command doesn't have options, but you can't just enter

```
expr
```

at the Wish prompt. There's no formula for `expr` to evaluate, right? Therefore, you must add an *argument* to the command — that is, information that the command can process, manipulate, or use in some way. Unlike options, arguments aren't built into the command — you can pass whatever information you want to the command. For example, all the following are valid `expr` commands:

```
expr 1 + 1
expr sin (3.14/2)
expr (sin (3.14/2) * 100)
```

In the first example, the argument of the command is the mathematical expression `1 + 1`. In the second example, the argument is `sin(3.14/2)`, and in the third example, the argument is `sin (3.14/2) * 100`.

Clearly, every possible mathematical expression can't be built into the basic `expr` command as an option — the Tcl/Tk crew would still be working on the arithmetic options if they had to hard-code every operation as an option.

What *is* built into the command is an expectation about what kind of information the parameter contains. For example, the `expr` command handles mathematical expressions, and if you pass it arguments like `expr 1 + fish`, the command returns an error message. This is not to say that all arguments must be mathematical expressions; however, you can use numbers as arguments, like

```
incr 15
```

or words, like

```
lsort apple banana cherry
```

Giving a command the wrong kind of data to play with always causes the interpreter to stop and ask you just what you were thinkin'.

Recognizing Tcl/Tk words

The use of the term *word* in the context of Tcl/Tk commands is a little bit different from the use of *word* in the context of human language. A word is simply a bunch of alphanumeric characters without spaces or a bunch of characters with spaces that are grouped together using special characters.

Combinations not found in English (or any human language)

Any string of characters that isn't interrupted by spaces is deemed a *word* in Tcl/Tk. All the following examples are Tcl/Tk words:

```
x
.x
.x1
cthulu
my_variable
the_wreck_of_the_edmund_fitzgerald
```

For that matter, almost any single character is a word in Tcl. The only characters that can't stand alone are the following:

```
"
\
{
[
```

These characters have special tasks to perform, as you see in the next few pages.

Grouped and substituted material

Two of the most important concepts in Tcl/Tk are grouping and substitution (which are covered in detail in Chapter 6). You can group several words together in several different ways so that the Tcl/Tk interpreter treats them as though they are a single word. You can also specify that certain parts of the command be replaced by new stuff when the command is executed. (This isn't nearly as esoteric as it sounds, and you find the specifics in Chapter 6.)

- ✔ **Curly braces:** Such as in {ram a lang a ding dong}
- ✔ **Double quotes:** Such as in "fee fi fo fum"
- ✔ **Square bracket:** Such as in [clock clicks]

Each character has its own special use. Here's a thumbnail description of each character's function:

Items between curly braces. When an item is wrapped within a pair of curly braces, the item counts as a single word, no matter what other characters are inside the curly braces. The following items are single words in Tcl/Tk syntax:

- ✔ {ram a lang a ding dong}
- ✔ {Carl "the nightstalker" Kolchak}
- ✔ {yabba dibba [sic] doo}

Items between double quotes. In the same way, items wrapped within a pair of double quotes are counted as a single word. The following are single words for purposes of forming Tcl/Tk commands:

✔ `"fee fi fo fum"`

✔ `"are you getting the hang of this?"`

Items between square brackets. Finally, items between square brackets count as a single word in a Tcl/Tk command, and they must be Tcl/Tk commands, too. The following are valid single words:

✔ `[clock clicks]`

✔ `[message .m -text "yabba dibba [sic] doo"]`

✔ `[expr 1 + 1]`

Constructing commands

You have a simple model for constructing valid Tcl/Tk commands: A command is a list of words separated by spaces or tabs. The first word is always a command name. That's it — really! Tcl/Tk is meant to be super-simple. Punctuation marks and other symbols like brackets, braces, and parentheses are always part of words rather than independent players in the command.

Note: Punctuation acts in a special way in three situations, and you may have already seen them in Chapter 4. Any guesses? If you guessed the # symbol, which marks comments when at the beginning of a line, the semicolon (;), which marks the end of a command, and \, which allows a command to continue on the next line, you are the winner. (Maybe # and \ aren't really punctuation, but they really aren't anything else, either.)

A Tcl/Tk command is structured as shown in the following code:

```
command-name option argument1 argument 2 . . .
```

Every built-in command uses a different set of options and arguments. Some commands require that you specify options, some require that you provide an argument, and many require both. Very often, commands allow for optional arguments or options that you can add as needed. The following examples are legal Tcl/Tk commands. Here are diagrams of each command with its basic component parts:

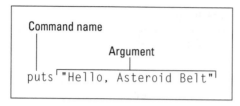

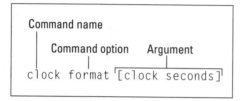

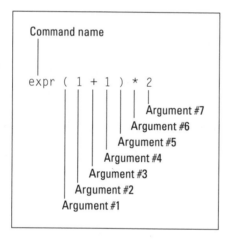

You have no a magical way to determine which options and arguments a particular command needs. When you can't remember the format of a command, you have two basic techniques at your disposal:

✔ Look it up

✔ Trial and error

Wish is distributed with complete documentation of Tcl/Tk in HTML format, so it's easy to find the "official answer," even if you're working on a laptop in Siberia. However, sometimes it's easy to guess what kinds of options and arguments a command is expecting.

Reading the documentation

The most recent version of the HTML-based Tcl/Tk documentation uses a separate HTML document for each command that Wish and the Tcl/Tk plug-in supports. Each documentation page includes all the basic information that you need to create a command:

- ✔ The command's name
- ✔ A synopsis of option and argument usage for the command
- ✔ Detailed descriptions of the command's options, if any
- ✔ Descriptions of the arguments used by the command
- ✔ Sample commands, with example arguments

To read a command's documentation, drag the documentation file from the documentation folder in the Wish distribution onto your favorite Web browser.

What Are Variables?

Hard-coding all the arguments (that is, putting in fixed values, like 12 or "Hello, Mars") is limiting. What if you want to use a value that needs to be calculated somewhere else in the program or you want to accept user input and then use that input as the argument to a command?

Enter the *variable.* You can think of a variable as a place to store information. A variable can store numbers, strings, lists of numbers or strings, or even more complex structures. You can alter the information stored in a variable whenever you want and recall its value whenever you need it.

Some languages, like C, C++, and Java, are pretty picky about variables. Each variable must be declared with a special command before you can use it, and any one variable can store only one kind of information. In fact, you need different kinds of variables to store different kinds of numbers. For example, an *integer* variable (which stores numbers such as 1, 2, or 3) can't hold *floating-point* numbers (such as 1.0, 2.0, or 3.0). You certainly can't store something like a string of characters (such as "fish" or "axolotyl") in a variable that is set up for integers.

By comparison, Tcl/Tk is a very easy-going language. Tcl/Tk really contains only two kinds of variables:

- ✔ **Scalars:** Can contain numbers (of all sorts) and strings.
- ✔ **Associative arrays:** Also just called *arrays* or sometimes called *hashes.* Can contain lists that have been indexed with numbers or any other indexing system that you can think up.

You can name a variable just about anything in Tcl; but by convention, variable names are usually a single word. The variable's name describes what the variable is supposed to contain. For example, if you create a variable that holds a random number, you'd probably name the variable randomNumber or random_number.

Using scalars to store information

Scalars are the basic kind of variable available in Tcl. Scalars store information like numbers and strings that don't need to have any sort of internal ordering. All the following examples are legal scalar values:

- 1
- 1.0
- one
- "one of these days, I'm going to look up scalar in the dictionary"

If that last entry looks like a list of words — and hence a list — it is. You can store a list in a scalar variable, and theTcl/Tk interpreter treats it as a list whenever appropriate. I told you Tcl/Tk is an easy-going kind of interpreter.

Remember our discussion of words? A word isn't a data type: It's merely a convention for grouping the parts of a command into logical units so that you can say things like "the second word of the command" without ambiguity. Words can contain any kind of data type: strings, numbers, lists, or whatever.

Setting and retrieving scalars

The basic command for storing information in a scalar is the set command. The command goes like this:

```
set variable-name new-value
```

So, to set a variable called my_number to the value 12, type

```
set my_number 12
```

To look at the value of a scalar after it is set, use the set command without adding the new-value argument, like this:

```
set my_number
```

Wish returns the current value of the variable, as in the following code:

```
% set my_number
12
```

You can use a scalar variable as an argument in a command; however, you must use *variable substitution* to cause the command to use the value of the variable rather than the name of the variable in the command.

Here's how this works. Suppose that you want to multiply the value of my_number by 2. Your first attempt may be something like this:

```
expr my_number * 2
```

This code structure is almost right, and it's the way that variables are handled in many common other programming languages. However, Tcl/Tk interprets this code as an instruction to "multiple the *string* my_number by 2" (rather than "multiply the *contents of the variable* my_number by 2"). Of course, the first example is a nonsensical request, so the interpreter returns an error message.

To instruct Tcl/Tk to use the *value* of the variable rather than the *name* of the variable, you add a dollar sign to the front of the variable's name, as shown in the following example:

```
% expr $my_number * 2
24
```

The little dollar sign makes all the difference! Now the interpreter knows to use the value of the variable rather than the variable's name when evaluating the command.

Note: You look at variable substitution a little more closely in the next chapter. Substitution is affected by grouping, and works differently inside different kinds of braces and brackets, even though each brace or bracket groups things into words in the same way.

Changing data types

The great thing about Tcl/Tk scalars is that they freely transform themselves into the appropriate data type. For example, when you last left my_number, it was the number 24, right? However, if you treat the number like a string — the character 2 followed by the character 4, Tcl/Tk follows suit. Observe:

```
% set my_phrase "It's been $my_number months since I seen
        my pappy!"
It's been 24 months since I seen my pappy!
```

Using associative arrays to store information

Associative arrays are a way of storing data that's organized as an indexed list. In many languages, arrays use numbers — and only numbers — to index the array. In Tcl/Tk, the array can use anything at all for indexing — numbers, strings, or any combination thereof.

Suppose that you want to create an array variable that contains basic information about a music CD. You may set up categories like this:

- ✔ Title
- ✔ Artist
- ✔ Category
- ✔ Stars

Call this array CD_info. To refer to the members of the array, use the array's name with the categories (or *indices*) in parenthesis after the name, like this:

```
set CD_info(title) "The Shape of Jazz to Come"
set CD_info(artist) "Ornette Coleman"
set CD_info(category) "Jazz"
set CD_info(stars) 5
```

Make sure that there's no space between the array's name and the left parenthesis.

You can retrieve the values using the same techniques that you use with scalar variables. Use the set command without a new value argument, like

```
set CD_info(title) "The Shape of Jazz to Come"
```

Likewise, you can use variable substitution in the same way that you do with scalar variables:

```
message .m -text "$CD_info(artist)"
pack .m
```

Tcl/Tk also provides the array command, which provides some special tools for manipulating arrays. For example, the gets option causes the array command to display the entire contents of the array, pairing each index with its value:

```
% array get CD_info
stars 5 category Jazz title {The Shape of Jazz to Come}
          artist {Ornette Coleman}
```

Similarly, when the array command is used with the names option, it returns the names of all the indices in the array:

```
% array names cd_info
stars category title artist
```

The size option causes the array command to return the number of indices in the array.

```
% array names cd_info
stars category title artist
```

In Chapter 7, where you look at looping constructs, you see how you can put this kind of information to use.

Chapter 6

The Olde Switcheroo: Substitutions and Grouping

*A*lrighty now, intrepid explorers . . . you have reached the inner sanctum of Tcl/Tk. Substitution and grouping are at the very heart of programming in Tcl. After you understand how substitution and grouping work, you have a firm grip on the rest of this book and on programming with Tcl/Tk. This chapter is really *the* most important chapter in the whole book. *Substitution and grouping* are the techniques that you use to put simple parts into complex instructions. Read carefully, type lots of code into Wish, and then try your code in mini-tclets.

Creating Substitutions

The basic idea behind substitution is pretty simple: Substitution is like using a kind of verbal shorthand in a natural language. For example, suppose that you write a note to yourself that says, "Call the landlord about the leaky ceiling." When you get around to calling your landlord, rather than look up the words "the landlord" in your phone book, you call a particular person with a particular name.

Or sometimes you can substitute the results of an action in a real-world setting. For example, if you ask someone to address an envelope with the address of the building that's on the corner of first and Main, that person doesn't write "the address of the building on the corner of First and Main" (unless she is a philosophy major). Instead, she looks up the address of the building you're looking for and then writes something like "100 Main Street." In this case, your friend substitutes the results of the command ("look up the address") for the command.

You can instruct the Tcl/Tk interpreter to perform similar types of substitutions in your tclets. The interpreter can replace designated parts of your Tcl/Tk command with the value of a variable (or the results of a command). You must explicitly instruct the interpreter to perform these substitutions, and you do so by marking the material to be swapped with special characters, which are described in the following sections.

Technically, three kinds of substitution exist in Tcl:

- ✔ Variable substitution
- ✔ Command substitution
- ✔ Backslash substitution

You find out about variable substitution and command substitution in this section. Backslash substitution doesn't quite seem to perform the same kinds of tasks as the other two, so I cover backslash substitution in its own section at the end of this chapter.

Performing variable substitution by using the dollar sign

Variable substitution swaps in (or substitutes) the value of the variable in place of the variable's name in a Tcl/Tk command. Most often, you will use variable substitution to look at the value of a variable, but sometimes, you will use it to change your commands as they are interpreted.

Basic syntax

Suppose that you set up a variable called `my_landlord` and give it the value `Mark`.

```
set my_landlord Mark
```

When you want the Tcl/Tk interpreter to use variable substitution to swap in the variable's value in place of the variable's name, you must put a dollar sign ($) at the front of the variable's name, like so:

```
message .m -text $my_landlord
pack .m
```

(The use of `message` and `pack` are described in detail in Chapter 2.)

When the Tcl/Tk interpreter sees the variable substitution marker (the dollar sign), the interpreter swaps in the value of the variable and then executes the command, as shown in the following code:

```
message .m -text Mark
pack .m
```

The interpreter has simply swapped in the *value* of the variable named `my_landlord` for `$my_landlord`. Without the dollar sign at the front of the variable's name, this swap won't take place.

Be sure to make good use of the dollar sign. The single easiest mistake to make when you write a Tcl/Tk program is forgetting to add the dollar sign when you reference a variable's value. It's especially easy to forget if you've spent a lot of time programming in other languages that don't use this convention. When you're trying to fix a tclet that doesn't work, one of the first things you should check is the proper use of the dollar sign.

Variable substitution isn't limited to swapping whole words for whole words, nor is it limited to any particular part of a Tcl/Tk command. You can perform variable substitution *anywhere* in the command. Watch this:

```
set x age
```

Now that the variable `x` has the value `age`, you can use variable substitution to swap the string `age` in the middle of a word. For example, take a look at the following code:

```
.message .m2 -text saus$x
pack .m
```

The interpreter reads the preceding code as

```
.message .m2 -text sausage
pack .m
```

In fact, you can perform this type of substitution inside the command name. When the interpreter sees

```
.mess$x .m3 -text "bacon"
pack .m3
```

The interpreter performs the substitution and evaluates the command, as shown in

```
.message .m3 -text "bacon"
pack .m3
```

You might use this kind of substitution when you're working with a bunch of similarly-named widgets, and you want to do something to each widget in turn. Say you want to create a series of message widgets named .m1, .m2, .m3, and so on, and you have created an index variable called current that you want to use to keep track of the widget that you're working on. If you set current to 1, like so

```
set current 1
```

you can create the widget .m1 by using variable substitution:

```
message .m$current -text "message widget \
number $current"
```

Since the value of current is 1, the interpreter makes the substitution

```
message .m1 -text "message widget number  1"
```

If the value of current were set to 2, the interpreter would use the substitution:

```
message .m2 -text "message widget number  2"
```

Thus, you can use the same line of code over and over again to create a series of different widgets; all you need to do is change the value of current before you re-use the code. (You'll see this technique applied in Chapter 7, which covers looping constructs — commands that are executed repeatedly.)

Limits on variable substitution

The variable substitution game has an interesting and important rule: The interpreter makes only one pass through each command to perform substitutions, so you can't perform variable substitutions within variable substitutions. For example, suppose that you create a variable called twoparts, and give it the value 10:

```
set twoparts 10
```

Then you create two variables to store the variable's name in halves, like this:

```
set x two
set y parts
```

Now, if you use xy in a command, the interpreter swaps in two for $x and parts for $y, to yield twoparts. Suppose that you then put another dollar sign up front, as shown in the following code:

```
message .m4 -text $$x$y
```

You may expect this code to swap in twoparts for xy and then swap in 10 for $twoparts. Although this theory may seem to be a good one, in fact, the interpreter performs only one substitution. The message in the preceding sample line displays $twoparts rather than twoparts's value of 10.

Creating command substitutions by using square brackets

Suppose that you want to add two numbers and put the result in a variable. To do so, you can use the expr command to add numbers and the set command to store a number in a variable. But how do you combine these commands so that the results of one command are used in another command? You can combine these commands by using *command substitution*.

When the Tcl/Tk interpreter finds a Tcl/Tk command enclosed in square brackets ([ ]), the interpreter substitutes the results returned by the command in the brackets for the stuff in the brackets. Remember my real-world example at the beginning of this section? You ask a friend to put the address of the building on the corner of First and Main on the front of an envelope. If you try to render this instruction with Tcl/Tk command substitution, the composite instruction will look something like the following code:

```
put [find the address of the building on First and Main] on
           the front of the envelope
```

Of course, the preceding example isn't real Tcl/Tk code, but it's real Tcl/Tk command substitution syntax. The Tcl/Tk interpreter looks up the address and swaps it in for the bracketed material, like this:

```
put 100 Main Street on the front of the envelope
```

Here's how you apply command substitution with real Tcl/Tk code to add two numbers and put the results in a variable.

```
Set sum [expr 25 + 25]
```

In the preceding code, the Tcl/Tk interpreter first evaluates the little command in the brackets `[expr 25 + 25]` and swaps the result into the whole line of code, like so:

```
Set sum 50
```

The interpreter executes this command, which sets the value of `sum` to 50.

Naturally, the stuff between the brackets must be a legal Tcl/Tk command because the interpreter tries to execute the command that appears between the brackets in order to find a result to swap in. If the stuff between a pair of square brackets isn't a legal command, the interpreter generates an error message, just as it does when the bracketed material appears on a line by itself.

One common way to use command substitution in your Tcl/Tk code is to embed a widget-creating command inside a `pack` command. When you create a message widget with Wish, the interpreter returns as its result the name of the widget. You can take advantage of this feature to combine the command that creates the widget *and* the command that displays the widget into one line of code, as shown in the following example:

```
pack [message .m6 -text "Hello, Ganymede"]
```

When the Tcl/Tk interpreter processes this line, it first executes the little command between the square brackets:

```
message .m6 -text "Hello, Ganymede"
```

The little command does two things: It creates a message that can be viewed on-screen, and it returns a name that you can use to refer to the widget in your Tcl/Tk code. After substitution, the big command looks like this:

```
pack .m6
```

After substitution, the interpreter executes the big command, displaying the message on the screen.

You don't need to limit yourself to one level of substitution: Little commands inside square brackets can contain little commands within square brackets, too. Instead of `"Hello, Ganymede"`, you can add a different command substitution as the text of the message widget:

```
pack [message .m7 -text [expr 12 * 12]]
```

When the Tcl/Tk interpreter reads this command, it starts by evaluating the command in the innermost set of brackets, namely:

```
expr 12 * 12
```

Remember, `expr` evaluates mathematical expressions, so Tcl/Tk does the math and uses the result (144, the product of twelve times twelve) to replace the innermost set of brackets:

```
pack [message .m7 -text 144]
```

Next, the interpreter performs substitution on the remaining square brackets. This little command,

```
message .m7 -text 144
```

creates a message that can be displayed on-screen — a message with text that is simply the number 144. The `message` command also returns the name of the message that it created, `.m7`, and uses this result to replace the command within the brackets:

```
pack .m7
```

Now, that the interpreter has finished making its substitutions, it can interpret the command, and display the message on the screen.

You can embed command substitutions with as many layers as your imagination allows. Keep in mind, though, that stacking several commands in the same line of code makes figuring out what's going on in the tclet really hard. When you look at code with three or four levels of embedded substitutions six months after you write the code, you'll kick yourself. Hard.

Grouping Text

As you discover in Chapter 5, a Tcl/Tk command consists of a list of words. In most cases, any particular argument of a command should be a single word. For example, the `label` command, which creates a simple text label to be displayed in the tclet The following code creates a label that contains the single word *gesundheit!*

```
label .l -text gesundheit!
pack .l
```

This system is all very nice for creating terse, one-word text labels, but your tclet's users are going to think you're mighty inarticulate if you can't muster up a phrase or a sentence every once in a while.

The secret to displaying more than one word in a label or, in general, making Tcl/Tk treat a group of words as one "word," is called *grouping*. As you see in Chapter 7, what you, as a speaker of a human language consider a word and what the Tcl/Tk interpreter considers a word are two completely different things. (My wife, who is a linguist, has a third, completely different notion of what a word is.) In Tcl, when you group words with curly braces or quotes, the whole shebang is considered a word when the interpreter is counting the number of words in the command. Thus, the following are all words, so far as Tcl/Tk is concerned:

- gesundheit!
- "gesundheit!"
- {bless you!}
- "bless you!"
- {pass the Kleenex, please}

Using this system, you can rewrite the label code with whatever text you want. Both

```
.label .12 -text {bless you!}
```

and

```
.label .13 -text "bless you!"
```

are correct.

I know your next question. If curly braces and double quotes both perform grouping, what's the difference between them? When should you use curly braces, and when should you use double quotes?

The short answer: When you group words by using curly braces, no substitutions can take place inside the braces. When you group words by using double quotes, you can perform substitution on the code that appears within the double quotes. Take a look at each of these two kinds of groupings in the following sections, and see what these differences mean in practical terms.

Grouping text by using curly braces

When you put stuff between a pair of curly braces, no substitutions of any kind take place between the braces. No variable substitutions, no command substitutions — the string appears exactly as you type it. (The curly braces themselves are discarded.)

Breaking quoted material across lines

Curly braces can swallow up everything between them and group all the code into a single word. I do mean everything, including breaks at the ends of lines. Code such as the following (with poetry swiped from Mr. T.S. Eliot's poem, "Gerontion") is perfectly legal Tcl:

```
set poem {Think
Neither fear nor courage saves
   us. Unnatural vices
Are fathered by our heroism.
   Virtues
Are forced upon us by our impu-
   dent crimes.}
```

From the interpreter's point of view, this whole command is *one line of code,* which is three words long (set, poem, and everything that appears between the curly braces). The interpreter considers the invisible line breaks after Think, vices, and Virtues to be part of the giant Tcl/Tk *word* between the curly braces — the line breaks are not end of line characters and not separators of commands.

In the following little tclet, you set some variables to see curly braces in action. The resulting labels are shown in Figure 6-1. You can see that the contents of the brackets appear in the string without any substitution.

```
set a {Can you buy a decent cigar for $1?}
set b {I like those macarena [sic] cigars}
set c {{After a good cigar, I like to nest curly braces
          inside each other }}

# pack labels, using variables a, b, and c as text strings
pack [label .l4 -text $a]
pack [label .l5 -text $b]
pack [label .l6 -text $c]
```

However, if you enter the first line of the preceding example code with double quotes rather than curly braces, as in the following example:

```
set a "Can you buy a decent cigar for $1?"
```

the interpreter assumes that you want to substitute $1 with *the value of the variable named* 1. As Dr. Freud said, "sometimes a cigar is just a cigar," and in this particular text string, $1 simply means *one dollar.* When we use the curly brackets to group the phrase,

```
{Can you buy a decent cigar for $1?}
```

the interpreter understands that the dollar sign is a dollar sign and not a request for variable substitution.

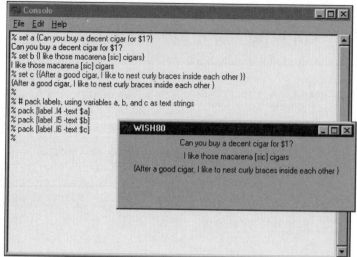

Figure 6-1:
This simple
tclet was
built by
packing a
series
of label
widgets.

Similarly, the interpreter does not handle the second line of code very gracefully if the text string is grouped with double quotes:

```
set b "I like those macarena [sic] cigars"
```

In this case, the interpreter tries to execute sic as a command. In this example, however, [sic] is an editorial comment, not a command for the interpreter to execute. (Tcl/Tk doesn't have a built-in command called sic, anyway, just in case you were wondering.) When the interpreter tries to evaluate the preceding line of code, it will return an error that tells you that *sic* is an unrecognized command.

Again, curly braces come to the rescue. When the phrase is wrapped up in curlies

```
{I like those macarena [sic] cigars}
```

the interpreter treats the special characters [and] as ordinary square brackets rather than as a request for command substitution.

Curly braces are used to group material into a single word. No substitutions take place inside the quoted material.

TECHNICAL STUFF

Brace Yourself

When you write procedures and fancy structures in Tcl/Tk that look like

```
procedure happy_answer {} {
    return "I'm sure glad to be a
    procedure!"
}
```

or like

```
if {1 == 1} {
    pack [label .1 -text "yes, one
    still equals one"]
}
```

you are taking advantage of the no-substitutions feature of curly braces. Every command in Tcl/Tk is just a bunch of words — Tcl/Tk words, that is — and the braces are there just to provide grouping. They're not part of the command itself.

Remember, Tcl/Tk uses the invisible end-of-line character to tell where a command ends. If that invisible end-of-line character is inside a pair of curlies, the end-of-line character isn't treated as a sign that the command is over; instead, the character is treated as just another character, like everything else inside curlies. Only a naked end-of-line outside a pair of curlies can indicate that a command is finished.

Grouping text by using double quotes

When you group words with a pair of double quotes, you can perform all types of substitutions between the double quotes. In fact, the substitution issue is the *only* difference between curly-brace grouping and double-quote grouping.

In many other programming languages, you see double quotes around *string arguments,* which signifies that the quoted material is a *string,* rather than the name of a variable or a command name. In such languages, such as C and Java, *every* part of the code that is meant to be interpreted as a bunch of characters, rather than as an instruction or a variable name, has quotes around it to signify that the string character is a special kind of data.

Adding quotes around everything that is meant literally as a bunch of characters, rather than as a command or variable name, is not necessary in Tcl/Tk. Although it's permissible to wrap a single word or character within quotes, it's not necessary. The code

```
label .1 -text "gesundheit!"
```

is treated in *exactly* the same way as the string

```
label .1 -text gesundheit!
```

Substitution — both variable and command substitution — work normally inside a pair of quotes. For example, without worrying about how you'd do such a thing, say that you've created a new Tcl/Tk command called DayOfTheWeek, which calculates and returns the current day of the week. At the Wish prompt, when you type the new command (don't type this into Wish — it's not a real command)

```
>DayOfTheWeek
```

the command returns Sunday or Monday or whatever, depending on when you happen to type the command. Now, say that rather than simply calling the command DayOfTheWeek, you use the command to store the day of the week in a variable and then use that variable inside a pair of quotes:

```
set today [DayOfTheWeek]
label .1 -text "Today is $today"
```

Say this little snippet of code is running on a Wednesday. The first line of code uses command substitution to swap in the result of the DayOfTheWeek command for the stuff in the square brackets, yielding the command

```
set today Wednesday
```

which sets the value of the variable today to Wednesday.

The second line of code uses variable substitution inside a pair of quotes. Because quoting allows substitution, the interpreter replaces the variable name $today with the variable's value, Wednesday, to yield:

```
label .1 -txt "Today is Wednesday"
```

In fact, because command substitution is permitted inside quotes, you could skip a step in the preceding two-line example. Instead of putting the results of DayOfTheWeek into a variable and then putting the variable between the double quotes, you could simply use command substitution inside the quotes like so:

```
label .1 -text "Today is [DayOfTheWeek]"
```

The interpreter evaluates the little command so that the command becomes

```
label .1 -text "Today is Wednesday"
```

Double quotes are used only to group the quoted material into a single word. You can perform substitution on the material between the quotes.

Protecting Special Characters with Backslashes

Suppose that you want to use the following sentence to appear as a label.

```
There are $count laptops on the market that cost less than
          $2000!
```

Now, suppose that you want to do variable substitution on $count, but you don't want to do variable substitution on $2000, which in this case means *two thousand dollars* rather than the value of a variable named 2000. If you group the whole sentence with curly braces, you disable the substitution of $count. Yet, if you group the whole string with double quotes, the interpreter tries to find a variable called 2000 and substitute its value in place of $2000.

To handle this kind of situation, Tcl/Tk provides a third kind of substitution, called *backslash substitution*. What happens is this: The interpreter replaces certain special combination of characters with other characters. It's called backslash substitution because each special character combination starts with the backslash character.

For example, in the preceding example string, you'd use the special character combination \$ in place of the dollar sign in $2000, like so:

```
There are $count laptops on the market that cost less than
          \$2000!
```

When the interpreter finds the \$ combination, the interpreter replaces it with a simple $. This substitution is the only one that takes place at this spot in the code: The interpreter doesn't interpret the resulting $2000 as a request for variable substitution.

```
There are 100 laptops on the market that cost less than
          $2000!
```

Although I know that there's a substitution taking place, to me it feels like the backslash prevents a substitution, protecting special characters like $ and [and r, and that's how I think of it. This is probably a bad thinking habit on my part, but it makes it easier to remember what's happening.

You can use backslash substitution for all the special characters that you've encountered so far:

 "

✔ { and }

> ✔ [and]
>
> ✔ ;

In other words, to get the character " after substitution, you'd use the sequence \ " before substitution. Similarly, you'd use \ { to get {, \} to get }, and so on.

For example, suppose that you want to store the semicolon character (;) in a variable called semicolon. Suppose that you enter the following code:

```
set semicolon ;
```

As described in Chapter 2, the Tcl/Tk interpreter thinks that the semicolon indicates the end of the command, and that you're trying to say

```
set semicolon
```

The preceding command isn't what you want to do at all — it's the command you'd use to retrieve the value of semicolon, which you haven't even set yet. You must use backslash substitution so that the interpreter reads the semicolon as a semicolon rather than as an indication that the command is over.

```
set semicolon \;
```

In a few cases, backslash substitution does not yield the same character that appears to the right of the backslash. You're already familiar with one such case . . . any guesses? That's right: The backslash character at the end of a line is, in fact, part of the whole backslash substitution conspiracy. When the interpreter finds the combination

```
\invisible-end-of-line-character
```

the interpreter swaps in a plain old space — the same kind you add with the keyboard spacebar. In other words, the code

```
set homophone "pear \
pair"
```

is exactly the same as

```
set homophone "pear pair"
```

The backslash effectively supresses the end-of-line character(s) that follow, so that as far as the interpreter is concerned, the two lines of code are a single line.

Chapter 7

Flow Control: Conditionals and Loops

*W*ith the tclet-building tools that you already have, you can build some powerful commands, and even some interesting little tclets. To create even more useful programs, you need to find out how to use flow control — the commands that are used to make decisions and repeat steps.

Structuring Your Program

The basic tools for controlling the flow of your programs — deciding which commands to execute and which commands to skip over — are conditionals and looping structures.

Flow control statements are special commands that allow you to structure the way that a tclet is executed.

Using *conditionals*, the tclet decides on the fly which commands to execute and which commands to skip.

With *looping constructs*, you can repeat commands as needed to handle repetitive tasks . . . and just about every problem can be viewed as a repetitive task.

Without flow control statements, the structure of a tclet is pretty straightforward: The interpreter executes the first command, and then the second command, relentlessly executing each command in exactly the order they are listed until it reaches the end of the tclet.

There *are* languages that are satisfied with this simple top-to-bottom organization. In fact, one of the most widely used languages today — HTML — does not offer any kind of flow control. As a result, HTML is easy to learn, but it's not very useful for creating dynamic or interactive pages. (That's why you're jazzing up your pages up with tclets, right?)

Conditionals (Or, If I Only Had a Brain . . .)

Conditionals are the decision-makers of Tcl. The basic conditional command, if, works pretty much the same way that the word "if" works in English. For example, you might say something like, "If I have enough money in my pocket, I'll buy a *latte.*" You follow the same basic procedure in Tcl conditionals:

- ✔ Test a statement to see if it's true.
- ✔ If it is true, execute the designated command or set of commands.
- ✔ If it is not true, skip the designated commands.

In a real-world decision, you may have a back-up plan: "If I have enough money, I'll buy a *latte;* otherwise, I'll buy a regular coffee." This approach also has an exact Tcl analog:

- ✔ Test a statement to see if it's true.
- ✔ If it's true, execute the designated command or set of commands.
- ✔ If it's not true, execute the designated alternate command or set of commands.

Sometimes, you even have a whole set of backup plans: "If I have enough money, I'll buy a *latte;* otherwise, if I have enough for a *café au lait,* I'll buy that; if I don't have enough for a *café au lait,* and if I have enough money for a deluxe coffee, I'll buy a deluxe coffee; if all else fails, I'll buy a regular coffee.

I won't cloud your mind with another bullet list that shows how Tcl handles this particular case; just know that you can use conditional statements to handle any such set of contingencies and that you'll find the specifics in this section.

Making decisions with if

The basic structure of the if *command*

The basic command that's used to make decisions is called, logically enough, if. Like any Tcl command, this one consists of the command name, followed by a bunch of words. In its simplest form, the command goes like this:

```
if condition set-of-instructions
```

This simple version of the if statement has three basic parts:

- ✔ The command's name
- ✔ A condition to be evaluated as true or false
- ✔ A set of instructions to be performed if the condition is true

Both the condition and the set of instructions need to be single words. In all but the most trivial cases, you need to use grouping to make the condition and instructions into single words.

Figure 7-1 is an example of the most trivial of cases. When you type **1** into Wish, Wish beeps at you. (It's probably annoyed that you're bothering it with such a silly command.)

Figure 7-1:
Code
statement
parts.

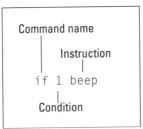

The interpreter regards every number except 0 as "true" when it evaluates the number as a true-or-false, so it interprets 1 as true. Consequently, it executes the one-word command beep. If you enter

```
if 0 beep
```

Wish maintains a stony silence. Remember, it considers 0 false, so it does not execute the instruction. This is how the if command works at the basic level.

In the real world, an if statement looks more like Figure 7-2:

```
 ┌─Command name
 │        Condition
 │  set x 5
 └─if ⌐{$x > 3}⌐ {
        message .m -text "x is still greater than three!"
        pack .m
    }
```
Set of instructions

Figure 7-2:
Adding
more
arguments
to a code
statement.

I used curly braces to quote the conditional and the commands. Because the interpreter executes the if command after it performs the substitution, be sure to protect the conditional and commands so that the if command can use them exactly as you've written them. When the interpreter executes the if command, it will do internal substitutions inside the condition word and the set of instructions.

Always use curly braces to group the words that make up an if command.

Evaluating the condition

How does the interpreter decide if the condition part of the if command is true or false?

You've already seen the basic way: if the condition is a number, the interpreter evaluates the condition as false if the number is 0 and true in all other cases. Of course, you shouldn't ordinarily use a plain number like 1 or 0 as the condition — doing so makes the if command always true or always false, respectively. There's no point to a conditional that never changes, right?

However, it's very handy to be able to put a variable or a command expression in the evaluation spot. For example, if you set the value of the variable x to 5, the following if statements will execute their instructions:

```
if $x {
    message .m2 "the value of x is not zero!"
    pack .m2
}
```

```
if [expr $x -4] {
    message .m3 "the value of x is not 4!"
    pack .m3
}
```

If you set the value of x to zero, the following if statements will *not* execute their instructions:

```
if $x {
    message .m4 "the value of x is not zero!"
    pack .m4
}
```

```
if [expr $x * 2] {
    message .m5 "the value of x is not zero !"
    pack .m5
}
```

You can also use mathematical expressions that can be evaluated as true or false as the condition of an if command. For example, the following if command will execute its instructions:

```
if {1 > 0} {
    message .m6 "pheww! one is still greater than zero !"
    pack .m6
}
```

But this command will not:

```
if {1 < 0} {
    message .m7 "warning: mathematics has experienced a
            systems failure"
    pack .m7
}
```

The basic operators that you use to create these kinds of expressions are pretty much the same as what you learned back in elementary school. Just in case that epoch of your education is a little foggy, Table 7-1 shows the most common operators. (All of the examples yield the value true, just in case you are wondering.)

Table 7-1	Equality Operators	
Operator	*Meaning*	*Example*
==	equal	1 == 1
!=	not equal to	1 != 0
>	greater than	1 > 0
>=	greater than or equal to	1 >= 1
<	less than	1 < 2
<=	less than or equal to	1 <= 2

Note: The only real ringer here is equal, which is designated with two equal signs, that is,

```
1==1
```

It's easy to forget to add the second

```
=
```

especially when you're just getting started. Always use

```
==
```

when creating an expression for a condition. Very often, you'll want to set up more than one condition in an `if` statement. Say you're using two variables, x and y, and you want to make sure that the value of *both* variables are greater than zero. You can combine conditions with Boolean operators. In this case, you use the Boolean operator `&&`, which returns true only if both expressions that it joins are true:

```
set x 1
set y 1
if {($x > 0) && ($y > 0)} {
    message .m8 "both x and y are greater than zero"
    pack .m8
}
```

Table 7-2 shows each of the Boolean operators and how they work. True and False refer to the truth or falsehood of expressions like $x > 0$ — by the way, you shouldn't use the words *true* and *false* themselves.

Table 7-2		Boolean (Logical) Operators	
Name	*Operator*	*Examples*	*Results*
And	&&	true && true	true
		true && false	false
		false && true	false
		false & false	false
Or	|	true | true	true
		true | false	true
		false | true	true
		false | false	true
Not	~	~true	false
		~false	true

Designating the instructions

After you build a condition for your if statement, you can start adding instructions for the statement to execute. Remember, an if command is structured like so:

```
if condition set-of-commands
```

The commands that the if statement executes are just plain old Tcl/Tk commands, grouped together with curly braces. By convention, the opening brace is on the end of the same line as the if command, and the closing brace is on it's own line at the end of the block:

```
if {$x} {
    # a commands to be executed
    # another command
}
```

The body of the if statement can contain *any* legal if Tcl/Tk command, including another if statement.

Adding an else *clause*

What about backup plans? To specify an alternate block of code to be executed, add an else clause to the basic if command. Here's the basic pattern:

```
if condition set-of-instructions else alternate-
                instructions
```

The alternate set of commands must be grouped into one word with curly braces, just as the basic set of instructions are grouped. Here's a real world example of an if . . . else construction:

```
set x 25
if {$x < 10} {
    message .m9 -text "x is less than ten!"
} else {
    message .m9 -text "x is greater than ten!"
}
pack .m9
```

If you look carefully, you'll see that the ends of lines 2 through 4 are all quoted with curly brackets in one way or another. In other words, there are no naked end-of-line characters anywhere inside the whole if command. When you're using else, be sure that it's sandwiched between one word's closing curly brace and the next word's opening curly brace, all on one line, like so:

```
} else {
```

This guarantees that the `if . . . else` command is in the proper form for all Tcl commands: a command followed by a bunch of words, terminated by an end-of-line. (This is becoming my Tcl mantra, isn't it?)

Adding an `elseif` *clause*

Several layers of `if` statements embedded inside each other can become ungainly very quickly. Consider the following:

```
set x 1
set y 1
set z 1
if $x {
    # do something interesting} else {
    if $y {
      #do something even more spectacular
      } else {
         if $z {
            #do something world-shaking
         }
      }
   }
}
```

As we say in the art department, *yuck*. Nesting each new `if` command inside the previous command's `else` clause makes this brace-happy and hard to balance. Because embedded `if`'s are very common but the code is so unpleasant, Tcl offers the `elseif` construction. As the name suggests, `elseif` collapses the construction

```
} else {
    if condition {
```

into the much tidier

```
} elseif condition {
```

Using `elseif`, you can rewrite the preceding nasty code as follows:

```
set x 1
set y 1
set z 1
if $x {
    # do something interesting
} elseif $y {
    #do something even more spectacular
} elseif $z {
    #do something world-shaking
}
```

Steamlining decisions with switch

Using a series of elseif constructions can make your code much cleaner, but sometimes you can use Tcl's industrial strength conditional command: switch.

Say that you're a restaurant cook, and it's your first day on the job. You don't know how to make any of the restaurant's specialty dishes, but you do have a cookbook. Suddenly, a waiter announces that a customer would like a tofu dog.

If the real-world cookbook were set up like an if . . . else construction, if would say something like, "If the customer wants a hamburger, put a hamburger patty on a bun and serve with pickle. Else, if the customer wants a gyro. . . ." Such a cookbook would go right into the garbage can the first time you tried to look up a recipe.

In a real-word cookbook, you'd scan the names of the recipes at the tops of pages. When you found "tofu dog" at the top of a page, you'd follow the instructions underneath to prepare the tofu pup.

The switch command works like the real-world cookbook. Here's the basic pattern:

```
switch string {candidate-string body candidate-string body}
```

The switch command has five basic parts:

- ✔ The command name
- ✔ Command options (not shown in the preceding pattern)
- ✔ A string to be matched
- ✔ A collection of candidate strings that it tries to match the first string against
- ✔ One set of instructions for each candidate string; instructions executed if candidate string matches first string

Figure 7-3 illustrates a switch statement in real Tcl code.

The interpreter runs down the list of candidate strings looking for a match. When it finds a match, it executes the *first* command in the block of commands that's paired with the matching string. The interpreter ignores all commands that don't match and all subsequent matches after the first one.

You can also do a search with regular expressions as candidate strings. To use regular expressions in a switch command, you need to use the -regexp option. (See Appendix A for a complete description of regular expressions

```
                    String to be matched

set x "tofu dog"
switch $X {
    hamburger   {label .1 -text "put a burger on a bun"}
    "hot dog"   {label .1 -text "cover hot dog with mustard"}
    sushi       {label .1 -text "cut fish and put on rice
with wasabi"}
    "tofu dog" {label .1 -text "slather tofu dog with miso"}
}
pack .1
    candidate strings                   instructions
```

Figure 7-3:
Elements of
a switch
statement.

and how to create them.) Here's a simple example, using regular expressions
that look for words that start with different letters:

```
set my_word cantaloupe
switch -regexp $my_word {
    {^[a-m]} { label .12 -text "the word starts with a-m"}
    {^[n-z]} { label .12 -text "the word starts with n-z"}
}
pack .12
```

The regular expression ^[a-m] finds words that start with any of the letters
from *a* to *m,* and the regular expression ^[n-z] finds words that start with *n*
through *z.* When the -regexp option is used with switch, the interpreter
uses the candidate strings as regular expressions — rather than for exact
character-by-character matching.

Around and Around and Around You Go: Looping Constructs

Personally, I hate repeating myself and doing things over again, but computer programs seem to love it. Humans can solve problems with human
tools like deduction and intuition: Computers usually solve problems by
repetition, and lots of it.

Actually, as programming languages go, Tcl/Tk is not so terribly loop-
obsessed as languages like C and Pascal. Many of the loops that you need to
handle user input, such as mouse movement and keyboard activity, have
been written for you, and they're hidden away inside the interpreter. Still,
you need a solid understanding of looping constructs to write working tclets.

Sooner or later, you'll get trapped in an infinite loop. In fact, it will probably happen quite a few times until you get the hang of writing looping structures. This is something to be proud of — it's an important part of the initiation into the world of programming.

To extricate yourself gracefully:

- ✔ If you're running a tclet in a browser, just close the browser window, and the problem will go away.

- ✔ If you're running Wish under Windows, press Ctrl+Alt+Delete. Select Wish in the Close Program dialog box, and click the End Task button. You don't need to restart if you're running Windows 95 or Windows NT.

- ✔ If you're running Wish under the Mac OS, you'll have to force-quit out of Wish. Press Command+Shift+Esc, and click OK in the "Force Wish to Quit?" dialog box. You should probably restart because the whole system usually bombs shortly after any forced quit.

Simple looping with for

Say that you'd like to create an array of buttons like the ones shown in Figure 7-4. If you enjoy typing, you can simply create all of the buttons by hand:

```
button .b1 -text "button number 1"
pack .b1
button .b2 -text "button number 2"
pack .b2
button .b3 -text "button number 3"
pack .b3
button .b4 -text "button number 4"
pack .b4
button .b5 -text "button number 5"
pack .b5
button .b6 -text "button number 6"
pack .b6
button .b7 -text "button number 7"
pack .b7
button .b8 -text "button number 8"
pack .b8
button .b9 -text "button number 9"
pack .b9
button .b10 -text "button number 10"
pack .b10
```

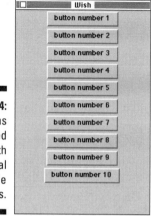

Figure 7-4:
Buttons
created
with
individual
code
commands.

Of course, entering the code for each of these buttons individually is a tremendous waste of your time. Using a looping construct, you can create the same set of buttons with just a few lines of code:

```
for {set index 1} {$index <= 10} {incr index} {
    button .b$index -text "button number $index"
    pack .b$index
}
```

This is the approach that wins friends and influences people. Now, take apart the `for` loop and see how it works.

Basic construct of the `for` *command*

A `for` command consists of five basic parts:

- ✔ The command name
- ✔ An initialization statement
- ✔ A test statement
- ✔ A re-initialization statement
- ✔ The body of the loop

Each of these parts is fairly complex, so curly braces are used to group each component into a single tcl word. Figure 7-5 shows how the code that made the buttons fits into this scheme.

Here's the sequence that the interpreter follows as it executes a `for` command:

1. **Sets up an index variable that keeps track of how many cycles the loop has gone through. (This is what the initialization statement is for.)**

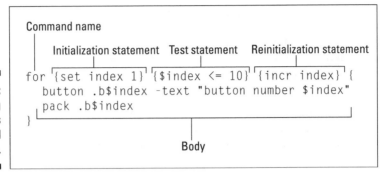

Figure 7-5:
Grouping
components
into Tcl
words.

Command name

Initialization statement   Test statement   Reinitialization statement

```
for {set index 1} {$index <= 10} {incr index} {
    button .b$index -text "button number $index"
    pack .b$index
}
```

Body

2. Evaluates the test statement.

If the test statement is true, the for statement executes the body of the loop. If the test statement is false, the for statement doesn't execute the body of the loop; instead, the interpreter skips Steps 3 and 4 and moves on to the next command.

3. Increments the index variable to show that the loop has completed another cycle.

This task is done by the re-initialization statement.

4. Goes back to Step 2.

The initialization statement

The *initialization statement* is a regular Tcl command. It's sole responsibility is to *set up* the counter that keeps track of the number of loops that the for command has gone through. The initialization doesn't keep track of the counter — it's only evaluated once, at the get-go.

You should wrap it up with curly braces to protect it from the substitution pass that swaps in new values for the whole for command. When the interpreter uses the initialization statement to set up the counter, it will strip off the braces and perform any substitutions that are necessary.

Normally, you set the counter to zero or one, because you're counting loops. It's up to you, though . . . the counter can be anything you want it to be. Very often, you'll use the counter's value throughout the loop. In the button-array building tclet, the counter is called $index. Notice that I use the counter inside the loop to name the buttons, to put the buttons' names in the button's text, and to pack the buttons.

The test statement

The interpreter uses the *test statement* to decide whether to execute the body of the for statement's loop. The test statement is built in exactly the same way as the condition of an if statement, and it behaves in pretty much the same way.

You find one important difference: If you set up the condition of an `if` statement in the wrong way, your tclet will simply do the wrong thing, and you will swear at your computer — no harm done. If you set up the test statement incorrectly, the `for` statement may keep on looping forever, causing you to bang on your keyboard with your fist. This is bad for your keyboard, and bad for your fist.

If you want the `for` loop to stop — and it should stop at some point, or the interpreter will never run the rest of your program — the test statement must eventually evaluate to false. You should look at the test statement very carefully to make sure it's correct.

In the button-making tclet example, the test statement, `$index <= 10`, simply checks to see how many times the loop has been executed. When the number of loops is 11, the statement evaluates as false, and the `for` statement kicks out of the loop.

What if you use `$index <= 0` as a test? The interpreter will simply continue adding 1 to the value of `$index`. Because you start at 1, `$index` will never have a value less than 0, and so `$index<=0` will never be false, and the loop will never stop. This is a Bad Thing.

Be sure to wrap up your test statement with a pair of curly braces to prevent substitution when the interpreter makes its first substitution pass on the whole `for` command. When it's time to evaluate the test statement as a test statement, the interpreter will perform the necessary substitutions.

Always double-check your test statement to make sure that it will eventually yield a value of false.

The re-initialization statement

After a loop counter is set up with the initialization statement, the counter is kept up to date by the *re-initialization statement*. The re-initialization statement is executed as a regular Tcl command after each iteration of the body of the `for` loop.

In the example tclet, I use the special command `incr`. The `incr` command merely adds one to the value of its argument, that is, the command

```
incr x
```

is *exactly* the same as the command

```
set x [expr $x + 1]
```

You can use whatever system you like to maintain the value of the counter value: You don't need to use `incr`, and you don't need to increase the counter by 1 for every iteration of the loop. For example, to create a set of even-numbered buttons like the ones shown in Figure 7-6, you must increase the counter by 2 rather than 1 after each loop:

```
for {set index 0} {$index <= 10} {set index [expr $index +
        2]} {
    button .b$index -text "button number $index"
    pack .b$index
}
```

Figure 7-6:
Testing
controls the
increments.

Again, be careful — you should make sure that the test statement will eventually evaluate as false. If you do something creative with the re-initialization statement, make sure that you account for it in the test statement.

The body of the loop

The *body* of the loop is where the work gets done. The commands in this part of the for statement are executed every time the interpreter evaluates the test statement as true. In the example tclet, the body of the loop is responsible for creating and displaying the buttons. You can put whatever kind of Tcl/Tk commands you like inside a loop, including another loop.

As mentioned in the discussion of the initialization statement, you can reference the value of the loop's counter inside the body of the loop. You can change the value, too, if you like, but be forewarned that this is an easy way to create infinite loops and other bizarre behavior if you're not careful. For example, this little snippet of code will never break out of the loop. (Don't run it, unless you don't believe me!)

```
for {set index 0} {$index < 10} {incr index} {
set index [expr $index - 1]
}
```

Fancy looping with foreach

You know you've been programming too long when you start to have favorite commands in a language. For reasons that I don't entirely understand, `foreach` is one of my favorite tools in Tcl. It's an elegant way to cycle through a collection of things — widgets, words, variables — and do something with each of them.

Say that you want to create a set of buttons like the ones shown in Figure 7-7. Each button is labeled with a day of the week rather than with a number. Because each label is unique, you can't easily create this set of buttons with a basic `for` command. I'm not going to demonstrate the tedium of creating each button individually, as you probably picked up on that the last time. Instead, I show you how easy it is to build the list with `foreach`:

```
set index 0
foreach current "Sunday Monday Tuesday Wednesday \
            Thursday Friday Saturday Sunday" {
    button .b$index -text $current
    pack .b$index
    incr index
}
```

Figure 7-7:
And on the seventh day, the programmer rested.

Take a closer look at `foreach` to see exactly what's going on here.

The basic construct

The `foreach` command has four basic parts:

- ↙ The command name
- ↙ The variable name used for each cycle of the loop
- ↙ The list to be processed
- ↙ The body of the loop

The interpreter executes the body of the loop once for every member of the list. In the example code, the loop is executed seven times because seven word are in the list. On each pass through the loop, the value of the variable is assigned to the next value in the list. In the example code, the variable is called current. During the first pass through the loop, current has the value Sunday; in the second pass, current has the value Monday; in the third pass, current has the value Tuesday . . . got it?

The name of the index variable

The name of the index variable can be whatever you like it to be. It doesn't need to be quoted with braces; because it's a variable, it has a one-word name or it's already quoted.

The list

The list argument of the foreach command can be any string of words separated by spaces or tabs. If a variable contains a list of words, go ahead and use it as this argument. For example, the following is a common use of foreach:

```
set my_list "avacados bannanas cucumbers"
```

```
foreach current $my_list {
    # do a vegtable thing
}
```

Likewise, you can use any command substitution that returns a list. Say you set up an array called car (see Figure 7-8) with indices like:

```
set car(color) white
set car(make) Honda
set car(model) Civic
set car(year) 85
```

(Now you know why I'm writing this book!) You can use the array names to get the list of the indices of the car array, and use this in the foreach command:

```
set counter 0
foreach current [array names car] {
    message .m$counter -text "car($current) = [set
            car($current)]" \ width 200
    pack .m$counter
    incr counter
}
```

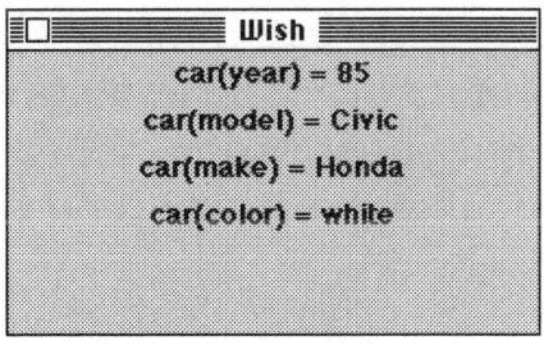

Figure 7-8:
If you
want the
car, write
the loop.

Flexible looping with while

The most flexible looping structure offered by Tcl is the while command. The while command doesn't provide counters or list-processing features; it simply repeats a loop until some programmer-designated condition is satisfied.

The basic pattern

The while command has just three parts:

- ✔ The command name
- ✔ The test statement
- ✔ The body of the loop

The interpreter processes the while command by evaluating the test statement. If the test statement is true, the body of the loop is executed. If the test statement is false, the interpreter skips over the body and moves along to the next command. This process is repeated until the test statement is false.

Here's an example of a while command in action. The results are shown in Figure 7-9.

```
set counter 0
while {$counter < 5} {
    incr counter
    button .w$counter -text "new button $counter"
    pack .w$counter
}
```

Figure 7-9:
While can
repeat
many
elements.

The test statement

The test statement in a while command is exactly like the test statement in a for command or the condition in an if command. The test statement should be wrapped in curly braces to prevent substitution. When it's time for the interpreter to evaluate the test statement, it will strip off the curlies and make any necessary substitutions.

Note: Be sure the test statement in a while command will eventually be evaluated as false. Logically, the test statement must use at least one of the variables altered in the body of the loop; if the statement uses only unchanging variables, it's truth value will never change.

The body of the loop

The body of a while statement loop contains the instructions that are to be executed with each iteration. Because no automatically-executed initialization or re-initialization statements are built into the command, you must do all the bookkeeping in the body of the command and set the variables used by the test statement. The example code uses the variable $counter to keep track of the number of passes through the loop, incrementing counter's value with the incr command in each pass.

Bailing out of a loop

Sometimes it's appropriate to bail out of a loop in the middle of a cycle. Tcl provides two subtly different emergency eject commands:

- ✔ break: causes the interpreter to exit the loop entirely.
- ✔ continue: causes the interpreter to exit the current cycle of the loop and jump to the start of the next loop cycle.

Changing your mind with break

The break command cancels the current loop command completely. The interpreter moves along to the next instruction in the tclet. Normally, you put the break command into a conditional statement so that you bail out of the loop only under certain conditions. Now, put a break command into the little while loop that built the buttons. The break command is called when the value of counter is 3, before the button is created, so the tclet will create only two buttons, as shown in Figure 7-10.

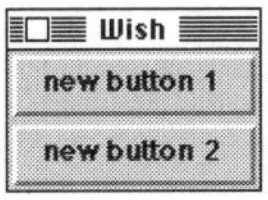

Figure 7-10:
The product
of the break
command.

```
set counter 0
while {$counter < 5} {
    incr counter
    if {$counter == 3} {
    break
    }
    button .w$counter -text "new button $counter"
    pack .w$counter
}
```

(Of course, you could have simply created only two button in the first place, but you wouldn't have seen break in action.)

Skipping a loop with continue

The continue command is only a little different than the break command. It skips the rest of the current iteration of the loop, but then it goes back to the top of the loop for the next pass. Change the break tclet just a tiny bit, and substitute continue for break. The tclet will skip over the part of the loop that builds button 3 but will pass through the loop again to create buttons 4 and 5.

```
set counter 0
while {$counter < 5} {
    incr counter
    if {$counter == 3} {
       continue
    }
    button .w$counter -text "new button $counter"
    pack .w$counter
}
```

See? Rather than stopping after the break command, the tclet finishes out the loop, skipping only the third pass through the loop. As you can see in Figure 7-11, button number 3 is missing from the array of buttons.

Figure 7-11:
Skipping
the third
pass omits
the third
button.

Chapter 8

I've Got a Little List!

*L*ists are everywhere! Grocery lists, top ten lists, little-black-book lists, even books of lists. Everybody uses them. I can list dozens of useful lists! But what is it that makes lists so useful? Well, lists can be ordered. You can use them to keep track of things that belong in a certain order, such as an alphabetical list (like a class roster) or a numerical list (like the top ten reasons why Tcl is better than Java). But it can be any order at all. Maybe you want to keep track of the order in which people choose your links. Maybe you want to provide users with a list of your most recently updated pages, in the order in which they've been updated. By the time you finish reading this chapter, I'm sure you will be able to list even more ways to use lists in your tclets.

Tcl provides a wide range of basic commands for processing lists. You can use simple commands to add things to list, access list elements, access information about lists, search lists, and sort lists.

Making a List

The best thing about using lists is that they are a compact way of referring to sets of stuff. A list is a way of taking a whole bunch of things and giving them one name. Take a grocery list. Every time you want to refer to what you must buy on your way home, you just say groceries, not milk, lettuce, cream cheese, and frozen apple pie. Such a list will not only save you time, it also will make it easier to hand the list — and, therefore, the job — off to someone else.

In Tcl you can make a list of strings, give it a name, and then treat that name as one variable for passing around in your tclet. In Tcl, you call each thing on a list an *element* of that list. When you want to get at the individual elements contained in the list you can use special commands to manipulate the list.

In Tcl you can create a list with the `list` command, as follows:

```
set groceries [list {milk} {lettuce} {cream cheese} \
{frozen apple pie}]
```

All this does is assign the output of the command

```
list {milk} {lettuce} {cream cheese} {frozen apple pie}
```

to the variable *groceries*.

Your best approach is to write the elements of the list in curly braces ({ }) so that Tcl knows which words belong together (like *frozen* and *apple* and *pie* belong together, but they don't belong with *cream* or *cheese*). Actually, you don't have to write single-string elements in curly braces, but it's a good idea to keep everything consistent.

Probably the most familiar way to make a list is simply to add items onto the end, just like you add items to a list on a sheet of paper. The `lappend` command appends elements onto a list, one by one. Try these commands in Wish so that you can see how the list changes with every successive command:

```
% lappend groceries milk
% puts $groceries
milk
% lappend groceries lettuce
% puts $groceries
milk lettuce
% lappend groceries {cream cheese}
% puts $groceries
milk lettuce {cream cheese}
% lappend groceries {frozen apple pie}
% puts $groceries
milk lettuce {cream cheese} {frozen apple pie}
```

In the preceding line, the curly braces are very important. If you don't include them, you'll get very confusing results, as shown here:

```
% lappend groceries cream cheese
% puts $groceries
milk lettuce cream cheese
```

Because you know that *cream* and *cheese* go together as one element, this result may not look like a problem. But Tcl doesn't know about cream cheese. If you sent Tcl to the store with this list, it would come back with *milk, lettuce, cream,* and *cheese,* which is not what you wanted at all.

In short, for making a list, you can use the `list` command if you already know a bunch of the elements that go in the list. Otherwise, you can use the `lappend` command to add elements one (or more) at a time on to the end of the list.

Moving Information

Are you wondering how to get information out of a list after you put the information in? That's where the ordering of the list becomes important. Each element in the list has a number called its *index.* As you may suspect, that index of an element simply indicates where in the list the element is located. You may think that the first element in the list will have the index 1, the second will have the index 2, and so on. Well, almost. In fact, like many computer languages, Tcl starts counting with 0, so the first element of a list has index 0, the second has index 1, and so on.

Accessing individual elements

Say that you decide to buy only the dairy products from the preceding grocery list. It so happens that you would be selecting the first and the third elements of the list, which have index 0 and index 2. In Tcl, you can extract these elements from the list by typing the following commands:

```
% lindex $groceries 0
milk
% lindex $groceries 2
cream cheese
```

`lindex` is just short for List Index, so by typing `lindex $groceries 0`, you are just asking Tcl to give you the element that is listed at index 0 in the list contained in the variable `groceries`. Remember that `groceries` is just the name of the list. To get at the *contents* of the list, you must use variable substitution, as with any other variable, and put a $ in front of it.

You can instruct the interpreter to give you a range of elements (say, from element 1 to element 3) by using the `lrange` command, which is short for List Range. (I'll bet you're starting to see a pattern here.)

```
% lrange $groceries 1 3
lettuce {cream cheese} {frozen apple pie}
```

Replacing Elements

Now that you know about the index of an element, you can easily replace one element with another (or even with a whole list of other elements). The command for this is . . . (drum-roll, please) . . . you guessed it! lreplace. The lreplace command is a little different from the previous commands because it actually changes the content of the list.

As a result, you must assign the output of the lreplace command to a new variable. Call it new_groceries. lreplace takes the list and replaces all the elements from the first index given (in this example, index 1) to the second index given (in this example, index 2) with the list of things at the end of the command. So, you can replace everything in the middle of the groceries list with one word, *cookies,* like this:

```
% set newGroceries [lreplace $groceries 1 2 cookies]
% puts $newGroceries
milk cookies {frozen apple pie}
```

As you can see, index 1 and index 2 of the list groceries is replaced with one element, cookies, which now has index 1 (and frozen apple pie has index 2). If you want to get rid of the pie also, you can type

```
% set newGroceries [lreplace $groceries 1 3 cookies]
% puts $newGroceries
milk cookies
```

thereby replacing everything from index 1 through index 3 (inclusive) with one element. If you only want to replace one element, you just set the first and last index to be the same as that of the element you want to replace, for example:

```
% set newGroceries [lreplace $groceries 2 2 \
{low cal cream cheese}]
% puts $newGroceries
milk lettuce {low cal cream cheese} {frozen apple pie}
```

It's also perfectly okay to replace with more than one element at a time:

```
% set newGroceries \
[lreplace $groceries 1 2 cookies cake {whipped cream}]
% puts $newGroceries
milk cookies cake {whipped cream} {frozen apple pie}
```

Inserting Elements

Knowing how to replace things, you can probably almost guess how to insert things into the list without removing anything that's already there. If you think that you can use a command like, say, List Insert, you're absolutely correct. But because you used `lreplace` for List Replace, call List Insert `linsert`.

You can use the `linsert` command to insert a new list member before any given element. As with `lreplace`, you must assign the output of the command to a new variable. *Unlike* `lreplace`, `linsert` requires only one index — that of the element before which you want to insert your new element(s).

For example, to insert *hamburger* into the groceries list between *lettuce* and *cream cheese,* just remember that *cream cheese* is the third element in the list, so it is at index number 2.

```
% set newGroceries [linsert $groceries 2 hamburger]
% puts $newGroceries
milk lettuce hamburger {cream cheese} {frozen apple pie}
```

Now `hamburger` is the third element of the list, with index 2, and `cream cheese` has been moved over to be the fourth element, with index 3. If you want to insert a whole bunch of stuff into the list before a given index, just add the items to the `linsert` command in the order that you want them to appear in the final list. If you want to add a bunch of picnic things before the hamburger, you type the following:

```
% set newGroceries [linsert $groceries 2 napkins charcoal \
{paperplates}]
% puts $newGroceries
milk lettuce napkins charcoal {paper plates} \
hamburger {cream cheese} {frozen apple pie}
```

In fact, you can insert a list into another list. You can do this two ways. The first is to simply use `linsert` to plunk your second list right down in the middle of the first. Say that you have one list, called `picnic_supplies`, that you want to add to our old friend `groceries`. First, look at what's in each list.

```
% puts $groceries
milk lettuce {cream cheese} {frozen apple pie}
% puts $picnic_supplies
plasticware {paper plates} napkins tablecloth \
{bug repellent}
```

Now, just `linsert picnic_supplies` into groceries, and save the resulting list with the name of, say, `picnic_groceries` (sort of a combination of both of the original lists).

```
% set picnic_groceries [linsert $groceries 3 \
$picnic_supplies]
% puts $picnic_groceries
milk lettuce {cream cheese} {plasticware {paper plates} \
napkins tablecloth {bug repellent}} {frozen apple pie}
```

Notice the extra { before `plasticware` and the } after `{bug repellent}`. These braces indicate that everything between them is a list in and of itself. If you type

```
% lindex $picnic_groceries 3
plasticware {paper plates} napkins tablecloth \
{bug repellent}
```

you get the entire contents of the list `picnic_supplies` as the element with index 3 of the list `picnic_groceries`.

Note: `lreplace` acts just like `linsert` — any inserted list will retain its original list structure within the new list.

On the other hand, say that you want to insert the `picnic_supplies` list into `groceries` in such a way that every element of `picnic_supplies` becomes one element of the resulting list. The tool to use in this case is the `concat` command. `concat` lets you stick two lists together, one on the end of the other. You have one special condition: The lists must be joined end to end — `concat` does not actually let you insert one list into the middle of another. Thus, the command simply sticks the elements of `picnic_supplies` right onto the end of `groceries`:

```
% set picnic_groceries [concat $groceries $picnic_supplies]
% puts $picnic_groceries
milk lettuce {cream cheese} {frozen apple pie} \
plasticware {paper plates} napkins tablecloth \

{bug repellent}
```

Chapter 9

Strings 'n' Things

· ·

In This Chapter

▶ Getting information about strings

▶ Comparing strings

▶ Changing strings

▶ Creating and parsing strings

· ·

The string is one of the basic building blocks of Tcl. *Strings* are sequences of characters (letters, numbers, symbols), with or without whitespaces (spaces, carriage returns, newlines, tabs, and so on). For example, this sentence is a string. So is this entire book (except for the pictures, I suppose). Even a single character, such as Q, can be a string.

Any text you see in a tclet is a string. Any text you type into a tclet is a string. (Even Tcl commands themselves are strings!) You should care a lot about strings because without them, even if your tclets look pretty, they will say nothing, and understand nothing.

In this chapter, you'll discover different tools for identifying strings, different ways to change the characters in a string, and even how to create and parse strings. String analysis and manipulation commands are crucial for this task, especially the very powerful tools called *regular expressions* (which are covered in detail in Appendix A) to easily get a lot of information about a string. Processing data on the fly is one of the major advantages of Tcl in your Web pages.

With the information in this chapter, you will be able to do all but the most complex processing. In fact, if you're inventive and don't mind writing a lot of code, you can combine the contents of this chapter with the contents of the chapters on Looping and Judgments and end up with tclets that match the performance of regular expressions. Remember, with Tcl, there's usually more than one way to do anything.

Checking out Strings

Lucky for you, strings are pretty easy to handle in Tcl/Tk. The most important attribute of strings is that strings can be stored in *variables* (locations for sharing and saving data).

Introducing the Ego-Matic!

If I had to type Alexander L. Francis every time I wanted to display my name, I would soon become very bored. Not because I find my name boring (I don't!) but because I hate to type the same thing over and over. When writing a tclet to display my name, I can put my name into a variable with the `set` command, like this.

```
set name "Alexander L. Francis"
```

After that, whenever I want to refer to myself, I can just call on the content of the variable name. For example, to put my name into a message widget called `ego`, I just use this command:

```
message .ego -text $name
```

Note: When a string contains whitespaces (spaces, tabs, carriage returns, new lines), be sure to enclose them in double quotes, like this:

```
set sentence "This is a string."
```

The quotes are not stored as part of the string. They are just signs to Tcl that there is one string between them. If your string does not contain whitespaces you can usually just use it, like this.

```
set sentence
   This_is_also_a_string.
```

(This is really just a particular example of the general principals of grouping, as presented in Chapter 8.)

You'll almost never do anything with raw strings (and they taste terrible!). Aside from assigning strings to be the output of commands or the content of message or label widgets, you'll probably never work with strings except within variables. For example, when your tclet is taking input from a user (such as from an entry box widget), you have to save the response in a *textvariable*. A textvariable is a fancy name for a variable that contains a string.

Of course, after a string is contained in a variable, you can't tell what it is. Just by looking at the command

```
puts $name
```

you have no way of knowing whether the output will be Alexander L. Francis, Hieronymous Bosch, or perhaps someone even stranger. Looking at the variable $name, you can't even tell whether the string in the variable will fit inside your message window or whether the user typed the kind of response your tclet expects.

When faced with a variable containing a new and unfamiliar string, the first thing you do is introduce yourself. (Perhaps then you can go out for coffee, or maybe have lunch.) After these preliminaries are observed, you can get down to the details:

✔ How long is the string?

✔ Does the string contain the characters you expect?

✔ Are the characters where you expect them?

Almost all of the commands for dealing with strings have the same format. First is the command `string`, which indicates that you are asking about a string. Your query is followed by the command for the characteristic of the string that you're asking about. For example, the command

```
string length $name
```

returns the length of the string called `$name`. This chapter treats such two-word sequences as though they are one command, though technically they are all variations of the single command `string`.

string length

As you might suppose, the command `string length` returns the length of a string. If you fire up your trusty Wish program, you can try the following tests on strings. To find the length of the string `"This is a string of unknown length"`, type the following:

```
string length "This is a string of unknown length."
```

According to Wish, this string is 35 characters long. This includes whitespaces and the period at the end, but *doesn't* count the quotation marks enclosing the string. To see how Tcl deals with strings contained in variables, first put the string into a variable called `unknown_string` using the `set` command, like this:

```
set unknown_string "This is a string of unknown length."
```

To find the length of the string contained in `unknown_string`, use the `string length` command as before, but this time use it on the variable `unknown_string`, like this:

```
string length $unknown_string
```

Remember that the dollar sign ($) tells Tcl to perform the command on the contents of a variable. If you accidentally leave it off, Tcl still computes the length of a string, but that string is the string unknown_string, which has only 14 characters (*u, n, k, n, o, w, n,* and so on).

string index

Now, maybe you don't care how long the string is, as long as it contains some particular character or symbol. For example, if you ask a yes-or-no question, you want to be able to treat all responses like "yes," "YES," "Yes," "y," "Y," "yeah," "Yup!," and even "Yes, certainly, thank you very much!" as the same. On the other hand, "no," "No," "nope," and "Never!" should also all be treated as one answer. Rather than check whether the user typed each of these possible answers, just check whether the user typed the first character of the string as a "y" or an "n."

As far as Tcl is concerned, a string is just a list of characters, in order. Because Tcl starts counting with 0, the first character in a list is character number 0, the second is number 1, the third is number 2, and so on. The number of a character in the string is called its *index*.

In the string "Yes," the character with index 0 is "Y," and the character "s" has index 2. Turn to Chapter 16 for more about using indexes.

The string index command is followed by the string to be analyzed, then followed by the index of the character to be returned. Therefore, to find the first character in a string called response, use the string index command to give the character at index 0, like this.

```
string index $response 0
```

String index shows you the character at a particular index. The next set of commands show you the indices of particular characters. It's pretty much the same kind of thing, only different.

string first

At times, you may want to find the first occurrence of a particular character or set of characters in a string. For example, you may have a couple of different strings that are each someone's e-mail address, for example, tweety@birdcage.com and sylvester@suffrin.succotash.org, but all you really care about is where they are located, not their names. Because the only information in front of the @ symbol is the name, finding the first occurrence of @ enables you to use the index of this symbol as a marker to indicate where to cut each string (using the `trim` commands discussed later in this chapter) so that you can store only the machine and domain names of each address.

The format for the `string first` command is `string first` followed by the character or string to be searched for (call this the *search string*), followed by the string in which to search (call this the *main string*).

For example, to find the first occurrence of the @ in a string called `address`, type the following.

```
string first @ $address
```

Figure 9-1 shows the results of this command on the two addresses `tweety@birdcage.com` and `sylvester@suffrin.succotash.org`. If there is no occurrence of a particular search string in the main string, `string first` returns the value `-1`, as shown in Figure 9-1.

Judging yes-no responses

If you haven't had experience with writing code to judge user responses, don't read this sidebar yet. However, if you are already thinking about this kind of thing, here is a tip on how to make your life a little easier.

When you ask a user to respond either "yes" or "no" to a question, you really need to check whether the response is one or the other, *not* both. In general, if one answer will have more of an effect than the other answer, your best option is to assume that the user will answer no, and just check whether they, instead, answered yes. For example, if you have a query like

```
"Download 157MB file to your
   hard drive? (yes or no?)"
```

you should start by assuming that the user doesn't want to do this. Then just check to see whether the response, in fact, starts with a "y" or a "Y." If it doesn't, whether or not they typed an answer starting with an "n" doesn't

matter. On the other hand, if your query is something like

"Mail you a check for $100 for visiting our site? (yes or no?)"

you could assume that the user does want the offer and check only whether the answer begins with an "n." If for some bizarre reason it does, don't send the check, of course. (Don't tell your boss I suggested sending out $100 checks.)

Of course, if you want to be doubly sure that your tclet responds to user input the way the user expects it to, you should check for both "y" and "n" responses. Though the `string first` command works fine for this, more elegant formats, called regular expressions, are available for doing this. If the "simple stuff" in this chapter doesn't help you do what you want the way you want, take a look at Appendix A, which has more about using these powerful tools.

Searching for strings

The first tag of the `string first` and `string last` commands can be any string, not just one character. That means you could actually search a string like "This is a test. This is only a test." to find the first occurrence of the string "test" like so:

`string first test $runaway`

If you enclose your search string in quotes, you can even include whitespaces, like this:

`string first "a test" $runaway`

Note that if the search string appears in the main string, the `string first` command will return the index in the main string of the first character of the search string.

When the variable `runaway` contains the string "This is a test. This is only a test." the command

`string first "test" $runaway`

and

`string first "test. This" $run-away`

return the same value, 10, because the first character of the first occurrence of both strings ("test" and "test. This") has the index 10. If the search string does not exist in the main string, Tcl will return a -1.

```
                         Console
% string length "This is a string of unknown length."
35
% set unknown_string "This is a string of unknown length."
This is a string of unknown length.
% puts $unknown_string
This is a string of unknown length.
% string length $unknown_string
35
% string length unknown_string
14
% |
```

Figure 9-1:
Ah, pursuit.

string last

If the `string first` command finds the first occurrence of a search string, you can bet that `string last` will find the last occurrence of a search string. `string last` is identical to `string first` in every way except that it finds the last example of the search string instead of the first. The syntax is exactly the same. The command

```
string last / "/usr/home/afrancis/TCL/tclets"
```

returns the index of the last instance of the string /. In this case, this command returns

string range

You have one more important thing to unearth about strings: how to cut a *substring* out of a main string. The string range command takes three arguments:

- ✔ The name of the main string to be operated on
- ✔ An index number for one end of the substring
- ✔ An index number for the other end of the substring

What string range does is return all the characters in a string from the index *x* to the index *y*. For example, take the string alphabet:

```
set alphabet "abcdefghijklmnopqrstuvwxyz"
```

the command

```
string range $alphabet 7 23
```

returns the string "ghijklmnopqrstuvw", which is all of the characters from *g* (index 7) to *w* (index 23), inclusive, as is shown by typing

```
string index $alphabet 7
```

and

```
string index $alphabet 23
```

as shown in Figure 9-2.

Figure 9-2:
String index
output.

```
% set response "You betcha!"
You betcha!
% string index $response 0
Y
% string index $response 5
e
% string index $response 10
!
% |
```

By the way, here's a handy little trick for grabbing the name of a directory from a string that consists of the entire path, using a combination of the string range and string last commands. The command

```
string range $cur_dir [string last $cur_dir /] end
```

returns the string

```
/tclets
```

if `$cur_dir` contains the string

```
/usr/home/afrancis/TCL/tclets
```

To get the part of a string that stretches from a certain index to the end of the string, you can substitute the word `end` for the second number of the `string range` command, like this:

```
string range $alphabet 23 end
```

which returns

```
wxyz
```

Comparing Strings

Now that you know your way around strings pretty well, you can move on to some more-sophisticated ways of getting information about strings. The commands in this section, `string match` and `string compare`, work much like the other commands in the `string` family except that they are able to do more-complex analyses on a string.

string compare

The `string compare` command is very simple. It just takes two strings, a *main* string and a *search* string, and compares them. If the two are identical, `string compare` returns 0. If even one character differs, `string compare` returns a -1.

The command `string compare` does not act like other matching commands, which return 1 if a match is made and 0 otherwise. Instead, `string compare` acts a little bit like the `string index` command, in that `string compare` returns a -1 if a character in the search string is not present in the main string (or vice versa). See Figure 9-3 for some examples of the `string compare` command.

Figure 9-3:
The string
compare
command
returns -1 if
the search
doesn't
match.

```
┌─────────────────── Console ───────────────────┐
│ % set address tweety@birdcage.com              │⇧
│ tweety@birdcage.com                            │
│ % string first @ $address                      │
│ 6                                              │
│ % set address sylvester@suffrin.succotash.com  │
│ sylvester@suffrin.succotash.com                │
│ % string first @ $address                      │
│ 9                                              │
│ % string first X $address                      │
│ -1                                             │
│ % |                                            │⇩
└────────────────────────────────────────────────┘
```

string match

The `string match` command, like the `string compare` command, will tell you whether the main string contains a series of characters that match the search string. Unlike `string compare`, however, `string match` does this by returning 1 if there is a match; otherwise it returns 0. For example

```
string match Alex "Alex"
```

returns a 1 because part of the main string consists of the characters of the search string. However,

```
string match Alex "alex"
```

returns a 0 because there is no sequence of characters *A, l, e, x* (remember, Tcl is case-sensitive!).

This command would be pretty boring if this is all `string match` can do. After all, you can just use `string compare` instead. However, `string match` is more useful because it matches whole classes of patterns, not just a specific search string.

The style of matching which `string match` uses is called *glob-style matching*, or *globbing*. Globbing is explained in more detail in Appendix A. In brief, glob-style pattern matching makes use of special characters called *wildcards*. These wildcard characters are symbols that can stand for whole sets of symbols, like a wild card in poker can stand for whatever you need to make a royal flush. The wildcards for globbing are shown in Table 9-1.

Table 9-1	Glob-Style Wildcards
Symbol	*Meaning in a Glob-Style Expression*
*	Matches any number of characters of any kind
?	Matches one instance of any character
[ ]	Encloses a set of characters, either a range, such as [a-z], or just any set, such as [xyzpdq]

These little doohickies are actually easy to use. If you want to be sure that you can deal with globbing like a pro, go ahead and read the section on glob-style pattern matching and regular expressions in Appendix A. However, globbing's not really all that difficult. Just try the following examples.

Pretend that your tclet contains a variable called `cur_dir` that holds a string passed from the URL. This string is simply the machine name and the current directory in which the URL and the tclet reside. You'll mimic this in this example by setting the `cur_dir` variable to be the current directory [on my Linux machine], named `turing`.

```
set cur_dir turing:/home/afrancis/TCL/tclets
```

Now, to see whether the string in the `cur_dir` variable contains any slashes, you can enter the following command:

```
string match *\/* $cur_dir
```

Notice that you must put asterisks (*) around the pattern you must match. This indicates to Tcl that you want to match any string starting with any number (including 0) of any character (represented by the first *) followed by the expression \/ which itself is followed by any number (including 0) of any character (represented by the second *). This example is shown in Figure 9-4.

Figure 9-4:
Asterisks
create a
pattern for
matching.

```
                    ■ Console ■
% set runaway "This is a test.   This is only a test."
This is a test.   This is only a test.
% string first test $runaway
10
% string first "a test" $runaway
8
% string first "test.  This" $runaway
10
% string first "blah" $runaway
-1
%
```

If you don't include the asterisks, as in the first matching attempt in Figure 9-4, string match \/ `$cur_dir` what you are asking Tcl to match is any string consisting of the pattern \/, alone. Similarly, in order to match one forward slash (/) you must put a backward slash (\) in front of it to indicate to Tcl that you want it to treat the / as the character / rather than as the symbol /, which has a special meaning for Tcl.

The second wildcard character is the question mark (?). This wildcard matches any single character. So the command string match ? `$input` returns a 1 if the variable input contains a single character. If not, it returns 0. You can use the ? wildcard in interesting ways. For example, if a string can be either "caps" or "cats", you can match both with the expression "ca?s" without also matching "cape" as would the expression "ca*". (Of course, this expression also matches "cans" and "cals" and any other string starting with "ca" and ending with "s" with any single character in between.)

The ? wildcard is also useful. If you want to match any two character strings like "aa" or "a1" or "12", you can use the expression "??" to do so.

Tcl can also match a range of characters, for example numbers. To do this, simply enclose the characters you want to match in square brackets ([ ]). For example, the command

```
string match {[0-9]} $input
```

matches any string in the variable input that consists of a single digit.

You must enclose the match string in curly braces ({ }); otherwise, Tcl will read the square brackets as an indication that the stuff between them should be interpreted as a Tcl command. Just as you can string multiple ?s together to make an expression that matches multiple-character strings, you can also string together expressions like [0-9] or [a-z]. For example, if you are expecting input for something like a game of Battleship, in which the commands are always a letter (between *A* and *J*) followed by a single digit, you can match only correctly formed commands with the string command match {[a-j][0-9]} $input.

Creating and Parsing Strings

So now you know pretty much all there is to know about investigating and manipulating strings. You even know the basic way of creating strings. (**Hint:** Put a bunch of text between double quotes, and, *voilá,* you've got a string!) However, you can do some really fun and useful things with strings (besides tying your shoes!). For example, it just may be the case that you will want to make a string that contains the values of variables but that you don't want to make a new string each time. Alternatively, you may have a string passed to your tclet that contains a lot of values for variables embedded inside it, and you may want to parse that string to extract the variables. Never fear — as usual — Tcl makes it really easy (well, easier than Java or C do, anyway) to do both these tasks.

The following discussion of the format command may seem a little complicated at first. Some day you may come across a situation in which it's important to be able to display variables in strings with extreme precision. At that time, the format command will come in very handy. Until then, however, you can probably get by just putting your variables directly into your strings, like this:

```
set name "Alex"
puts "Hello, my name is $name"
```

If you need to put formatting marks into your strings, you can use the backslash codes (mostly \t for tab and \n for newline are of use here). For example:

```
puts "Welcome to my tclet.\nThanks for visiting.\n\t- Alex"
```

creates a three-line output in which the last line starts with a tab, like this:

```
Welcome to my tclet.
Thanks for visiting.
    - Alex
```

If you want more control than this over how your variables come out in strings, read on!

format

The `format` command is one of the most useful ways of creating strings. In brief, the `format` command gives a recipe for making a string, complete with special holes left for the value of variables. These holes are tailored to fit only certain variables and to cut other variables to fit. (I think this analogy is getting out of hand.)

The recipe is followed by a list of the variables whose values will be fit in those holes when the tclet is operational. The `format` command is most commonly used when it matters what the value of a variable looks like. For example, maybe you just want to display the whole-number part of a decimal number like 12.735, or you want to truncate it to be 12.7.

In the `format` command, the recipe for the string is in quotes (so it can contain whitespaces) and the list of variables to fill the special holes are placed in order following the close quote. For example, the following format command creates a string which gives the results of a simple addition problem:

```
format "The sum of %d and %d is %d" $first $second \
[expr $first + $second]
```

Of course, this command assumes that the variables `first` and `second` were previously defined. Assuming that the variable `first` is given the value 42 and the variable `second` is given the value of 37, the string resulting from this `format` command should look as follows:

```
The sum of 42 and 37 is 79
```

Notice a couple of things about this command. In the string recipe, the places where the numbers appear in the result string are occupied by the cryptic symbols %d. This is how to specify the holes where the values of the variables will fit.

Be sure to note that, for formatting, Tcl cares which kind of thing is stored in a variable. This is important because in most places, whether you assigned a number or a string to a variable doesn't matter, but it does matter here (at least sometimes). The way you signal to Tcl that you are specifying a place to insert the value of the variable is with the % symbol.

If you want to put a % symbol in your string so that it appears as a %, escape the special meaning of % by preceding it with a backslash (\).

The % symbol is followed by a recipe for how you want that expressed value to look. First and foremost, this recipe consists of a special code telling Tcl which kind of variable fits in this slot. As far as Tcl is concerned, there are three main kinds of variables. The kind used in this example is called an *integer* (but normal folks may call integers whole numbers). Some examples of integers are 1, 19, 754, -33, 156, and so on. Integers can be *signed* (either negative or positive) or *unsigned* (always positive), and range either from 0 to XXX (unsigned) or from -XXX to +XXX (signed). The code for signed integers is d, and the code for unsigned integers is u, so %d signals to Tcl that the value of the variable that goes in this place in the string should be expressed in the resulting string as a signed integer, whereas %u says the same thing for an unsigned integer.

The second kind of variable in Tcl is a *floating point variable,* which most people may call a *decimal variable.* Basically, a floating point variable is an integer plus a fractional component expressed as some number of digits after a decimal place. For example, 5.125 is a floating point number for 5 and $^1/_8$). The code for a floating point number is given as f, so %f says to Tcl to display the contents of a variable as a floating point number. You can also have Tcl display your floating point number in scientific notation, (for example, 1.5e+8 is an expression for "1.5×10^8") using the code e instead of f after the % sign.

The third kind of variable is a *string.* Strings are the only kinds of variable that can contain nonnumeric symbols such as letters or punctuation marks. However, a string can contain number characters as well, as mentioned earlier in the section on matching strings. The code for a string is s, so to insert a the value of a variable that contains a string of any length into your formatted string, use the expression %s. The expression %c also puts a single character into a formatted string, but it requires that the variable contain an integer. The %c expression then signals to Tcl that Tcl should display the character that has the ASCII value of that integer. For example, the command

```
format "%d %c" 101 101
```

returns the string

```
101 e
```

which shows that the ASCII value of the character e is 101.

Because the most common reason to use the format command is to get Tcl to display your variables in exactly the right manner, you can even specify the way in which the variable is displayed. By putting a number between the % symbol and the d, u, f, e, s, or c code, you can tell Tcl how wide to make the field in which the value is to appear. For example, the following command shows three numbers in different sized fields. Note that all these examples include vertical pipe symbols (|) placed at the beginning and the end of the string to show where any leading or trailing whitespaces are.

```
format "|%10d %20d %5d|" 13 27 96
```

The first number, 13, is shown in a field 10 characters wide, at the rightmost edge of the field. The second number, 27, is shown in a field 20 characters wide, at the rightmost edge of the field; and the third number, 96, is shown in a field 5 characters wide, at the rightmost edge of the field, like this:

```
|        13                   27    96|
```

If you want to display your numbers at the left edge of the field, simply put a dash (-) between the % symbol and the number expressing the width of the field. For example, you can make the same string as before, but with a dash after each % symbol like this.

```
format "|%-10d %-20d %-5d|" 13 27 96
```

Now the resulting string looks like this:

```
|13         27                   96   |
```

With a floating point variable, you may not want to express all of the decimal places. If you precede the f or e code with a number that has a decimal point in it, you can ensure that the floating point that is displayed has only as many digits after the decimal point as the value of the number after the decimal place. This really pretty simple to pick up from examples. The command

```
format "|%8.3f|" 12.34567890
```

returns the string

```
|  12.346|
```

As you can tell from where the | symbols, which delimit the beginning and end of the formatted string, the resulting string is 8 characters wide (that's due to the 8 after the % symbol), and the floating point number has 3 decimal places (that's from the .3 after the 8). Also, because there is not a - (hyphen) between the % and the 8, the number is at the right edge of the field. If you write

```
format "|%-8.3f|" 12.34567890
```

the result looks like this:

```
|12.346  |
```

Of course, there's always the possibility that the number in the variable has *fewer* decimal places than you want to display. Never fear, Tcl will cope with this situation just fine. For example, the command

```
format "|%-10.5f|" 12.34
```

results in the string

```
|12.34000  |
```

which clearly has 5 decimal places. Tcl cleverly filled in the missing digits with zeros.

You can make Tcl do this in front of the number as well. For example, when putting numbers in alphabetical order (see the chapter on sorting for more detail) the numbers 0, 1, 2, 3, 4, 5, 6, 7, 8, 9, 10, 11, 12 are sorted into the order 0, 1, 10, 11, 12, 2, 3, 4, 5, 6, 7, 8, 9.

This is clearly not acceptable for many things. If you want to get your numbers in numerical order with an alphabetic sorter, the easiest way of doing it is to pad the single-digit numbers to be two-digit numbers starting with 0. This way, the numbers 00, 01, 02, 03, 04, 05, 06, 07, 08, 09, 10, 11, 12 are sorted into the order 00, 01, 02, 03, 04, 05, 06, 07, 08, 09, 10, 11, 12.

If your list to be sorted includes three-digit numbers, just pad the single-digit numbers with two zeros and the two-digit numbers with one zero. To use the format command to pad integers with preceding zeros, use the same strategy as to get floating point numbers to show a specific number of digits. That is, give the field width followed by a period followed by the number of digits to be displayed, including all zeros. For example, to pad an integer out to 3 digits at the rightmost edge of a 10 character field, use the following command:

```
format "|%10.3d|" 1
```

scan

Now that you know so much about formatting strings, *parsing strings* should be a snap. The trick to parsing a string correctly is knowing what format the string has. If you're not sure, you still have ways to do it (there are *always* multiple ways to do *anything* in Tcl), but they require a little bit of knowledge about programming. (For example, you can take a look at Chapter 8 for a different way to do some of the same tasks as are covered here.)

By *knowing what format a string has,* I don't mean that you must know what kinds of sets of characters the string contains. You need to know, at least, what kinds of variable values you want to pull out of the string, and where in the string they are located. Remember the three basic kinds of variables in Tcl: integers, floating point variables (or *floats* for short), and strings? Well, those same guys are what you need to parse a string with scan.

The scan command works pretty much like the format command, but in reverse. Where format puts variables into a string according to a recipe that includes special symbols indicating where in the string to put each variable, scan takes a string as input, and cuts it into pieces and saves those pieces in variables. The recipe for cutting up a string with scan looks very much the same as the recipe for putting a string together with format.

For example, remember the use of the command

```
format "The sum of %d and %d is %d" $first $second \
[expr $first + $second]
```

to create the output string that looked like this:

```
The sum of 42 and 37 is 79
```

Now, reverse the process by scanning this string to extract three integer variables.

```
scan "The sum of 42 and 37 is 79" "The sum of %d and %d \
is %d" first second sum
```

In this case, this command takes the input string "The sum of 42 and 37 is 79" and extracts from it the values 42, which is put into the variable first, 37, which is put into the variable second, and 79, which goes into variable sum. However, the recipe string "The sum of %d and %d is %d" can also work just as well on the string "The sum of 1 and 2 is 3" or even "The sum of 5 and 2 is 0" (a string is a string, even if the arithmetic in it is wrong!). In this last case, the variable first will have the value 5, the variable second will have the value 2, and the variable sum will have the value 0.

The scan command is very useful for getting information out of strings that are passed to your tclet from the URL. For example, the usual way of getting a list of variables into a tclet is in a string with the form "var1=val1,var2=val2 . . .", and so on. For example, the string

```
"cur_dir=/home/afrancis/TCL/tclets/"
```

is a message to the tclet that the variable cur_dir should have the value

```
/home/afrancis/TCL/tclets/.
```

On the CD-ROM that comes with this book, you can find a procedure called get_args.tcl that will pull all the variable-value pairs out of a string like this and store them in an embedded array. (See Appendix B for more about the CD.) However, if you know that you will be passing a string consisting of only three pairs of variables and values, you can use the following sequence of commands to extract them using the scan command:

```
set input "first=12,second=56,third=01"
scan $input "%5s=%d,%6s=%d,%5s=%d" a x b y c z
```

This command pulls out the five-character string first and saves first in the variable a. Then it pulls out the integer 12 and saves it in the variable x. The next variable, b, receives the value second (a six-character string), and so on. You should notice a couple of things about the recipe for the scan command. First, if you want to capture multiple strings from a single string input, you must specify how long the substrings are. If you don't, Tcl will assign the value of the rest of the input string to that variable, like this.

```
set input "first=12,second=56,third=01"
scan $input "%5s=%d,%s=%d,%s=%d" a x b y c z
```

The variable b receives the whole rest of the string as its value, and none of the variables in the list after b (for example, y) receive any value at all. The one time you don't have to do this is when each string that you want to pull out of a string is separated from the other by whitespaces (spaces or tabs). For example:

```
set bday_list "Wally    10/17/58
Carl    2/29/64"
scan $bday_list "%s %s %s %s" name1 date1 name2 date2
```

puts each fellow's name and birth date in separate variables. Even though the name and birth date of each guy are separated by a tab and the entries for each guy are separated by a newline, scan knows to treat tabs and newlines as though they are spaces.

Figure 9-5 shows one final advantage of knowing how to use the scan and format commands. With them you can take in data in one format, and change it around and write it back out with a minimum of trouble. By carefully using both scan and format, I got the original data pattern, which looked like this:

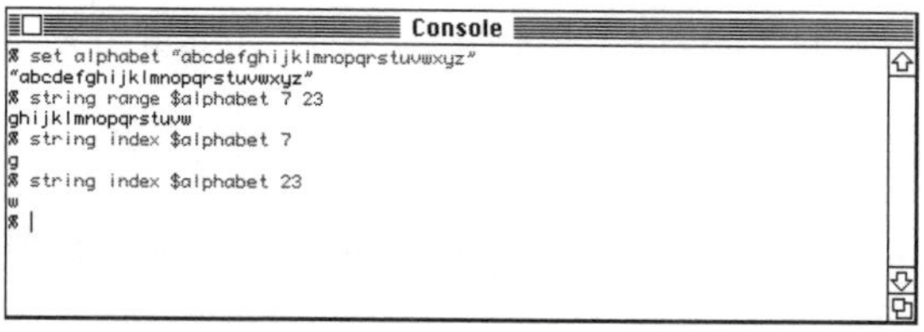

Figure 9-5:
The original
data
pattern.

```
Wally    10/17/58
Carl    2/29/64
```

to come out looking like this:

```
Carl 2/29/64    Wally 10/17/58
```

Chapter 10

Procedures and Functions

In This Chapter

▶ The basic parts of a procedure

▶ The `return` command

▶ Local and global variables

▶ The `upvar` command

*E*verybody's a back seat driver, especially when it comes to programmers. Fortunately, the definition of the Tcl/Tk language isn't a closed book. You can make up your own Tcl/Tk commands, using Tcl/Tk to write a description of what the new command does.

Tcl's original claim to fame is that it is extensible using the C language. When the need arises, you can write new Tcl commands in C and recompile Wish so that it recognizes the custom commands as built-in commands. As you may suspect, doing so is a little complicated, and we don't cover it in this book. You don't need to know how to extend Tcl in order to create top-notch tclets; in any case, you can't use extended Tcl in tclets for Web pages.

Writing Your Own Commands

There are some very good reasons to write your own commands — it's not just something you do to show off.

Streamlining your program

Sometimes you'll want to create your own commands just to make your program look a little more organized. For example, you can specify commands to be executed when a button is pushed, like so:

```
button .b -text "self-destructing button" -command \
{destroy .b}
pack .b
```

(You will look at the procedure for adding commands to buttons again when button widgets are covered in detail.) In the preceding example code, the embedded command, `destroy .b`, is easy to throw into the line that creates the button. But what if the command that is attached to the button is several lines long, like this?

```
destroy .b
label .l -text "Boom!"
pack .l
```

You *can* put these commands in the button command, like so:

```
button .b -text "self-destructing button" \
-command {destroy .b; label .l -text "Boom!"; pack .l}
pack .b
```

You can see how this approach may get old fast. Squeezing a whole block of code into one command makes it easy to make typos and makes the resulting code hard to read. It's much easier to wrap up the code that the button uses into a new command definition, like so:

```
proc boom! {} {
    destroy .b
    label .l -text "Boom!"
    pack .l
}
```

After the procedure is rebuilt, you can rewrite the original button command much more simply, like so:

```
button .b -text "self-destructing button" -command boom!
pack .b
```

Reusing code throughout a tclet

Using procedures allows you to use the same basic routine in different contexts throughout a program. This makes programs easier to create (if nothing else, you do less typing) and change.

For example, suppose that you established a standard "look" for all the buttons in a tclet — chose a particular font for the labels and a set of colors to be used for the label and the background. The code that you use to create an individual button looks something like this:

```
button .b -text "prototype button" \
-font "*-helvetica-bold-*-*-14-*-*-*-*-*-*-*" \
-foreground white -background black \
-width 40
pack .b
```

To create three or four buttons that use the same basic style, you can simply repeat the code again and again:

```
button .b1 -text "File" \
-font "*-helvetica-bold-*-*-14-*-*-*-*-*-*-*" \
-foreground white -background black \
-width 40
pack .b1
button .b2 -text "Edit" \
-font "*-helvetica-bold-*-*-14-*-*-*-*-*-*-*" \
-foreground white -background black \
-width 40
pack .b2
button .b3 -text "View" \
-font "*-helvetica-bold-*-*-14-*-*-*-*-*-*-*" \
-foreground white -background black \
-width 40
pack .b3
button .b4 -text "Special" \
-font "*-helvetica-bold-*-*-14-*-*-*-*-*-*-*" \
-foreground white -background black \
-width 40
pack .b4
```

You can see the resulting tclet in Figure 10-1. This cut-and-paste code doesn't seem like the most elegant solution, does it? If this code seems redundant, it is. Wrapping up the repeated code in a procedure is much more practical, like so:

```
proc make_button {button_name button_label} {
    button $button_name -text $button_label \
    -font "*-helvetica-bold-*-*-14-*-*-*-*-*-*-*" \
    -foreground white -background black \
    -width 40
    pack $button_name
}
```

Now you can create each stylized button with one line of code, like so (see results in Figure 10-1):

```
make_button .b1 "File me!"
make_button .b2 "Edit me!"
make_button .b3 "View me!"
make_button .b4 "Special!"
```

Figure 10-1:
Stylized
buttons
created
with one
line of code.

Reusing code in new tclets

After you write a few lines of code to solve a problem, you can use the same code to solve the same problems in other situations. For example, say that you want to display a text message in a message window. This task is a pretty simple one that can be accomplished with a few line of code, as you've now seen many times:

```
message .m "Hey there, web surfer! Welcome to my site." \
-width 200
pack .m
```

The easiest way to reuse this snippet of code is to simply cut and paste these two lines from the old tclet into the new tclet. The preceding code doesn't depend on anything else that's happening inside the tclet: It just dumps its message on the screen.

However, simply cutting and pasting doesn't take care of one possible snag: What if you're pasting this code into a tclet that already has it's own message widget (or widget of any kind, for that matter) called .m? Remember, each widget must have its unique name. Say that you have a little two-line tclet like this:

```
message .m "Welcome!"
pack .m
```

Pasting the lines from the first tclet into this second tclet yields the following program. If you try loading it in a Web page or sourcing it with Wish, you get an error message about the duplicated widget names.

```
message .m "Welcome!"
pack .m
message .m "Hey there, web surfer! Welcome to my site." \
-width 200
pack .m
```

This collision can be fixed quickly by changing the names of one of the variables. You can simply change the name of one of the widgets to .m1, and the problem is solved.

This can get complicated quickly, however. What if your message depends on the name of a variable, like this:

```
message .m "Hey there, $user_name! Welcome to my site."
```

Now you need to make sure that the variable name $user_name that you used in the pasted-in code is set correctly somewhere else in the tclet that you're pasting the code into. This assumes, of course, that you're not already using the variable name $user_name to store a value that is different from the one that you plan to use in your message widget.

By now you can probably see that "simple" cutting and pasting can get complicated quickly, especially when the code that you want to reuse contains more than one variable name or widget name. These little tweaks can take a long time and a lot of patience — you probably won't catch all the changes you need to make the first time that you try to adjust the program.

If you write a new command, however, many of the problems with variable names disappear. The variables used by a procedure are hidden from the rest of the program, so you can put your old code inside the definition of a new command called display, like so:

```
proc display {display_text} {

    #if message widget .m already exist, \
    change its contents to display_message
    if [winfo exists .m] {
        .m configure -text $display_text

    # otherwise, create a new message widget with
    # the display_widget
    } else {
        message .m -text $display_text -width 150
```

(continued)

(continued)

```
      pack .m
   } ;# close the if block
} ;# close the procedure block
```

Create the new command

```
display " Hey there, $user_name! Welcome to my site."
```

in the new tclet. Furthermore, you can cut and paste this procedure into new tclets — and it won't need any modification at all. (It even takes care of the widget name issue.)

Building a proc *Command*

Creating your own commands is as easy as wrapping up a series of basic Tcl/Tk commands inside a proc command. The basic structure is as follows:

```
proc procedure-name arguments body
```

As with all Tcl/Tk commands, a proc command consists of a list of words. Curly braces are used to group complex arguments and complex bodies into single words. (The interpreter will strip off the curlies and perform all necessary substitutions after the first substitution pass.)

Procedures versus functions

To write your own commands, you use the Tcl command proc to wrap up a block of ordinary Tcl/Tk commands. If you pick up a book on programming, you'll see that most languages distinguish between two kinds of commands: functions, which return a value, and procedures, which simply carry out a task and leave things at that.

Tcl doesn't really make this distinction. Commands that are really procedures and commands that are really functions are both defined with the proc command. Still, knowing the difference helps you more easily make decisions about how to handle creating your own commands.

A procedure simply does something; it returns an empty string as its value. For example, you may write a procedure that does the following:

✔ Sets all the variables in your tclet to their default setting.

✔ Displays a widget on-screen.

✔ Creates a widget in a standard style.

A function, on the other hand, returns a value. The value that's returned can be of any form; the important part is that some output value is returned.

Here's how a typical procedure breaks down into its component parts:

```
proc put_message {widget_name the_message} {
    if [winfo exists $widget_name] {
        $widget_name configure -text $the_message
    } else {
        message $widget_name -text $the_message \
        -width 100
        pack $widget_name
    } ;# end if
}
```

Now you can take a closer look at each of these parts.

Arguments for the procedure

The argument portion of the proc command lists the names of the variables that the procedure will use. For example, in the preceding example procedure, the argument is as follows:

```
{widget_name the_message}
```

In this example, the procedure will use two arguments: a variable called widget_name and a variable called the_message. These variable names don't need to have anything to do with any of the other variables in your program — you can call the arguments anything you like. (See "Using Global and Local Variables," later in this chapter, for more information.) When you call the procedure somewhere else in to program, the interpreter automatically assigns values to the variables in the argument based on the way that the arguments are used to call the procedure. For example, if you call the procedure by entering

```
put_message .m "Hello, Luna"
```

the interpreter assigns values to argument variables like so:

```
widget_name == .m
the_message == "Hello, Luna"
```

If you call the procedure with the code

```
put_message .another_widget "Hello, Saturn"
```

the interpreter will assign the values to the variables as follows:

```
widget_name == .another_widget
the_message == "Hello, Saturn"
```

If you call a procedure with few arguments than are specified in the `proc` command's argument section, the interpreter will return an error, like so:

```
% puts_message .3rd_widget
no value given for parameter "the_message" to "put_message"
```

Similarly, if you pass too many arguments to a procedure, the interpreter chokes:

```
% put_message .4th_widget hello, Halley's Comet
called "put_message" with too many arguments
```

You don't need to use *any* arguments in your procedure if you don't want to. However, if you don't use an argument, you must put the empty string in the `proc` command so that the interpreter doesn't think that the procedure's body is an incredibly long list of arguments. Here's how to specify the empty string as an argument:

```
proc no_args {} {
    # do something interesting!
}
```

In this case, you call the procedure `no_args` with just the command name, like so:

```
no_args
```

The body of the procedure

The body of the procedure is where the action takes place. In the `put_message` procedure, the body of the procedure is

```
{
    if [winfo exists $$widget_name] {
        $widget_name configure -text $the_message
    } else {
        message $widget_name -text $the_message \
        -width 100
        pack $widget_name
    } ;# end if
}
```

You can put any Tcl/Tk command you like into the body of a `proc` — even, strangely enough, another proc command. (You have are no practical reasons to define a procedure inside another procedure . . . at least with simple little tclets.)

If you regularly peek at other folk's tclets' source code, you may see tclets that *call themselves.* This is called *recursion,* and it's perfectly legal, as long as the procedure eventually goes through a pass wherein it doesn't call itself. It's a fundamental law of computer science that every task that can be handled by recursion can be handled by some looping structure (for example, a `while` or `foreach` command) and every loop can be handled with recursion. If you find them hard to figure out, you *don't* need to write recursive routines.

The return *command*

If your new procedure is a function — that is, it creates some sort of result — you need a way to send the results of the procedure back to the rest of the tclet that called it.

For example, say that you create a little procedure that finds the average of two numbers, like so

```
proc avg {x y} {
    set the_avg [expr ($x + $y) / 2 ]
}
```

Now say that you want to use your new command in conjunction with command substitution, like so

```
message .m1 -text "the average of 13 and 47 is \
[avg 13 47]" -width 100
pack .m1
```

This works just fine because the last command in the procedure is a set command, which returns a value. However, suppose the procedure adds up a list of numbers, like so

```
proc sum_list {list_o_values} {
    set sum 0
    foreach x $list_o_values {
        set sum [expr $sum + $x]
    }
}
```

Try the new command with command substitution:

```
set my_list "1 2 3 4 5"
message .m2 -text "the sum of $my_list is \
[sum_list $my_list]" -width 250
pack .m2
```

The results, pathetic as they are, are shown in Figure 10-2. The message mysteriously leaves off after the word *is.* What's going on here?

Figure 10-2:
Not the
greatest,
is it?

Here's the problem: The last line of the procedure is `for` command. Because the `for` command doesn't return a value, it returns an empty string, not the results of the last command in the `for` loop. You must add a special command to the procedure to cause it to return a value. This command is called, logically, `return`, and it's used like this:

```
return value
```

Here's how to add the `return` command to the `sum_list` procedure so that `sum_list` returns a value:

```
proc sum_list {list_o_values} {
    set sum 0
    foreach x $list_o_values {
        set sum [expr $sum + $x]
    }
    return $sum
}
```

Now you can call the `sum_list` command with command substitution. The following code is unchanged since your last attempt. (Be sure to destroy the `.m2` widget before you reenter this in Wish.)

```
set my_list "1 2 3 4 5"
message .m2 -text "the sum of $my_list is \
[sum_list $my_list]" -width 250
pack .m2
```

Figure 10-3 shows the improved results. The interpreter has swapped in a result for the `sum_list` procedure (for `[sum_list $my_list]`) instead of throwing in the empty string.

Figure 10-3:
The
interpreter
makes
everything
better.

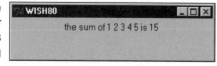

Using Global and Local Variables

Variables in a procedure exist in a slightly different world than the variables in the rest of a tclet. The variables that you create and use inside the body block of the procedure command are created and destroyed every time that the procedure is destroyed, so changes to a procedure variable named something like x don't affect changes to a variable called x in the body of the tclet (or in other procedures).

Take a look at how this works in a tclet. You may want to try this in Wish so that you can see the results right away. First, you create a little procedure that sets the value of the variable x to a value of 0:

```
proc set_x {} {
    set x 0
}
```

Now set the value of *x* outside the procedure:

```
set x " certainly not the number zero!"
```

Next you call the procedure:

```
set_x
```

Now you get the value of *x*":

```
puts "the value of x is $x"
```

Based on what you see in the procedure, you'd expect this to yield "the value of x is 0". But because the procedure creates and uses its own variables, the x in set_x doesn't affect the x in the body of the tclet. So Wish returns

```
% puts "the value of x is $x"
the value of x is certainly not the number zero!
```

Just to make what's happening clearer, tweak the procedure just a little by adding a line of code that shows what's happening inside the procedure, as follows:

```
proc set_x {} {
    set x 0
    puts "the value of x inside the procedure is $x"
}
```

Here's what you get when you call the new version of set_x:

```
% set_x
the value of x inside the procedure is 0
% puts "the value of x in the body of the tclet is $x"
the value of x in the body of the tclet is certainly not
                zero!
```

Changes to a variables inside a procedure *don't* affect variables with the same name in the body of a tclet.

This rule also applies to the arguments that are passed to a tclet. For example, make a new variable, called *y:*

```
set y "whatever y is"
```

Now change set_x again so that it takes a parameter. Notice that I switched the order of the lines inside the body so that you can get a readout of the argument's value *before* you set the argument to 0:

```
proc set_x {x} {
    puts "the value of x inside the procedure is $x"
    set x 0
}
```

Remember, the argument is really just a variable that the procedure uses internally. Even though the argument is called x, you can pass any variable to it that you like:

```
% set_x y
the value of x inside the procedure is whatever y is
0
% puts "the value of y is $y"
the value of y is whatever y is
% puts "the value of x is $x"
the value of x is certainly not zero
```

See? Passing y as an argument didn't change the value of y in the body of the tclet. A procedure doesn't change anything in the body of the tclet, no matter what variable names or argument names are used in the procedure.

Local variables

The variables that you use inside a procedure are called *local variables* because they're used only inside the procedure, and not anywhere else in the tclet. By default, all variables that you create inside a procedure are local variables. When you call the procedure, the variable is created, and when the procedure is finished, the variable is destroyed.

As a result, you can't store anything inside a local variable between calls to the procedure. Take a look at this code:

```
proc leftovers? {} {
    #if x already exists, print its value and add one to it
    if [info   exists x] {
        puts  $x
        incr x
    #if x doesn't exist, create it with a value of zero
    } else {
        puts "starting over"
        set x 0
    }
}
```

Now you call the `leftovers?` procedure a few times to see what happens:

```
% for {set index 0} {$index < 3} {incr index} {
>    leftovers?
> }
starting over
starting over
starting over
```

Each time the procedure is finished, the local variable x is destroyed. As a result, the test to see whether x already exists (the command substitution [info exists x] always yields a false answer, and the variable x is re-created from scratch.

Global variables

You may suspect that the *local-ness* of local variables may sometimes be a nuisance. What if you want to take a look at the variables in the body of a tclet from inside a procedure or store information between the passes of a tclet?

Well, you use the opposite of a local variable — a *global* variable. A global variable has the same name and variable anywhere in a tclet — in any of the tclet's procedures or in the tclet's main body.

Thanks to the `global` command, you can store information between calls to a procedure.

To create a global variable, you use the `global` command *inside* a tcl procedure. (Using global in the body of a tclet is legal but doesn't yield useful results.) Global just lets the interpreter know that a variable in a procedure refers to the variable with the same name in the body of the program. In general, the format for the `global` command is

```
global variable-name1variable-name2 . . . last-variable-
         name
```

To see how this works, rewrite the `set_x` procedure using the global command:

```
proc set_x {} {
    global x
    set x 0
}
```

Now you just make sure that you have something other than zero in `x` in the body of the tclet:

```
% set x "anything other than zero"
anything other than zero
puts "the value of x is $x"
the value of x is anything other than zero
```

Now you call the `global`-fied version of `set_x`:

```
% set_x
0
% puts "the value of x is $x"
the value of x is 0
```

Because you used the `global` command to tell the interpreter that the procedure's `x` was the same `x` used in the rest of the program, the interpreter changed the value of `x` in the body of the tclet in the procedure's `set x 0` line.

Part III
Widget Science

In this part . . .

1n this part, you discover *widgets* — buttons, scrollbars, and other Macintosh- and Windows-type devices that enable users to interact with your tclet. (After all, that interactivity is what separates tclets from plain old HTML, which sits on the screen like a big lump.)

In Chapter 11, you get to meet each member of the family of widgets. (Don't worry, it's an informal introduction so it's okay to wear casual clothes.) Next, you find out about the features that all widgets have in common. You also learn about *binding* (making widgets responsive to the user) and *geometry managers* (making widgets show up on screen).

Chapter 11

What Is a Widget?

- ▶ The widget lineup
- ▶ Configuring widgets
- ▶ Event Binding
- ▶ Displaying widgets
- ▶ Widget inheritance

*B*y now, you've created a bushel of little experimental widgets, but I haven't explained exactly what a widget is. A Tk widget, like a real-world widget, is a little object that's handy to have around. You can think of widgets as being like the tools in a Swiss Army knife: No tool can do everything, but you're likely to find a tool in there that does what you want (or in a pinch, can be jerry-built to do what you want).

This chapter covers the basics of widget management and gives you an overview of the topics that are covered in the next few chapters.

Widget Basics

A *widget* is a software tool, such as a button or a scrollbar, that is written and packaged to be easy to use. All the complicated business of creating an on-screen object is hidden away inside the Tcl/Tk interpreter. All you need to do is specify the way that you want the widget to appear and behave.

A widget is a GUI component

For all practical purposes, you can think of a widget as being a GUI component. *GUI* (usually pronounced "gooey," as in "gooey chocolate cookies") stands for graphic user interface. Does that explanation clear things up for you?

In compuspeak, a *user interface* is simply the way that the user of the program can control what the program does. If you were around in the bad old days before the Mac and Windows 95, you may have worked with a command-line interface (such as DOS) that required you to enter commands at a prompt or type numbers to choose things from menus. As we say in 1997: "Ugh!"

A *graphic user interface* is simply the familiar point-and-click approach used by Windows 95 and MacOS applications. You can do things such as choose commands from drop-down menus, click buttons or hypertext links, skip around inside a text document by repositioning the cursor with the mouse, and draw shapes in drawing programs. I suspect that using Windows-style applications is old hat now for almost all of you.

Although GUI-based programs are easy to use, they can be difficult to program. Just drawing a widget (such as a scrollbar) on-screen can take dozens of lines of code in a language such as C, and keeping track of user activity and updating the widget to reflect what the user's doing with the widget is a real headache.

Fortunately, when you create Tcl/Tk widgets, all the work has been done for you. That is, you don't need to draw the widget by hand; rather, you create it with one line of code and plunk it down on-screen with another line. After you put a widget on-screen, the Tcl/Tk interpreter keeps track of updating it for you. If the user clicks a button, the button flashes and moves to show that it has been clicked. If the user drags the knob of a slider widget, the interpreter takes care of moving the knob. (This is why I love Tcl/Tk — I don't have to write this bookkeeping code by hand when a computer program can do it for me.)

A widget is a window

It's also helpful to think of a widget as being a tiny window on-screen. When you look through the window into cyberspace, you can see the GUI component that you selected to occupy the window.

No, I'm not completely nuts. The reason why it's helpful to think of widgets as an on-screen window is that, in general, any kind of widget can contain any other kind of widget. Widgets can't contain in every possible situation, but it's true enough to remember as a rule. A user interface created with Tk is like a stained-glass window, with many little windows that combine to form the big window.

To see how this works, create a big square button by using Wish, as follows:

```
button .b -background white
pack .b
```

Now add a second button inside the first button:

```
button .b.b2 -background blue
pack .b.b2
```

You can see the result in Figure 11-1: The blue button is created right in the center of the white button. If you play around with this tclet in Wish, you see that you can click each button independently. If you click the edge of the white button, only the white button reacts, but if you click the blue button, the blue button responds.

Figure 11-1:
A tclet that
contains a
button-
within-a-
button.

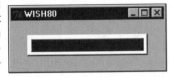

As you can see in the section "Displaying Widgets," later in this chapter, this system of windows within windows allows you to specify exactly how the widgets are laid out within a tclet.

A widget is an OOP object

If you've done much reading about programming, you've probably heard about something called OOP. *OOP* (pronounced as in "Oop! Those curly brackets aren't balanced!") stands for *object-oriented programming,* which is all the rage in programmer culture, if "programmer culture" isn't too much of an oxymoron.

Object-oriented programming means different things to different people, but most people would agree that it means that the behavior of a snippet of code is modeled on a real-world object, and you don't need to know how a particular software object works to use it.

Well, Tk widgets are like real-world objects. You can move the knob on a slider, for example, and you can measure the position of the slider's knob against the slider's scale. You don't need to know what the interpreter's doing to use the slider in your tclet.

Don't get the idea, however, that Tcl/Tk is an object-oriented language, because it's not. You're using objects that have already been defined by the Tcl/Tk interpreter — you can't define new widgets with Tcl/Tk commands. (Rocket-scientist programmers can create new widgets by extending the interpreter with code written in the C language.)

Creating and Configuring Widgets

When you create a widget, all you really need to specify is the kind of widget that you want to create (button, text, canvas, and so on) and a name for the widget. You can also specify options to customize the widgets, but options are never strictly necessary. The general pattern for this kind of command is as follows:

```
command-name widget-name -option1 value-of-option1 \
        -option2 value-of-option2
                    .
                    .
                    .
            -lastoption value-of-last-option
```

Each widget uses its own command name. You create buttons with the `button` command, text widgets with the `text` command, scrollbars with the `scrollbar` command, and so on.

Widget names always begin with a dot (.) and consist of one Tcl word. All of the following are valid widget names:

- `.b`
- `.b1`
- `.button`
- `.button-number-1`
- `.my-little-button-with-the-very-long-name`
- `.b.b2`
- `.b.button-within-a-button`

Widget options always use a hyphen (-) at the beginning of the option name. Each widget-building command uses a slightly different set of options, but many widgets share several options, such as these:

- Width of the widget
- Height of the widget
- Foreground color
- Background color
- Text label
- Font used for text displays

Each option must be accompanied by a one-Tcl-word-long option value. If you use the -text option with the label command, for example, you need to provide the text. This value goes directly after the option's name, like this:

```
-text foo
```

or

```
-text "what exactly does 'foo' mean?"
```

or

```
-text [lindex"fee fi foo fum" 2]
```

You can string together options for a command in any order that you like. All the following examples are equally correct. The command

```
button .b -text "pow!" -width 100 -height 100
```

yields exactly the same widget as the command

```
button .b -width 100 -height 100 -text "pow!"
```

and the command

```
button .b -height 100 -text "pow!" -width 100
```

In fact, any ordering of options is perfectly legal. The Tcl/Tk interpreter isn't fussy about this kind of thing.

If you like, you can skip the options altogether. Commands such as button .b, message .m, and scrollbar .s are perfectly legal, although buttons and labels that don't contain any text or other distinguishing features look a little strange.

After you create a widget, you can change its configuration as you please. (You get a glimpse of post-creation widget customization in Chapter 5.) Whenever you create a widget, you also create a Tcl/Tk command with the same name, and you use this command to change the widget later.

Suppose that you build a label widget, like this:

```
label .1 -text "my widget text"
```

As soon as the `label` command is executed by the interpreter, a new command, called `.l`, is created. Each widget-based command includes a `configure` option, such as the following:

```
.l configure -text "new text for the same widget"
```

Using the widget-name command with the `configure` option, you can change any widget options that you want. Simply add the options as you would if you were creating the widget from scratch. As is the case with widget options, order doesn't matter — you can specify options in any order. All the following examples are valid uses of the `.l configure` command:

```
.l configure -text "even newer text for the same widget" \
    -foreground white -background black
.l configure -foreground white -background black \
    -text "even newer text for the same widget"
.l configure -font "*-avenir-bold-*-*-100-*-*-*-*-*-*" \
    -foreground white -background black
```

The Widget Lineup

Now that you know what widgets are, you're ready to get down to specifics and meet the individual widgets. Some of these widgets have been introduced in previous chapters, but some of these guys are appearing here for the first time.

Toplevels and frames

Toplevels and *frames* are special widgets that you use to organize the way that your widgets appear on-screen. Neither toplevels nor frames do anything flashy by themselves; instead, they act as containers for other widgets.

Toplevels

A toplevel widget is a special case. When you're using Wish, a toplevel looks like an ordinary GUI window. (The display window in Wish, for example, is really just a toplevel widget.) When you create a tclet for a Web page, however, the toplevel is merely a square region inside the Web page. Figure 11-2 shows a series of toplevels in Wish, and Figure 11-3 shows a toplevel in a Web-page tclet.

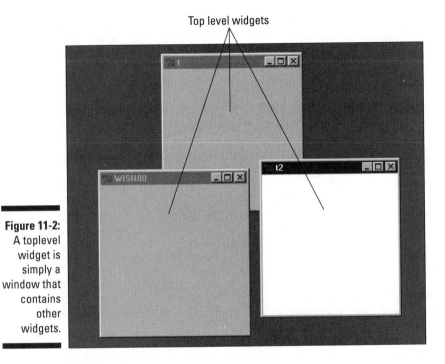

Top level widgets

Figure 11-2:
A toplevel
widget is
simply a
window that
contains
other
widgets.

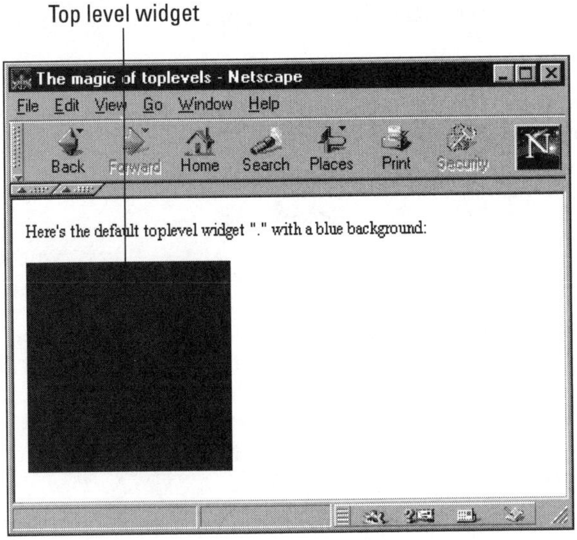

Top level widget

Figure 11-3:
On a Web
page tclet,
a toplevel
widget
is simply
a square
area.

You can create as many toplevels as you want in Wish, like so:

```
toplevel .t
toplevel .t2 -background white
```

You can't create toplevels in tclets that are embedded in Web pages. New toplevels are a potential security risk — bad guys may use a toplevel to imitate something like a password-entry dialog box and fool users into revealing private information.

When you write a tclet for a Web page, however, you are provided with one toplevel widget, called . (period), that the plug-in creates automatically. You can configure this toplevel widget as you like, as follows:

```
configure . -background white
```

Every tclet — whether it's created with Wish or for a Web page — automatically contains the . (period) toplevel widget. In fact, the little dot that you use when you create widgets with names such as .b or .my-little-widget-with-the-really-long-name actually signifies that the widgets you create are inside the default window.

Frames

Frame widgets are invisible; they're used to group a set of widgets in one unit. As you see in Chapter 16, frames are invaluable for making widgets go where you want them to go.

You can look at frames in detail in Chapter 16, but for now, you get a little taste of how you can use frames to stack buttons in a square. (To see how things change from step to step, your best option is to try this procedure in Wish.)

1. **Create the frame for the left column of buttons, and add a few buttons inside the frame, as follows:**

```
frame .left
button .left.a1 -text A1
button .left.b1 -text B1
pack .left.a1 .left.b1
```

Notice that none of the buttons has actually appeared in the Wish window yet; you've packed the buttons into a frame, rather than into the display window. You can display the frame and the buttons that it contains, like so:

```
pack .left -side left
```

2. **Create another frame (called, surprisingly, `right`), and add buttons to this frame, like this:**

```
frame .right
button .right.a2 -text A2
button .right.b2 -text B2
pack .right.a2 .right.b2
```

3. Add the new frame to the display, as follows:

```
pack .right -side right
```

Figure 11-4 shows how this code works out in the real world: The buttons are packed into the frame from top to bottom, and the frames are packed side by side, so that the buttons form a square.

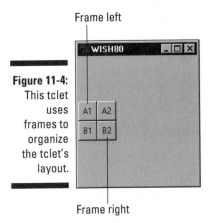

Frame left

Frame right

Figure 11-4:
This tclet uses frames to organize the tclet's layout.

Buttons

In previous chapters, I use quite a few button widgets. *Button widgets* are stylized squares that perform a Tcl/Tk command when the user clicks the button. If no command is specified, the button does nothing when it's clicked.

Buttons widgets are created with the button command, like so:

```
button .b -text "Hit me!"
```

Figure 11-5 shows a few buttons and the button commands that created them.

The most interesting (and practical) of the special options that you can use to customize the button command is the -command option, which allows you to specify a set of Tcl commands to be executed whenever a button is clicked. Creating a self-destructing button is easy, as the following example shows:

```
button .b -text "don't click me!" -command {destroy .b}
```

When this button is clicked, the interpreter executes the command specified in the command option (destroy .b). In this case, the command simply destroys the button.

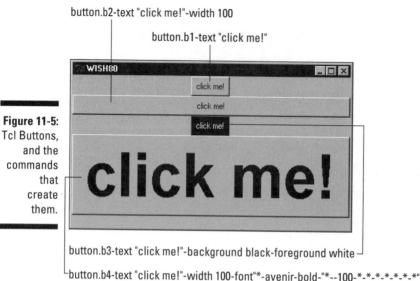

button.b2-text "click me!"-width 100

button.b1-text "click me!"

Figure 11-5:
Tcl Buttons,
and the
commands
that
create
them.

button.b3-text "click me!"-background black-foreground white

button.b4-text "click me!"-width 100-font"*-avenir-bold-"*--100-*-*-*-*-*-*"

You don't need to limit yourself to one command, of course; you can put as many commands as you want between the curly brackets that group the command in a single word. You can use the following code to create a counter button that keeps track of the number of times that it has been clicked:

```
set counter 0
button .b -text $counter \
    -command {
        incr counter
        .b configure -text $counter
    }
```

See Chapter 15 for more on buttons and the finer points of button-making.

Checkbuttons and radiobuttons

Checkbuttons (usually called checkboxes in the world outside Tcl/Tk) and radiobuttons should be familiar to most readers who have spent some time working with Windows- or Mac-based applications. Both checkbuttons and radiobuttons allow readers to choose options with a click of the mouse.

Checkbuttons

A *checkbutton* allows the user to answer yes-or-no and true-or-false questions by clicking a little square. Figure 11-6 shows a series of checkbuttons in a typical context.

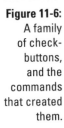
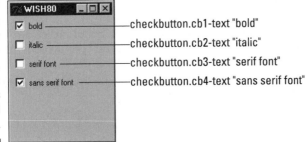

Figure 11-6:
A family
of check-
buttons,
and the
commands
that created
them.

Checkbuttons are created with the checkbutton command, like so:

```
checkbutton .cb -text "Want to be on our mailing list?"
```

You can customize checkbuttons with several special options, including the following:

- command: Allows you to specify a set of commands to be executed when the user clicks the checkbutton.
- variable: Allows you to specify the name of a variable that stores the on-or-off status of the checkbutton.

See Chapter 20 for more about checkbuttons.

Radiobuttons

Radiobuttons (usually spelled as the separate words *radio buttons* outside the world of Tcl/Tk) allow the user to select one option from a set of two or more options. (Almost everyone routinely encounters radiobuttons in everyday applications.) Only one radiobutton in any given set can be selected at any time.

Look at the set of radiobuttons shown in Figure 11-7. These buttons allow users to specify the Web browser that they are using. The Windows radiobutton is currently highlighted. If the Mac radiobutton is clicked, its selector box becomes highlighted, and the Windows radiobutton becomes deselected.

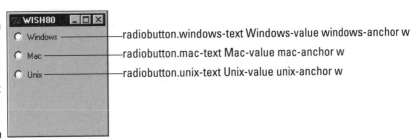

Figure 11-7:
Radiobuttons,
and the
code that
created
them.

Radiobuttons, which are created with the `radiobutton` command, are a little tricky to work with. Although you can create individual radiobuttons without using any command options, creating a set of radiobuttons requires that you assign each radiobutton a value with the `-value` option, like so:

```
radiobutton .windows -text Windows -value windows -anchor w
radiobutton .mac -text Mac -value mac -anchor w
radiobutton .unix -text Unix -value unix -anchor w
pack .windows .mac .unix
```

Label, message, and text widgets

To the naked eye, label, message, and text widgets all look very similar; all three are used to display text messages to the user. A few basic differences exist, however:

- ✓ **The user can edit the text in a text widget.** Text in a label or message widget, however, can't be edited directly.

- ✓ **Label widgets are meant to display single lines of text.** By default, text is displayed centered and without line breaks.

- ✓ **Message widgets are meant to display blocks of several lines of text.** By default, text is displayed in several lines of flush-left text.

Figure 11-8 shows how these widgets differ.

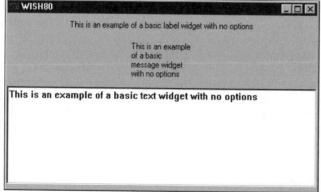

Figure 11-8:
Labels,
message,
and text
widgets are
all slightly
different.

In each widget, the text to be displayed is exactly the same. The top widget, a *label*, displays the text in one unbroken line and is created with the following command:

```
label .l -text \
"There is no emperor but the emperor of ice cream"
```

The middle widget, a *message,* breaks the text into several lines and is created with the following command:

```
message ,m -text \
"This is an example of a basic label widget with \
no options"
```

The bottom widget is a *text* widget. Notice that, by default, the widget has a large border. If you're entering these commands in Wish, go ahead and try to edit the text in the text widget, just as though you're using a text editor or word processor. You'll find that you can edit the text, and you can even use many standard text-edit shortcuts, such as double-clicking on words to select them.

The text widget is created with the following lines of code:

```
text .t
.t insert 1.0 \
"This is an example of a basic label widget with no \
options"
```

See Chapter 19 for more about text-based widgets.

Entry widgets

Entry widgets are simple boxes that users can type text in; they're exactly like the textboxes commonly seen in HTML forms. Entries probably are the easiest way to pass text information between the user and your tclet. Figure 11-9 shows an entry widget in action. (The text to the left of the box is actually a separate label widget, not part of the entry widget.)

Figure 11-9:
You can use entry boxes to collect user input.

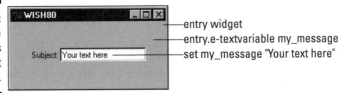

— entry widget
— entry.e-textvariable my_message
— set my_message "Your text here"

Entry widgets are created with the `entry` command, like so:

```
entry .e
```

The text to be displayed in an entry widget doesn't go in a `-text` option; rather, the entry widget has a special relationship with a variable called a `textvariable`. When you use the `textvariable` option like this:

```
entry .e -textvariable my_message
```

Everything that the reader types in the entry widget `.e` is stored in the variable `my_message`, just as though you put it there with the `set` command. Similarly, when you change the value of `my_message` with `set`, as follows:

```
set my_message "Your text here"
```

The new value (in this case, `Your text here`) is displayed automatically in the entry widget.

Note: Several widgets use `textvariables`, but only entry widgets allow the user to change the value of the widget's `textvariable`.

Listboxes

Listboxes are a special way to display a series of text strings. Each string is displayed in its own line of text, and the user can select the entire line by clicking it anywhere. (If you've ever used a file dialog box in Windows or MacOS, you've seen a listbox in action.) Figure 11-10 shows a listbox created with Tcl/Tk.

Figure 11-10:
You use listboxes to display lists of things. Surprise!

The `listbox` command simply creates an empty listbox; no options allow the contents to be specified when the widget is created. The contents of a listbox are added after the listbox is created, like so:

```
listbox .lb
foreach index "bread milk butter eggs" {
    .lb insert end $index
}
```

Turn to Chapter 22 for the specifics on listboxes.

Scrollbars

You've certainly seen scrollbars before; they appear in almost every window that contains an image or a word-processing document. *Scrollbars* are the controls that allow you to pan around inside a document. You can operate a scrollbar by clicking the arrows at either end or by dragging the little box in the middle (called the *scroll box*) to either end of the scrollbar.

Although you can create a freestanding scrollbar like the one shown on the left side of Figure 11-11, scrollbars usually are used in conjunction with text widgets or canvas widgets (which display images). The textbox on the right side of Figure 11-11 shows the traditional use of scrollbars.

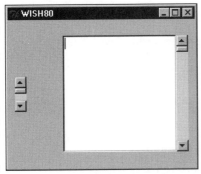

Figure 11-11: Scrollbars are often used as teammates of textboxes and other widgets.

Scrollbars are created with the `scrollbar` command, like so:

```
scrollbar .sb
```

The scrollbar's option is the tool that's used to connect the scrollbars to a text widget. Text and canvas widgets have built-in tools for interacting with scrollbars (see details about scrollbars in Chapter 17).

Scales

Scales are my favorite widgets; they're something like scrollbars, but they're designed to allow users to enter data by moving a slider around. You may have encountered scales in your system control panels; these scales allow you to adjust the volume of your speakers or the brightness of your screen. Figure 11-12 shows a few scale widgets created with Tcl/Tk.

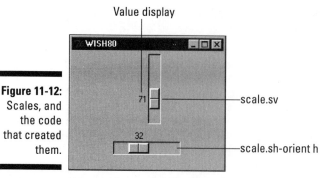

Value display

Figure 11-12:
Scales, and
the code
that created
them.

scale.sv

scale.sh-orient h

To really appreciate the beauty of scales, cook up a few in Wish, as follows:

```
scale .sv
scale .sh -orient h
pack .sv .sh
```

Notice that when you drag the sliders around with the mouse, the Tcl interpreter takes care of everything, including updating the value display and moving it to synchronize with the slider.

You can configure almost every aspect of a scale, including the following:

- ✔ Horizontal/vertical orientation
- ✔ Whether the position value is displayed
- ✔ Whether the scale is calibrated with tick marks
- ✔ The starting and ending values for the scale

Check out Chapter 17 for more about scales.

Canvases

Canvas widgets allow you (or a user) to show your artistic side. A *canvas widget* is a blank stretch of screen that you can decorate with special commands. You can draw, write, or even display image files in a canvas widget. Figure 11-13 shows a canvas widget that I used to draw two simple geometric shapes.

By itself, a canvas widget is blank, like a new painter's canvas. Canvas widgets are created with the `canvas` command, as follows:

```
canvas .c
```

Figure 11-13:
You can use
canvas
widgets
to display
all kinds
of graphics.

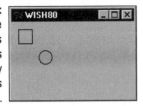

After you create the widget, you can draw in it by using commands based on the canvas widget's name. (Remember that a new command is created every time you create a new widget.) If you create a canvas widget called .c, you can draw a rectangle, like so:

```
.c create rect 10 10 30 30
```

Or you can draw a circle, like so:

```
.c create oval 40 40 60 60
```

You find out how to paint in Tk canvases in Chapter 18.

Finding Documentation about Widget Options

Almost all Tk widgets have some standard attributes. Every widget has a size and color, for example. Most widgets also display some sort of text, and you can configure the text style — the point size and typeface of the text — when you create the widget. Chapter 14 describes the most common properties, which are shared by a wide range of widgets.

The most complete description of the command options for each widget is included in the HTML documentation that's distributed with the Wish application. Each widget is described in its own HTML page; the radiobutton widget, for example, is described in the file radiobutton.html. Just drag the HTML document into your Web browser. Each widget's documentation includes the following:

- The name of the command
- A synopsis of how the command is constructed
- A list of the basic options that the widget supports, with detailed descriptions of common widget options described in the HTML file options.html

✔ A list of options that are specific to the widget, with detailed instructions for using these options

If you're using Linux or another UNIX-based platform, you may also want to look at the Wish man pages. Just enter **man Wish** at the system prompt.

Event Binding

The beauty of widgets is that they don't just sit on-screen. The user can interact with widgets by clicking them, dragging them, typing text in them, or whatever seems like the intuitive thing to do.

The beauty of Tcl/Tk is that when users interact with widgets, widgets do things by themselves — buttons execute commands, scrollbars move text within a text window, and so on. As the programmer, you participate in the process of responding to user activity on three levels:

✔ **Level One:** You do nothing. Widget behavior that gives feedback to the user (such as the way buttons flash or the way the slider of a scrollbar or scale moves when it's dragged) are built into the widget.

✔ **Level Two:** You specify a set of commands for the widget with the -command option. Most widgets are tied to an obvious user action — you click a button or drag a scale, for example. Commands specified in this way are executed when the obvious thing happens to the widget.

✔ **Level Three:** You set up a relationship between any user event and any widget, and you specify the command that takes place when the widget and the event come together. You can, for example, specify a command to be executed when the mouse passes over a label or message (even if the user doesn't click the widget) or create two different sets of commands for a button — one set for regular clicks and one set for shift-clicks.

An *event,* in Tcl/Tk parlance, is anything that the user of the program does while the tclet is running. While the interpreter is executing a tclet, it always has one ear to the mouse and keyboard, and whenever the user does anything (moves the mouse, clicks a mouse button, presses a key, or holds a key down, for example), the interpreter takes note.

Often, the interpreter ignores events. No widget is automatically configured to respond to mouse movements for example; if you simply skid the mouse around inside a tclet (without dragging), nothing happens. Likewise, if you click a label widget, nothing happens; by default, labels don't recognize mouse clicks.

You can configure a label widget so that it responds to motion over the widget and displays the number of events that it has detected. Here's how:

1. **Create a variable called** hits **that stores the number of mouse-motion events that the label has detected, as follows:**

```
set hits 0
```

2. **Create the label, specifying that it display the value of the variable** hits **instead of a canned text string, like this:**

```
label .l -textvariable hits -width 50
pack .l
```

3. **Use the Tcl/Tk command** bind, **which creates connections between widgets and events. Enter the command in Wish (or as a line of tclet code), as follows:**

```
bind .l <Motion> {incr hits}
```

Don't worry about the pattern of the bind command right now — you can find more about it in Chapter 13.

Unfortunately, the names of events in Tcl are case-sensitive, and unlike all of Tcl/Tk's other special words, event names start with uppercase letters. Be sure to type Motion, instead of motion or MOTION, or this example won't work.

Now every time the interpreter detects mouse motion over the widget .l, it executes the command incr hits. Because hits is a textvariable, every time it is incremented, the display of the label is updated automatically.

If you move the cursor over the label widget, the value displayed by the widget changes as you move the mouse. If you hold the mouse still over the widget, nothing happens, but if you scrub the mouse in little circles, the value continues to climb. If you move the mouse around elsewhere in the display window, however, nothing happens; the bind command is specific to the label widget instead of to the event.

Events exist for almost every user activity (including combination events such as dragging the cursor while holding down the Shift key), and you can bind any event to any widget, giving you complete control of the way that your widgets behave.

Displaying Widgets

The last subject in our general coverage of widgets is adding widgets to your tclet's layout. Earlier chapters have made extensive use of the simplest command used to add widgets to a layout: the `pack` command. I've really only scratched the surface of `pack` so far; like most commands, it has a series of options that can fine-tune the way that `pack` puts widgets on-screen. You can add buttons from left to right, add space between buttons, cause buttons to expand to fill all available space, and so on. See Chapter 16 for the fine points of `pack`.

Tcl/Tk offers commands besides `pack` that can display widgets. The `grid` command, for example, also adds widgets to the layout, but it uses a different system for specifying where widgets should be placed, as in the following example:

```
label .l -text "the secret command!"
grid .l
```

Check out Chapter 16 for more about `grid`.

Properly speaking, the `pack` command controls a special assistant genie called the packer, and the `grid` command controls the gridder. These assistant genies, which work for the interpreter, are called *geometry managers*. Other geometry managers exist besides the packer and the gridder, but you don't really need them to create snazzy Web-page tclets.

Although frames are really widgets like any other widgets, Chapter 17 is set aside for a special discussion of using frame widgets to organize the rest of the widgets in a tclet.

Chapter 12

Name, Rank, and Serial Number: Standard Widget Features

. . . .

In This Chapter

▶ Customizing colors

▶ Planning proportions

▶ Bending buttons

. . . .

*T*cl has a lot of widgets, and the appearance of every widget can be configured in at least a few different ways (some widgets can be tweaked so many ways, it can get kinda crazy). Lucky for you (and me), John Ousterhout, the guy who invented Tcl, decided that most widgets should be primarily defined by certain basic features.

In fact, he made life even easier for us by making sure that every widget starts with a *default value* for all of these basic features. You don't even have to specify these features. However, if you are a rugged individualist, you'll probably want to start playing around with the features (that is, the widget attributes) in this chapter in order to get your tclets looking just right. (***Note:*** In later chapters on individual widgets, you can read about widget-specific options.)

Keep in mind that not every widget has all of the features described in this chapter. And remember that some widgets have more (lots more) features than this chapter describes. The options in this chapter are special because you can depend on them to work pretty much the same way, no matter what widget you try to configure.

Sprucing Up with Color

Adding a bit of color can really spruce up a tclet, especially in the monotonous gray world of the Web. You can specify the color of a widget in terms of two characteristics: the widget's background and foreground.

background

The *background color* of a widget is the color of the widget itself, including the border and the shadows cast by the border (if any) — you read more about what those things are a bit later in this chapter. The standard background of a widget is the omnipresent, utility gray of the Web universe. Just changing the background color of a button can make it stand out quite a bit. For example, the following code just makes a bunch of buttons.

You can either type the code into Wish or use the file `grey_buttons.tcl` found on the CD-ROM that comes with this book. See Appendix B for more about the CD.

```
frame .f1
frame .f2
button .f1.b1 -text "Door #1"
button .f1.b2 -text "Door #2"
button .f2.h1 -text "Help!"
button .f2.q1 -text "Quit"
pack .f1 .f2 -side top
pack .f1.b1 .f1.b2 -side left
pack .f2.h1 .f2.q1 -side left
```

The result should appear like the display in Figure 12-1, which looks quite functional, albeit pretty darn boring.

Figure 12-1:
Buttons
made
by Wish.

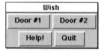

Quick use of the configure command can liven things up a bit:

```
.f2.h1 configure -background red
.f2.q1 configure -bg blue
```

The preceding code results in a display like the one in Figure 12-2.

The `configure` command just changes the values of the options specified in the command. Thus, the preceding code says, in effect, "change the background of the fields `.f2.h1` and `.f2.q1` from whatever they were to red and blue, respectively."

Figure 12-2:
Background
colors
added to
the Wish
buttons.

You can abbreviate the feature -background as -bg and save yourself some typing, and some space on the line. As your widgets become more complicated, shorter feature names are useful because you then have more space on a line to fit the values of the features (such as text, different fonts, widths, heights, and so on).

foreground

As you may have noticed in the previous example, black text looks good only against backgrounds of certain colors. Against other colors, such as blue, black text can be hard to read. Luckily, you're not stuck with black text any more than you're stuck with gray backgrounds. You can change the color of the text of a widget (among other things) by changing the color of the widget's foreground. The foreground of a widget consists of anything that appears on top of the background — usually text or bitmap characters.

The -foreground option works just like the -background option. (You can even abbreviate it as -fg.) For example, to change the text of the .Quit button in the previous example to white, type the following:

```
.f2.q1 configure -foreground white
```

or

```
.f2.q1 configure -fg white
```

The results should end up looking like Figure 12-3. The type on the buttons is now white.

Figure 12-3:
A white
foreground
added to
the Wish
buttons.

The configure command

The `configure` command is very helpful for trying out different looks for your widgets while using Wish. To change the configuration of any widget feature, just type the name of the widget, followed by the command option `configure`, followed by the feature you want to change and the new value for that feature.

The old value of that feature is instantly replaced with the new value. For example, to change the background color of a button widget named `.warning_button` to red, type

```
.warning_button configure -
   background red
```

Be careful not to color the foreground and background of widgets with colors that are similar in shade (such as a white background and a yellow foreground or a black background and a blue foreground). If users display your tclet on a black-and-white monitor, the interpreter will just use black for all the dark colors and white for all the light ones, making your black-and-blue widget all black, and totally unreadable.

Custom colors

If you're a lover of the X Windows UNIX color palette and you just have to have a button whose background is PaleVioletRed and whose text is a delicate shade of PapayaWhip, you can do it easily with Tcl/Tk. One easy way is to use the color names, as in the following example:

```
.f1.b1 configure -bg PaleVioletRed
.f1.b1 configure -fg PapayaWhip
```

The Display window should now look something like Figure 12-4.

As though hundreds of tasty colors like PapayaWhip and BlanchedAlmond aren't enough, Tcl/Tk lets you make up your very own colors. You can specify the exact amounts of red, green, and blue to mix to create any shade you like.

Figure 12-4:
The Display
window.

To specify a color, you put a set of hexadecimal numbers (see the sidebar "Expressing custom colors") in the same place that you would put the name of a color — for example, right after the -bg tag. You must add a # sign to the front of hex numbers, like so:

```
.f1.b2 configure -bg #0f0
```

for a good, solid, traditional green, or

```
.f1.b2 configure -bg #000
```

for basic black, or

```
.f1.b2 configure -bg #888
```

for a 50 percent shade of gray.

Actually quite a few other widget features are available that you can color. However, because most of these are specific to only a few widgets, I won't go into excruciating detail here. Table 12-1 provides a good idea of the basic widget parts that can carry a hue.

Table 12-1	Colorful Widget Features
Feature	*Attribute*
-activebackground	Widgets: buttons, menus, scrollbars and scales. The color the widget's background becomes when you click on it.
-insertbackground	Widgets: canvas, entry, text. The color of the background of the cursor where data is inserted.
selectbackground	Widgets: canvas, entry, listbox, text. The background color of a selected region.
activeforeground	Widgets: buttons and menus. The color a widget's foreground becomes when the widget is clicked or otherwise activated.
selectforeground	Widgets: canvas, entry, listbox, text. The foreground color of a selected region.
highlightcolor	Widgets: Every one which can respond to being clicked on (not listbox, menu, or message). The color of a widget that is currently activated with the tab key.
selectcolor	Widgets: Checkbutton and radiobutton. The color of the symbol that indicates a button has been selected.
troughcolor	Widgets: Scale, slider. The color of the trough through which the slider moves.

Tweaking Size

Besides color, size is probably the most obvious thing you may want to tweak in a widget. We've already mentioned size a couple times in passing (for example, in Chapter 2), but here's the whole story, in all its gory detail.

The natural state

Widgets are born with a *natural* size, so you don't need to specify the size if you don't want to. Usually, the natural size of a widget is just about big enough to get the job done — message widgets are just big enough to hold the text you put in them, buttons are just big enough to hold the text label, and so on. This makes tclets really easy to get working without worrying about how they look. But eventually, you'll want your widget's layout to look good. For example, just using the code

```
message .msg -text "Tcl/Tk is a lot of fun!"
button .b -text "Continue"
pack .msg .b
```

to create the tclet in Figure 12-5 does the job, but it's certainly not going to win any tclet beauty contests.

Figure 12-5:
A functional
tclet using
defaults.

You can improve the whole thing immensely just by getting the text to appear on one line, as in Figure 12-6. This is done by changing the width feature.

Adjusting width

Almost every widget has a width, and you can change it to your heart's content. For example, to make the widget in Figure 12-6 look like the one in Figure 12-5, you just type the following line:

```
.msg configure -width 240p
```

Figure 12-6:
The
configure
command
added
to the
preceding
figure.

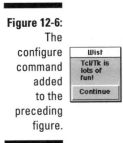

Now, I bet you're wondering how I knew that 240p was a good width, and you're maybe even just a wee bit curious about what the heck that p stands for, right? Never fear, as with most Tcl things, the answer is quite simple.

Tcl is so clever, it can specify distances on the screen in many different measurements:

- Centimeters
- Inches
- Millimeters
- Printer's points ($^1/_{72}$ of an inch)
- Pixels

It's kinda backwards. You specify which of these measurement units you are using by putting the first letter of the measurement after the number which says how many of the units you want to use. For example, 2.5c stands for 2.5 centimeters. As you may remember from studying the metric system in the late 70s, 2.5 centimeters is just about an inch, which you write in Tcl as 1i. According to the arcane mathematics of the metric system, 2.5c also happens to be exactly the same as 25 millimeters, which supposedly would be written as 25m.

From my deep store of irrelevant trivial facts, I know that one inch equals about 72p. Let's try a quick demo to check confirm my brainstorm. (The demo is on the CD-ROM that comes with this book as frame_width_wide.tcl.)

```
frame .f -bg white -width 5c -height 5c
pack .f
frame .f.a -width 2.5c -height 1c -bg red
frame .f.b -width 25m -height 1c -bg blue
frame .f.c -width 1i -height 1c -bg green
frame .f.d -width 72p -height 1c -bg black
pack .f.a .f.b .f.c .f.d -padx 1m -pady 1m
```

Wow! If you tried this demo, you know that there's something wrong with the m specification — actually, it appears that 1m must stand for 10 millimeters, not 1 mm as claimed. Not exactly obvious, but easy to fix, with the following change to the configuration of the second frame widget (here's our old friend the `configure` command again!).

```
.f.b configure -width 25m
```

The three specifications are about as close as anyone can tell. (The corrected example is on the CDROM as `frame_width_narrow.tcl`.)

The final measurement is pixels. A pixel's exact size depends on the monitor the tclet is displayed on. Pixels is the default option used whenever you give a size feature a value without any letter following it. For example,

```
.frame f.e -width 102 -height 1c -bg yellow
```

creates a frame the same size as the other on my Mac monitor. On my Linux system, which has a different sized screen,

```
.frame f.e -width 75 -height 1c -bg yellow
```

matches the screen size.

In general, my advice is to pick a method and go with it. Keep all your widgets in the same system and you'll be sure that widgets with the same width specification (such as 72p) will be the same width (usually — see the sidebar, "Dealing with the width of widgets containing text").

Specifying height

Height works just like width, except in the vertical direction. (Wow, what a deep concept!) That is, you can specify height in terms of centimeters (c), 10s of millimeters (m), inches (i), printer's points (p) and pixels (no tag) just as you specify width. As with width, different widgets will act more or less strange in response to your commands. Just as some widgets do not have really have a width, some widgets do not have height. Let's try tweaking the -height of some frame widgets to see what happens.

```
frame .f -bg white -width 5c -height 5c
pack .f
frame .f.a -width 2.5c -height 1c -bg red
frame .f.b -width 25m -height 1c -bg blue
frame .f.c -width 1i -height 1c -bg green
frame .f.d -width 72p -height 1c -bg black
pack .f.a .f.b .f.c .f.d -padx 1m -pady 1m
```

Dealing with the width of widgets containing text

As you'll find out from reading the chapters on individual widgets, some widgets (such as sliders) do not have width. Because those are pretty high-level types of things, we won't deal with them yet. However, even when working with relatively simple widgets, you may find that the geometry packer will fiddle around with your width specification. In certain cases the rude little machine may even appear to ignore your commands entirely.

If you come across something strange, take a look at the chapter on the widget that you're creating. Chances are, there's something funny about that kind of widget, and you have to appease it is some special way (I usually try begging and pleading first, followed by offers of flowers and candy). Message widgets especially seem to have a mind of their own. For example, look at the results of the following code (from `message_width.tcl` on the CD-ROM), which are displayed in the figure in this sidebar.

```
message .msg -width 10c -text
    "10 cm red bar" -bg red -fg
    white
pack .msg
% frame .f -width 10c -bg black
    -height .5c
pack .f
```

Obviously, the 10 cm red bar is not 10cm wide — at least, it's not as wide as the black bar, which is probably just about 10 cm wide. On the other hand, changing the width to 1 cm with the configure command,

```
.msg configure -width 1c
```

also does not seem to have quite the expected effect, though it does change the appearance of the widget to that in the figure in this sidebar.

Notice that, along with specifying width and background color, which should be quite familiar to you now, this example also specifies the height. For simplicity's sake, all of the frames in this example are the same height (1 cm) but you can try making a display that is the equivalent of turning this example on its side, with the following code (from `frame_height.tcl` on the CD-ROM):

```
frame .f -bg white -width 5c -height 5c
pack .f
frame .f.a -width 1c -height 2.5c -bg red
frame .f.b -width 1c -height 25m -bg blue
frame .f.c -width 1c -height 1i -bg green
frame .f.d -width 1c -height 72p -bg black
pack .f.a .f.b .f.c .f.d -padx 1m -pady 1m -side left
```

The results should look like Figure 12-7.

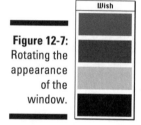

Figure 12-7:
Rotating the
appearance
of the
window.

Adding Borders

Up until now we've dealt with pretty flat displays. Flat widgets are useful, but they're not very distinctive. Adding borders can help you set off your widgets from each other and from the background of the rest of your page. Borders help important messages stand out better, make it easier for users to figure out where they should or should not click, and generally just add style to your tclets. There are two main -border attributes that you can adjust: -relief and -borderwidth.

relief

The -relief option specifies how much a widget stands out (or in) from the level of the page. Of course, because your computer screen is smooth (I hope), relief relies on a visual illusion: certain edges of the widget are lightened, and others darkened to simulate highlights and shadows. Besides the *flat* (no relief) settings (the default for frames), -relief can be set to *raised* (the default for button widgets), *sunken, grooved,* or *ridged.*

For example, try using the following commands to change the border relief on the frames from the previous example: (Or just source the example `reliefs.tcl` from the CD-ROM.)

```
.f.a configure -borderwidth 4 -relief raised
.f.b configure -borderwidth 4 -relief sunken
.f.c configure -borderwidth 4 -relief groove
.f.d configure -borderwidth 4 -relief ridge
```

The results should look something like Figure 12-8.

Figure 12-8:
Selected
shading
creates
raised-
appearing
areas.

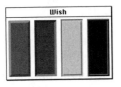

As you may be able to tell from comparing Figure 12-8 with Figure 12-7, all Tcl/Tk does to make a raised button is make the left and top edge of the widget lighter, and the right and bottom edges darker. A sunken widget use the opposite lightening/darkening schemes. Grooved and ridged patterns are somewhat more complicated, but they also just involve selectively lightening and darkening parts of the widget.

borderwidth

The `-borderwidth` feature determines the width of the part of the widget which is made darker or lighter by the relief command. By making `-borderwidth` larger, you can make the relief look more dramatic (sunken widgets look deeper, raised widgets look taller, and the edge patterns of grooved and ridged widgets look more extreme). For example, look at the effects of the following commands on the previous example (or source `reliefs_more.tcl`), as shown in Figure 12-9.

```
.f.a configure -borderwidth 10
.f.b configure -borderwidth 10
.f.b configure -borderwidth 10
.f.c configure -borderwidth 10
.f.d configure -borderwidth 10
```

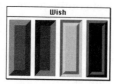

Figure 12-9:
Borders
enhance
selected
areas of
the display.

The width of the borders is usually expressed in pixels (without a letter-tag), but you can use any format you want, using the same abbreviations you used to specify height and width.

Using Bitmaps

If plain text messages just won't do, Tcl/Tk gives you the option of putting simple pictures onto your widgets instead of (or in addition to) text. These pictures are called *bitmaps,* because they consist of a map of bits — basically a set of pixels which are either one color (the background) or another color (the foreground color).

To display a widget with one of the internally defined bitmaps, you just have to put the name of the bitmap after the -bitmap feature.

```
frame .f -width 10c -height 1c -bg grey
pack .f
label .f.error -bitmap error -fg red -bg white
label .f.hourglass -bitmap hourglass -fg black -bg white
label .f.info -bitmap info -fg blue -bg white
label .f.questhead -bitmap questhead -fg brown -bg white
label .f.question -bitmap question -fg green -bg white
label .f.warning -bitmap warning -fg red -bg white
pack .f.error .f.hourglass .f.info .f.questhead .f.question
.f.warning -padx 2m -pady 2m -side left
```

Chapter 13

Binding

● ●

In This Chapter

▶ Simple binding with the `-command` option

▶ Flexible binding with the `bind` command

▶ Roundup of basic Tcl/Tk events

● ●

All righty, now that you have an idea how to create Tcl scripts and Tk widgets, put 'em together and attach your scripts to your widgets. The result is pretty magical — your tclet comes alive and looks very much like a real world, Windows-style, user-friendly application.

The `-command` *option*

Many of the basic Tk widgets support the `-command` option. The easiest way to attach a set of commands to the widget is to simply include the command as part of the code that you use to create the widget in the first place.

Review of the `-command` *option*

The `-command` option is just like any other widget option: You can add the `-command` option at any point in the sequence of options that you add to a widget command. The basic pattern is

```
widget-creating-command -command commands-to-be-executed
```

The commands to be executed by the widget must consist of one Tcl word, just like the commands embedded in the body of a Tcl if, for, or proc command. All of the following lines of code are valid uses of the -command option in a widget-building command:

```
button .b1 -text "self-destructing button" \
-command {destroy .b1}
button .b2 -text "self-replicating button" \
    -command {
        button .b3 -text "self-replicating button"
        pack .b3
    }
button .b3 -text "extremely fertile button" \
    -command {
        for {set i 1} {i < 5} {incr i} {
            pack [button .sub-b$i -text "button $I]
        }
    }
```

The bind *command*

You don't need to limit yourself to attaching commands to widgets that support the -command option, or to the default events that are already set up for you. Tcl/Tk is a flexible language, and you can bind any event to any widget, period. In fact, you can create as many bindings as you like in a tclet, and the same widget can have several different bindings.

For instance, say that you want to set up a little tclet like the one shown in Figure 13-1. This tclet is a basic text box accompanied by a row of buttons with mysterious-sounding names. Underneath the buttons is a little status readout. In fact, this readout is a label widget that gives the user a little more information about what each button does.

Like all Tcl/Tk commands, a bind command consists of a list of Tcl words. The basic pattern goes like this:

```
bind widget-name <event-name> command
```

The parts are all pretty easy to understand:

- bind is the name of the command.
- widget-name is the name of the widget that you want to create a behavior for.

- ✔ event-name is the mouse or keyboard event that you want the widget to respond to. A list of ready-made events is built into Tcl/Tk — a handy table appears in the following "Event name" section.

- ✔ command is a set of Tcl/Tk commands, grouped together with curly braces. The idea is exactly the same as a block of commands embedded in a -command option, or in an if or proc command.

Look at each of these parts in detail.

Widget name

The widget-name argument to the bind command is the widget's name, exactly as it appears in the command that created the widget. (Widget names are always a single Tcl/Tk word anyway, so you don't have to worry about grouping it with braces).

Any widget, including the toplevel widget ". ", is fair game. Furthermore, you can use the special designation all, which binds the specified event to all of the widgets in the tclet. (See Chapter 11 for an overview of all of the Tcl widgets.)

You can bind only *one* widget at a time. The following command, which has two widget-name arguments, is *not* legal and generates an error message.

```
bind .button1 .button2 <Motion> {#do something wonderful}
```

When you set up a binding between a widget and a mouse event, the command executes when the event takes place inside the widget's borders. For example, set up a little motion-detector widget with the following code:

```
set overall 0; set b1 0; set b2 0; set b3 0
.configure -background white
label .overall -textvariable overall -width 25
button .b1 -textvariable b1 -width 25
button .b2 -textvariable b2 -width 25
button .b3 -textvariable b3 -width 25
pack .overall .b1 .b2 .b3 -pady 5
bind . <Motion> {incr overall}
bind .b1 <Motion> {incr b1}
bind .b2 <Motion> {incr b2}
bind .b3 <Motion> {incr b3}
```

When you first load this tclet, the screen image should look something like Figure 13-1. The label on top changes every time the tclet detects motion anywhere in the toplevel widget — in other words, anywhere in the tclet. The three buttons change when motion is detected inside them. (All four widgets display zero when the tclet starts up.)

After you start moving the mouse around, you see that the label changes, no matter where the cursor is. However, each button changes only when the cursor is inside its gray boundary.

Figure 13-1:
You can create a "motion detector" tclet to see how binding works.

If you look closely at the code, you see that all four of the bind commands use the same event specification: <Motion>. In other words, it's not that the different labels are responding to different events; rather, a label responds only to an event that takes place inside its own turf.

Keyboard events are a little trickier. a keyboard event is never really inside a widget. You can't really say that a keystroke on your keyboard takes place anywhere on screen. (Your keyboard and screen are completely separate units, right?)

However, you *can* say that a particular button is *active*. This concept is familiar for most of you — things like buttons and entry boxes are highlighted to show you that they're the currently selected widget. If you hit the return key, the current button activates, just as if you had clicked it; if you type, the letters appear inside a highlighted entry box.

Tcl/Tk allows the user to specify an active widget. To see how this works, press the Tab key while the motion detector tclet is running. A black border appears around the top button to show that you've selected it as the active button. (You can see the black border in Figure 13-2.)

If you press the Tab key a few more times, you see that the border jumps between buttons, so that each of the buttons becomes active in turn. (You also notice that the label *doesn't* become active; I talk about that in a second.) Here's the rule for binding widgets to keyboard events: *A widget responds to a keyboard event only when the widget is active.*

Figure 13-2:
The black border around the button widget indicates that the button is active.

See how widget activation works by adding some keyboard bindings to the motion-detector widget. You don't need to change any of the current bindings: You can put the new bindings right on top of the old ones. Go ahead and add the following code to the motion-detector tclet. (If you're doing this in a Web page, you need to reload.)

```
bind . <Key> {incr overall}
bind .b1 <Key> {incr b1}
bind .b2 <Key> {incr b2}
bind .b3 <Key> {incr b3}
```

The only difference between this little block and the previous set of bindings is that now the event that the widgets are interested in is <Key> — which represents any keyboard activity.

Now, take the cursor out of the tclet so you know that it's not responding to motion. Start typing on your keyboard — type anything you like. You'll see that the readout of the top label changes every times that you press a key on your keyboard. If one of the bottom buttons is active, the readout of the active button changes, too. Hit the Tab key to change the active button, and start typing. Now, the readout in the new active button changes.

Event name

You've probably noticed by now that events use a special kind of punctuation, namely, pointy brackets, like this:

```
<Motion>
```

You use pointy brackets exclusively to indicate event-names, and, like curly brackets, they serve to group any material that they contain into one Tcl word.

You can find ready-made events for just about every kind of transaction that can take place between a user and a tclet. In fact, there are some pretty esoteric events that can take place only on certain platforms, like the `<Gravity>` event under Unix. (Don't ask.) Table 13-1 summarizes the most common event types that you may find in the context of a Web page tclet.

Table 13-1	Events for Web Page Tclets
Name	**Description**
`<Button>`	The user presses the mouse button (but does not necessarily release it).
`<ButtonRelease>`	The user releases the mouse button.
`<Enter>`	The cursor moves into a widget's territory.
`<FocusIn>`	The Tab key activates the widget.
`<FocusOut>`	The Tab key deactivates the widget.
`<Key>`	The user presses any key on the keyboard (but does not necessarily release it).
`<KeyRelease>`	The user releases any key on the keyboard.
`<Leave>`	The cursor leaves the widget's territory.
`<Motion>`	The cursor moves around inside the widget.

Here are a few special shortcuts, abbreviations, and special cases:

- You can distinguish between the left and right mouse buttons by specifying `<Button-1>` and `<Button-2>` respectively. You can use the abbreviation `<1>` for `<Button-1>` and `<2>` for `<Button-2>`, if you like.

- You can specify a particular key by putting it between the brackets. For instance, if you want to bind a widget to the X key, you can specify the event `<Key-x>` or `<KeyRelease-x>`. You can use the abbreviation `<x>` for `<Key-x>` if you like.

Focus! Focus!!

Now, I said that you can bind any widget to any event, and it's true. But how can you bind a keyboard event to a label widget, if the user can't activate the label with the Tab key? Good question.

The user can't make the label key active, but *you,* the programmer, can, by using the special command `focus`. To make a label called `.1` active, just use the command:

`focus .1`

`focus` isn't restricted to label widgets; you can use it with any kind of widget you like. The `focus` command doesn't put a black border around widgets that wouldn't be activated by the Tab key.

You may never need to use the `focus` command, but it's there for you if you ever need to bind something like a label or message widget to the keyboard.

✔ Actually, if you want to bind to a particular key, you don't even need the pointy brackets, you can just use the name of the key; for example:

```
bind all x {#do something interesting}
```

rather than

```
bind all <x> {#do something interesting}
```

You can make things even more complicated, if you like, by binding widgets to combinations of events, rather than to simple events. The following combinations are typical combination bindings:

✔ Pressing the S key while holding down the Alt key

✔ Dragging the mouse while holding down the Control key

✔ Double-clicking with the mouse

To specify a combination event, you attach a modifier name to the name of the event with a hyphen, like so:

```
<Modifier-Event>
```

Create a readout label whose display changes when you double-click on the label. First, you create the widget and add it to the tclet:

```
set readout 0
label .readout -textvariable readout -width 25 \
-background white
pack .readout
```

Now, create the binding. The modifier for a double-click is simply called *Double*. Add the modifier to the basic mouse-click event tag to name the event:

```
bind .readout <Double -1> {incr readout}
```

The standard Tcl event-modifiers that make sense in the context of a Web page appear in Table 13-2.

Table 13-2	Standard Event Modifiers
Name	*Key*
Alt	On Windows, the Alt key; on the Mac, the ⌘ key
Control	The Control key
Double	Double-clicking the modified mouse button
Lock	The Caps Lock key
Meta	On Windows and the Mac, the Option key; elsewhere, the Meta key
Shift	The Shift key
Triple	Double-clicking the modified mouse button

The following are all legal event combinations:

- ✔ <Shift-L>
- ✔ <Alt-L>
- ✔ <Double-L>
- ✔ <Control-Z>
- ✔ <Control-Q>
- ✔ <Control-Shift-Z>

Command

The command block of a `bind` command is pretty much like the command blocks you've seen so far in Tcl/Tk constructions like `for` commands and `proc` commands. The commands should be grouped together to prevent substitution when the interpreter makes the first pass through the whole bind command; when it's time for Tcl/Tk to look at the block as if it were a group of commands, the interpreter strips off the curly brackets.

One special thing goes on inside the command block of a `bind` command that doesn't happen elsewhere: *event substitution.* (That's not the official name — there really isn't a name for this particular wrinkle in Tcl/Tk syntax — but event substitution works for me.)

Here's how it works: when the % character appears in the command block of a `bind` command, the interpreter swaps in special information about the event that triggered the block. The % character doesn't mean anything by itself. You use it with other characters so that you can specify the different kinds of event information that interests you.

For instance, when you use the combination %x in the command block, the interpreter swaps in the x coordinates of a mouse event. Similarly, %y swaps in the y value of the mouse event. If you clicked the mouse at a point that is 25 pixels from the left edge of the tclet, and 30 points from the top, then Tcl/Tk can take a command like

```
label .l -text "mouse click at %x, %y"
```

and perform substitutions like this:

```
label .l -text "mouse click at 25, 30"
```

To see this kind of substitution in action, update the hit counter tclet you created earlier in this chapter, and make it into a hit-tracker tclet. First, you create a label as a readout:

```
set readout "no motion detected"
label .readout -textvariable readout
pack .readout
```

Now, create a binding between the whole toplevel widget and any mouse motion. Whenever the widget detects motion, the tclet updates the message in the label widget with information about where the motion event occurred. The following line of code shows just how easy it is to set up the binding:

```
bind . <Motion> {set readout "motion at %x, %y"}
```

Enter the whole tclet into Wish, or load it as a tclet into your Web browser. When you move the cursor around inside the tclet, the readout label changes continuously with updates on the position of the cursor.

There are other kinds of event substitution. The combination %K swaps in the key value of any keyboard event — if you press the F key, it swaps in *f,* if you press Shift+F, it swaps in *F,* and so on. You can see it at work in your motion tracker tclet by adding another line to handle keyboard activity:

```
bind . <Key> {set readout "Keyboard activity: %K"}
```

The combination %W displays the name of the widget that's responding to the event. To see this work, you need to add a few more widgets to the event-tracker party:

```
for {set ctr 1} {$ctr <= 5} {incr ctr} {
    label .l$ctr -text "label $ctr"
    pack .l$ctr
}
```

Now, you bind every widget to the mouse-click event. When any widget detects a click, it updates the readout with its own name:

```
bind all <1> {set readout "Click inside widget %W"}
```

There are many other event-substitution combinations besides %X, %Y, %K, and %W, but they're pretty esoteric, and most don't reflect the kind of events that take place in a Web page. If you're really interested, see the bind.html file in the Wish documentation for more details.

Chapter 14

Geometry Managers

So far, you've been using a simple version of the `pack` command to plop widgets down in a tclet layout. In fact, you can use the `pack` command and a new layout command, called `grid`, to position your widgets exactly where you want them.

Making a game plan

Before you start building a complicated tclet layout, cranking out `pack` and `grid` commands, it's best to develop some idea of how you want the application to look. Call me low-tech, but I prefer to think out designs with pencil and paper, or with a layout program such as Adobe PageMaker or NetObjects Fusion, before I start coding.

You can work out these issues by trial and error while you're coding, but frankly, trial and error is frustrating and time-consuming. Even Wish, which is built for this kind of trial and error, is not as flexible as a plain old No. 2 pencil. (Wish is a great tool for refining your design, however, after you've got the basic skeleton on-screen.)

Note: While I'm pontificating about design, let me add that you should be thinking about laying out your tclet according to some sort of grid. I'm not suggesting you use a grid to organize your layout so that I have an excuse to talk about the grid command; rather, I'm suggesting it because it makes your tclet look better. Trust your old Uncle Tim on this one. The tclet looks better when everything's lined up with something.

Choosing a geometry manager

So why does Tcl/Tk have three geometry managers, when both do pretty much the same thing? The packer, the grid, and the place geometry managers are separate entities, because each has its own particular strengths.

The packer, which is the original geometry manager, is quite flexible; you can give it some fairly simple guidelines, and it works out the details of the layout for you. The packer is well suited for simple layouts that contain only a few widgets or that don't need an elaborate design.

On a more practical note, the packer has been around forever, and it's the geometry manager that most old Tcl/Tk hands are used to working with. Most of the information that you'll find about Tcl/Tk outside this book (in online tutorials and the like) uses the packer to create layouts — even complicated layouts. Also, many of the tclets that you find in other folks' Web pages use `pack` exclusively.

The `grid` geometry manager, which is a fairly new addition to the Tcl/Tk world, is handy for creating layouts that use many widgets laid out in a complex grid. If you want to create something like a form, or something that looks like a traditional Windows or Mac application, the `grid` geometry manager probably is the way to go.

The third, seldom-used geometry manager is called the `place` geometry manager. You can use the `place` geometry manager to position widgets on the page by means of absolute coordinates. A command like this one puts a widget called `button` exactly 20 pixels from the left edge of the tclet and 20 pixels from the top:

```
place .button -x 20 -y 20
```

Adapting tclet layouts for the Web

Both `pack` and `grid` have some special command options that deal with issues that don't arise in a Web-page tclet — such as what happens to the widgets (their size and relative positions) when the user resizes the tclet's window. Because Web-page tclets stay the same size throughout their lifetimes, the commands that deal with resizing aren't critical to creating a good-looking Web tclet. Just quietly pretend that these issues don't exist.

Also, some layout commands deal with multiple top-level widgets. Because you can't create new top-levels in the plug-in version of Tcl/Tk, you can safely disregard these commands; they're useful only in extraordinary cases anyway.

Although the use of exact pixel coordinates allows perfect precision, keeping track of the coordinates is a great deal of work, and a good-looking layout can turn into a disaster if the window is resized. This chapter doesn't discuss the place command in detail, but you can look it up in the place.html file in the Wish documentation, if you're interested.

Mixing geometry managers

Using more than one geometry manager in a tclet is perfectly legal. You can use one geometry manager to add widgets to a big frame widget and then use another geometry manager to display the frame in the tclet — it's your tclet.

When you're using different geometry managers to add tclets to the same top-level or the same frame, however, you run the risk of widget collision. A geometry manager knows about only the widgets that it has been given to pack. The packer doesn't know about the widgets that the grid geometry manager is taking care of, and it blithely puts its own widgets on top of the grid manager's widgets.

Using frame widgets

No matter which geometry manager you use to solve a layout problem, you'll probably need to use frame widgets for that purpose from time to time. A frame is really just a rectangular region, and using frames to group a set of related widgets is handy.

I cover the use of frames to create good-looking tclets in Chapter 16, but they're so essential to organizing layouts — especially when you're laying out with the packer — that I mention them occasionally in this chapter's discussions of the geometry managers.

Adding Widgets with pack

I'm sure that you've noticed that when pack adds a widget to an empty Wish display window, the window shrinks so that it's exactly the same size as the newly added widget. So that you can better see what really happens when you add things with the packer, use a special pack command option called propagate to turn off this auto-shrinking feature.

Fire up Wish and enter this command:

```
pack propagate . false
```

Now make a bunch of empty label widgets to play with. This way, you can use pack to add the widgets to the layout whenever you like without stopping to make a new label every time. Make about 10 label widgets, so that you have plenty of building blocks. Make the labels black (so that you can see them) and number them (so that I can refer to them in the figures). The following code will make ten numbered label widgets for you to use as building blocks for your layout experiments:

```
for {set ctr 1} {$ctr <= 10} {incr ctr} {
    label .l$ctr -text $ctr -background black \
    -foreground white -width 5 -height 3
}
```

In general, pack uses a simple rule for positioning widgets: *Put the widget at the edge of the space that's left over in the tclet.* Add the first label:

```
pack .l1
```

As you can see in Figure 14-1, label #1 appears at the top edge of the tclet, because none of the tclet's territory has been claimed. See how the space is divided into label #1's turf and unconquered territory?

Figure 14-1:
pack
places the
widget at
the top
edge of any
unclaimed
territory.

If you add a second widget, it appears at the edge of the territory not claimed by label #1 (that is, directly below label #1). Here's the code to add a second widget:

```
pack .l2
```

Figure 14-2 shows the new division of territory among label #1, label #2, and unclaimed real estate.

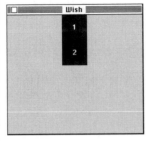

Figure 14-2:
The second widget is added to the top edge of real estate not claimed by the first widget.

Now suppose that you want to start packing labels sideways. The new widget appears in the center *of the unclaimed area,* not in the center of the entire widget or to the side of the label #2. Here's the code to add the third widget at the left side of the tclet:

```
pack .l3 -side left
```

Figure 14-3 shows the result of this move. As you can see, label #3 has carved out a little territory for itself on the left side of the screen, and the label itself appears in the middle of the vertical space that was left over after label #2 was packed.

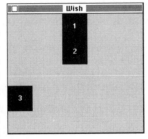

Figure 14-3:
when the -left argument is used with pack, the widget is added at the left side of the containing widget.

Now resume packing from the top. Can you predict where the next widget goes? The top edge of the unclaimed territory is still directly below label #2, but the unclaimed territory is a little narrower now, because label #3 has claimed its space on the left edge. As a result, widget #4 must scoot a little to the right so that it's in the middle of the free area. Here's the code to add widget number 4:

```
pack .l4
```

As you can see in Figure 14-4, label #4 isn't quite aligned with labels #1 and #2, because not much horizontal space was left after label #4 was packed.

Figure 14-4:
Widget #3,
on the left,
eats up
horizontal
territory, so
widget #4
doesn't
quite align
with
widgets #1
and #2.

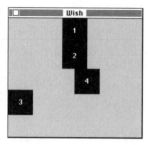

The -side *option*

You just saw the -side option in action. Let me take a moment to state formally that -side determines which edge of the remaining space the current widget is added to. The following table shows the possible values that you can assign to -side:

Option + Value	Results
-side left	Puts the widget at the left edge of the unclaimed territory
-side right	Puts the widget at the right edge of the unclaimed territory
-side top	Puts the widget at the left edge of the unclaimed territory (the default)
-side bottom	Puts the widget at the left edge of the unclaimed territory

Removing widgets

You don't need to destroy widgets to remove them from the layout; you can tell the packer to remove a widget from the display without actually destroying the widget. If you want to reuse these widgets, simply erase them, like so:

```
pack forget .11 .12 .13 .14
```

This particular code clears the tclet of these four widgets. In general, the formula is

```
pack forget widget-name
```

A handy way to remove all the widgets from the window at the same time is to use this simple command:

```
foreach x [winfo children .]
    {pack forget $x}
```

This command is especially handy when you've been experimenting in Wish and want to clear the board so that you can start again.

The -padx *and* -pady *options*

Often, you want to add a little space between widgets. The widgets in Figures 14-1 through 14-4, for example, are all butting up against one an- other, and it's hard to tell where one widget ends and the next begins. To add a little space between widgets, you can add the -padx and -pady options to the pack command. -padx adds horizontal space; -pady adds vertical space.

Start again by putting down a label without any special treatment, as follows:

```
pack .11
```

Now add a new widget and give it a little air with the -pady option, as follows:

```
pack .12 -pady 10
```

As you can see in Figure 14-5, you now have 10 pixels' worth of space between label #1 and label #2. The packer added space to both the top and bottom of label #3. If you add a third widget without the -pady option, label #3 is still separated from label #2.

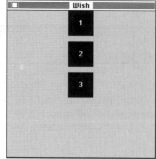

Figure 14-5:
The -pady
option adds
vertical
space
between
widgets.

The -padx option works exactly the same way with horizontal space. Here's some code that shows -padx in action:

```
pack forget .l1 .l2 .l3;
#to remove the last round of labels
pack .l1 -side left
pack .l2 -side left -padx 10
pack .l3 -side left
```

As you can see in Figure 14-6, this time label #2 is buffered by 10 points of horizontal space on each side of the widget.

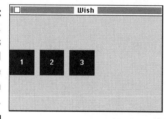

Figure 14-6:
The -padx
option adds
horizontal
space
between
widget.

The -ipadx *and* -ipady *options*

Sometimes, you want to add some space inside widgets to fatten then up, rather than adding space between widgets. You accomplish this task by using the -ipadx and -ipady options. (You can think of i as being an abbreviation for *interior* or *inside*.)

Internal padding adds extra space to a widget no matter what size is specified in the widget's -width and -height options. Internal padding is just a way to add a little more size to the widget after the widget has been created.

Figure 14-7 shows the result of internal padding. Label #1 has been fortified with 25 points of horizontal padding, and label #2 sports 25 points of vertical padding. Here's some code that demonstrates how internal padding is added with -ipadx and -ipady:

```
pack .l1 -ipadx 25
pack .l2 -ipady 25
```

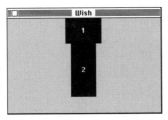

The -anchor *option*

You use the -anchor option to specify where a widget is positioned within the space that the packer allots to it.

As illustrated in Figure 14-1 earlier in this chapter, when you add a widget with the packer, the widget claims the entire width (or height) of any unclaimed territory. By default, the widget is centered at the edge of its own territory.

It doesn't need to be that way, however. A widget can be anchored at any of the four corners or four sides, or at the center of its turf. To specify the place where the tclet should be anchored, you use (naturally) the -anchor option. The argument of the -anchor option is one of the eight compass points (n for north, nw for northwest, w for west, and so on) or center for italic.

Try packing one of your label widgets at the left (western) edge of its territory, like so:

```
pack .l1 -anchor w
```

Now put the second widget in the center of its territory, like so:

```
pack .l2 -anchor center
```

Finally, put a third widget at the eastern edge of its territory, like so:

```
pack .13 -anchor e
```

Figure 14-8 shows these widgets anchored in the specified positions.

Figure 14-8:
The
-anchor
widget
allows you
to specify
where the
widget is
to be
positioned
within the
available
territory.

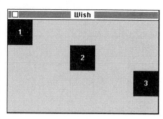

The -fill *option*

Sometimes, you want a widget to fill out its entire territory, rather than occupy the middle or an edge. To cause a widget to fill out its entire allocation of space, you can pack it by using the -fill option.

The -fill option has four possible values:

x	Fills the available horizontal space
y	Fills the available vertical space
both	Fills the available horizontal and vertical space
none	Doesn't fill (the default)

Use the -fill option to show the territories that the widgets actually stake out for themselves. So that you can easily see where each widget begins and ends, change the colors of the widgets slightly, as follows:

```
.12 configure -background #333
.13 configure -background #999
.14 configure -background #ccc
```

Now pack the widgets, using the -fill option. Add a horizontal fill to the widgets that you add to the top and bottom (#1 and #3), and add a vertical fill to the widgets that you add to the left and right (#2 and #4). Here's the code that adds the widgets:

```
pack .l1 -side top -fill x
pack .l2 -side left -fill y
pack .l3 -side bottom -fill x
pack .l4 -side right -fill y
```

As you can see in Figure 14-9, each widget has filled out its allocated territory.

Figure 14-9:
The -fill
option
specifies
that the
widget fills
out the
available
territory.

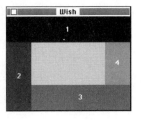

The -expand *option*

Now and then, you'll want a widget to use more territory than it needs. You may want to center the widget in the remaining unclaimed territory or even have it fill the empty space. To cause a widget to use all the unclaimed territory, rather than stake out just a slice, use the -expand option. This option takes either of two arguments: yes, which causes widgets to expand to fill the unclaimed territory, and no (the default), which causes widgets to claim territory in the usual way.

If you want to center one widget in an open window, for example, you pack it with the -expand option. Because the widget's territory is now as tall as the entire available vertical space, not just as tall as the widget, the widget is centered in the remaining space. Here's the code that adds the widget:

```
pack .l1 -expand yes
```

The -expand option is commonly used along with the -fill option, so that a row of buttons fills an entire window snugly. Experiment with using -fill and -expand together, (using labels, because you've already made a batch of them) in your window. Here's some example code that uses both -fill and -expand:

```
pack .l1 .l2 .l3 .l4 -side left -expand yes -fill both
```

Figure 14-10 shows the result. Because you used -expand, each button claims its own share of the total space; because you used -fill, each button fills its territory.

Figure 14-10:
When
you use
-fill and
-expand
together, the
widget is
displayed
using all of
the available
territory.

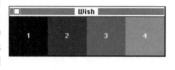

The pack configure *trick*

You can always change a widget's packing options after the fact by using the configure option of the pack command. The general pattern goes like this:

```
pack configure widget-name1 widget-name2 . . . \
-newoption1 value -newoption2 value . . .
```

(If this pattern looks familiar, it's because the code is exactly like the code to change a widget's options after a widget has been made.) Suppose you decide that you really didn't want the buttons in Figure 14-14 to fill out and touch one another, and you want to try packing them with the -expand option off. It's this easy:

```
pack configure .l1 .l2 .l3 .l4 -expand no
```

Changing the configuration this way affects only the specified options. The -fill both and -side left options that were specified in the original command don't change; only the -expand no option changes. As you can see in Figure 14-11, the resulting labels now use only part of the available vertical space in the window.

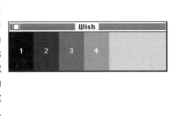

Adding Widgets with grid

The grid geometry manager is the snazzy new way to build tclets in
Tcl/Tk. As its name suggests, the grid geometry manager makes adding
widgets in a regular grid easy. The grid command supports many of the
options used by pack (such as padx and -ipadx), a well as some special
options of its own.

Before you start working with the grid manager, change the labels. (I'm a
little bored with the black ones, and I'd like to make it easy to see which
figures are about the packer and which are about the grid manager.) Make
all the labels white and the background a little darker. Here's the code to
swap the label and background colors:

```
for {set ctr 1} {$ctr <= 10} {incr ctr} {
    .l$ctr configure -background white -foreground black \
    -width 3 -height 2
}
. configure -background #777
```

The -row *and* -column *options*

When you simply add widgets with grid and no options, the widgets are
added in a vertical row that's centered in the available area. Here's some
code that demonstrates the simplest way to add widgets to a layout with
grid:

```
grid .l1 .l2 .l3
```

Figure 14-12 shows labels that have been laid out in this simple way.

Figure 14-12:
These
widgets
have been
added to the
tclet with
the grid
command.

The grid manager allows you to add padding between widgets with -padx and -pady, and add internal padding with -ipadx and -ipady, just as you would with the pack command. (You don't even need to clear the grid — just repeat the command with the new options.) For instance, to add a little internal padding to the widgets that you put down with the last line of code, you'd use the command:

```
grid .l1 .l2 .l3 -pady 5 -ipadx 10
```

Just to avoid confusion, set the padding back to zero before you go on. Here's the code to remove the extra padding:

```
grid forget .l1 .l2 .l3
```

The grid manager starts to get interesting when you specify rows and columns for widgets. Create a little 2 x 2 grid of widgets, as follows:

```
grid .l1 -column 1 -row 1 -padx 2 -pady 2
grid .l2 -column 2 -row 1 -padx 2 -pady 2
grid .l3 -column 1 -row 2 -padx 2 -pady 2
grid .l4 -column 2 -row 2 -padx 2 -pady 2
```

Figure 14-13 shows the result: two neat rows of labels. If you wanted to create a similar effect with the packer, you need to pack each row of labels into a frame and then pack the frames in a separate pass.

Adding a new label anywhere you want by using a new grid command is easy. To add a new widget outside the table you just created, you'd use code like this:

```
grid .l5 -column 1 -row 3 -padx 2 -pady 2
```

Figure 14-13:
The grid manager makes it easy to lay out widgets in a tidy little table.

Shuffling widgets around by using `grid` is easy, too. Without removing label #1 from the layout, you can move it with another `pack` command. Here's how:

```
grid .l1 -column 3 -row 3 -padx 2 -pady 2
```

Note: Actually, you can repack a widget with `pack` without removing the widget first, but it's just not as handy or cool as instant `regridding` is.

Figure 14-14 shows the result of this last set of moves. The label #5 appeared right where you specified (column 1, row 3) and label #1 jumped to its new home without causing the entire table to collapse.

Figure 14-14:
Rearranging widgets displayed by the grid manager is easy.

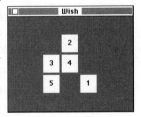

You have two more basic principles to remember, as you see in the following sections.

Principle 1

A column is as wide as the widest widget in the row, and a row is as tall as the tallest widget in the row.

Widgets that are smaller than the rest of the column or row are centered in the available space. Here's the code that fattens up label #4. Try it, and see what happens:

```
grid configure .l4 -ipadx 5 -ipady 5
```

Figure 14-15 shows the new layout. Column 2 is now as wide as its widest member (label #4), and label #2 is centered vertically in the column. Likewise, row 2 is as tall as label #2, and label #3 is centered in the row.

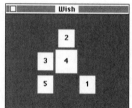

Figure 14-15:
Grid columns and rows automatically resize themselves to accommodate their biggest members.

Principle 2

Empty rows and columns collapse.

If you skip a column or row, you *don't* create any blank space: The grid manager acts as though the column or row doesn't exist. Skip column 4 completely and grid a new widget in column 5, as follows:

```
grid .l6 -column 5 -row 1 -padx 2 -pady 2
```

Figure 14-16 shows the result of this command. (Actually, I resized that gruesome-looking label #4 when you weren't looking; it didn't change as a result of the last command.) Although you specified column 5, the widget is in what looks like column 4.

Widget #5 really is in column 5 — column 4 has collapsed, because there's nothing in it. (If you make many tables in HTML, you're familiar with this phenomenon.) You can restore column 4 and put widget #5 in its rightful place by putting another widget somewhere in column 4. Here's an example of code that adds a widget to column 4:

```
grid .l7 -column 4 -row 2 -padx 2 -pady 2
```

Figure 14-16:
The grid manager is an empty column; the widget that looks like it's in column four is actually in column five.

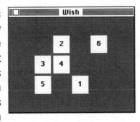

Figure 14-17:
Adding a widget to an empty column expands the column.

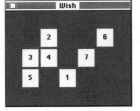

The -rowspan *and* -columnspan *options*

Tabular grids, with a fixed number of rows in each column, and and a fixed number of rows in each grid, can be restrictive. To knock down the walls between rows and columns, you can use the -rowspan and -columnspan options.

The argument of the -rowspan option is a number. When you grid a widget by using -rowspan, the grid manager reserves this number of rows for the widget's use. Naturally, -columnspan works in the same way with columns.

Add a widget to row 1, column 3 of your little grid, using the argument -rowspan 2, and add another widget to row 3, column 4 with the argument -columnspan 2. Here's how:

```
grid .18 -column 3 -row 1 -rowspan 2
grid .19 -column 4 -row 3 -columnspan 2
```

As you can see in Figure 14-18, the grid manager reserves rows 1 and 2 for label #8 and positions the label in the center of the allocated space — right between the two rows. Label #9 was allocated two columns, so it's positioned right in the center of columns 3 and 4.

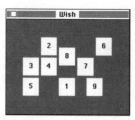

HTML experts and aficionados probably will recognize -rowspan and
-columnspan. These attributes work pretty much the same way as they do
in HTML <table> tags.

The -sticky *option*

The grid geometry manager doesn't have -fill or -anchor options like
the packer's, but it does have an option called -sticky that rolls up -fill
and -anchor into one package.

The -sticky option takes four basic arguments:

n   Causes a widget to stick to the top of its available space

e   Causes a widget to stick to the right of its available space

s   Causes a widget to stick to the bottom of its available space

w   Causes a widget to stick to the left of its available space

So far, the sticky system is pretty much the way that the -anchor option
works. There's a crucial difference, however: You can combine as many of
the arguments as you want in the same command. The following suggests a
few possible combinations, and what they look like:

-sticky ne   Makes the widget stick to the top-left corner of its
                space

-sticky ew   Makes the widget stretch across the available horizon-
                tal space, sticking on both the left and right side

-sticky nsew   Makes the widget stick to each of the four edges of the
                available space, filling the space completely

Remember that any combination of arguments is valid.

To see the use of multiple compass points with the sticky option in action, first create the board of widgets and then build a new 5 x 5 grid. Here's the code:

```
# wipe the board
foreach x [winfo children .] {grid forget $x}

#build a ring of widgets
grid .11 -row 1 -column 1 -padx 2 -pady 2
grid .12 -row 1 -column 2 -padx 2 -pady 2 -ipadx 25
grid .13 -row 1 -column 3 -padx 2 -pady 2
grid .14 -row 2 -column 1 -padx 2 -pady 2 -ipady 25
grid .16 -row 2 -column 3 -padx 2 -pady 2 -ipady 25
grid .17 -row 3 -column 1 -padx 2 -pady 2
grid .18 -row 3 -column 2 -padx 2 -pady 2 -ipadx 25
grid .19 -row 3 -column 3 -padx 2 -pady 2
```

Figure 14-19 shows the resulting ring.

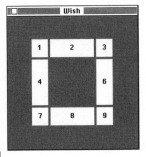

Figure 14-19:
You'll use this ring of widgets as a laboratory to explore the uses of the `-sticky` option.

Now `grid` label #5 into the ring by using different `-sticky` options, just to see what happens. First, put the label down without any `-sticky` options to see the default behavior. (Add a little padding, for consistency with the other widgets.) Here's the code that adds a widget without stickiness:

```
grid .15 -row 2 -column 2 -padx 2 -pady 2
```

Figure 14-20 shows that label #5 appears just where you'd expect it to: centered in row 2 and centered in column 2.

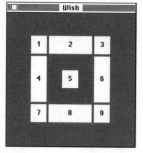

Figure 14-20:
By default, a widget is added in the horizontal and vertical center of its grid cell.

OK, now get the -sticky thang going. First, make label #5 stick to the top edge of its territory by specifying n as the -sticky argument. Here's how:

```
grid configure .l5 -sticky n
```

Figure 14-21 shows the result.

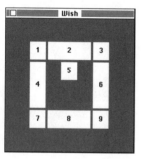

Figure 14-21:
Using -sticky n causes the widget to adhere to the top of its grid cell.

Next, stretch the label by making it stick to both the east and west edges of its grid cell. Here's the code that changes the -sticky option's value to ew:

```
grid configure .l5 -sticky ew
```

Figure 14-22 shows the result.

Finally, stretch the label by making it stick to each of the four edges of its cell.

```
grid configure .l5 -sticky ewns
```

Figure 14-23 shows the result.

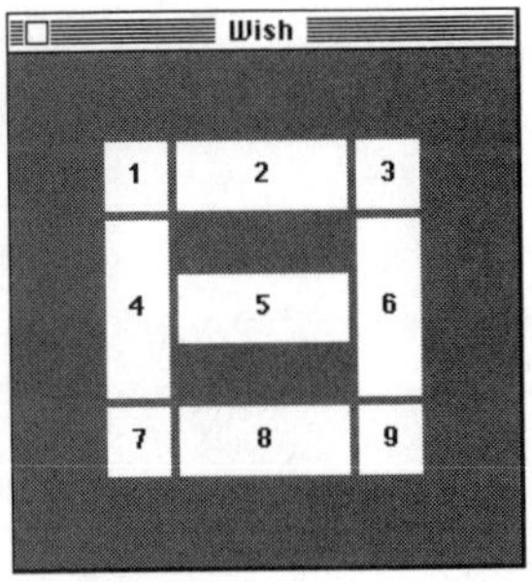

Figure 14-22:
Using
-sticky ew
causes the
widget to
stretch
horizontally
across its
cell.

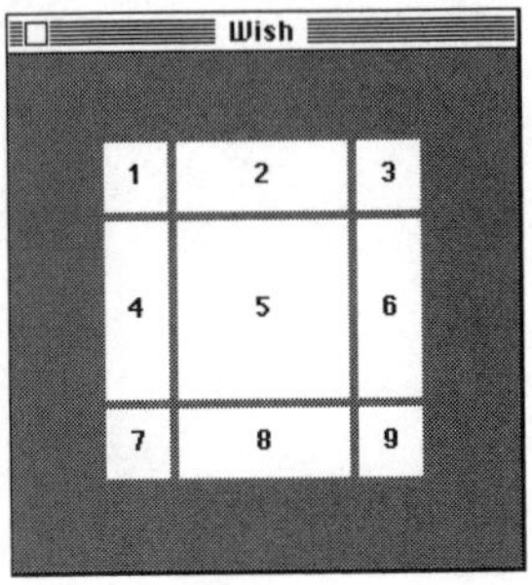

Figure 14-23:
Using
-stick
ewns
causes the
widget to fill
out its
table cell.

You can use many other combinations of edges with Wish — as many as 15 combinations, actually. Go ahead and experiment all you want with the ring-o'-widgets tclet, which you'll find on the CD-ROM in the file ring.tcl.

Part IV
Tclet Cookbook

The 5th Wave — By Rich Tennant

"I couldn't get this 'job skills' program to work, on my PC, so I replaced the mother-board, upgraded the BIOS, and wrote a program that links it to my personal database. It told me I wasn't technically inclined and should pursue a career in sales."

In this part . . .

Now that you've met the widgets and spent some time with them, it's time to make some tclets. You start by looking more closely at each of the basic widgets and use them to create some interesting tclets. Next, you figure out how to make tclets Web-savvy and how to download Web pages inside a tclet. You also learn how to control Web browsers, such as Netscape Communicator and Microsoft Internet Explorer, with a tclet.

Chapter 15

Button, Button, Who's Got My Button?

*B*uttons are the primary way for users to interact with a tclet, so they're very versatile. A Tcl/Tk button, like a button on your calculator, washing machine, or personal computer, is simply a mechanism for telling a computer chip to respond in a certain way. The response can be to execute a set of commands that the programmer (you!) defined. Examples of such command mechanisms include the "on" button on a radio, which starts power running through the circuits of the device; and the Q key on a typewriter, which makes a particular piece of metal strike the ribbon and paper.

As a computer user, you probably already have a good grasp of what a button is. After all, you use them a lot, both as physical buttons on your computer and in their virtual form on your Web browser and other "point-and-click" computer applications.

Tcl/Tk buttons aren't especially complicated. Button widgets have a few other features besides the standard ones that I discuss in Chapter 12. What makes buttons interesting, however, are the commands they call — and those are up to you, the tclet writer.

Button Features

Chapter 12 covers features that all widgets, including buttons, share. The features that are most useful for creating buttons appear again in Table 15-1.

Table 15-1	**Common Widget Features for Buttons**	
Feature	*Commands*	*Examples*

Color	`button .b -background`
	`white -text "A white`
	`button."`
		Insert Color (old fig1501) here

Text	`button .b -text` `"Click Here!"`	Insert Text (old fig1502) here
Bitmap	`button .b -bitmap` `questhead`	Insert Bitmap (old fig1503) here

Anchors	`button .b -anchor nw`
	`-width 50 -height 50`
	`-bitmap info`
		Insert Anchors (old fig1504)

Borders	`button .b -borderwidth`
	`15 -relief raised -text`
	`"border = 15"`
		Insert Borders (old fig1505) here

Relief	`button .b -relief groove`
	`-borderwidth 5 -text`
	`Relief = groove`
		Insert Relief (old fig1506) here

Size	`button .b -borderwidth 5 \`
	`-width 10 -height 10 -text`
	`"width 10, height 10"`
		Insert Size (old fig1507) here

Cursor	`button .b -height 10` `-width 10 -cursor shuttle`	Insert Cursor (old fig1508) here

Activebackground	`button .b1 -text "On"`
	`--activebackground white`
	`button .b2 -text "Off"`
	`-activebackground white`
		Insert Active background (old fig1509) here

Activeforeground	`button .b1 -text "On"`
	`-activeforeground`
	`whitebutton .b2 -text`
	`"Off" -activeforeground`
	`white`
		Insert Active foreground (old fig1510) here

The last three examples in Table 15-1 merit more attention. When you've got a button that does something, advertising that fact is a good idea. The cursor command "advertises" in a powerful way — it changes the appearance of the cursor when the cursor passes over the button. (It may be hard to tell from the example that the little shuttle icon is the cursor, and not some bitmap stuck on the button.) Changing the cursor isn't an obvious detail, but such unusual details make the difference between an okay program and a great program.

The -activeforeground and -activebackground commands should, strictly speaking, be part of the Color example. However, the -activeforeground and -activebackground commands are also useful with buttons when you want the user to know that a button is clickable. The commands change the colors of either the background or foreground of a button when the user places the mouse directly over the button. Like the cursor command, the -activeforeground and -activebackground commands are a good way to indicate that clicking on the mouse button has some effect.

The most important part of a button may be the -text feature. You use this feature to label the button with something informative about what the button does. Just put in the -text command somewhere after the button name, and follow it with the text you want to display on the button. Something like "Click here for more information" is great, but "Info" works also.

In the end, however, no matter how good your button looks, the button's gotta *do* something. I like to think of buttons as being able to do two kinds of things: execute commands and change parameters. Of course, this distinction is almost totally artificial, because you have to use a command to change a parameter. The real difference is whether the command is built into the button or whether you have to write it yourself. Checkbuttons and radiobuttons have built-in functions, which I talk about a little later in this chapter. To make a regular button do something, you have to write a command for it to carry out.

Using both bitmaps and text with buttons

Note that a button can display either text or a bitmap on it, not both. If you try to have both, as in the following lines of code,

```
button .b -text "Help" -bitmap
   info
```

or

```
button .b -bitmap info -text
   "Help"
```

Tcl/Tk displays only the bitmap. If you want both a bitmap and a text label on the button, put the bitmap on the button using the -bitmap feature, and put the text in a label next to the button, like this:

```
button .b -bitmap info -width 30
   -height 20
label .l -text "Click for Info"
pack .b .l -padx 5
```

The results should look like the accompanying figure.

Executing Commands

A regular button can do just about anything Tcl/Tk can do, because a regular button runs a Tcl/Tk command when someone clicks on it. When you use a regular button, you have to write the command that it carries out. You do this by using the -command feature. For example, clicking on the following button just quits Tcl. Not a particularly interesting button by itself, but it may be useful as part of a bigger tclet.

```
button .quit -text "Exit!" -command exit
```

The commands that a button carries out can get more complicated than this, and can involve multiple steps. For example, the following button actually creates and displays two more buttons (both of which have just quit Tcl, but have different text on them). The two buttons show up in a frame, which appears below the button that created it. Figures 15-1 and 15-2 show the before and after versions of this tclet.

```
button .b -text "Make two more buttons" -command {
  frame .f
  button .f.b1 -text \"exit\" -command exit
  button .f.b2 -text \"quit\" -command exit
  pack .f
  pack .f.b1 .f.b2 -in .f -side left -padx 2 -pady 2
}
```

As long as you can write Tcl/Tk commands that do what you want, you can make a button whose sole purpose in life is to carry out the command. Checkbuttons and radiobuttons are more specialized, so they have some different features. However, all three types of button work on exactly the same principle — when you click on one, something in the tclet changes.

Take a look at a regular button, such as one in a calculator. (For the complete calculator, take a look at calc1.Tcl/Tk on the CD-ROM included at the back of this book.) The following code has pretty much the same effect as the code that executes when you click on the key labeled "3" on the calculator tclet called calc1.Tcl/Tk on the CD-ROM.

```
button .three -text "3" -command {
  if {$done == "YES"} {
    set output ""
    update idletasks
  }
  append output 3
  update idletasks
  set done "NO"
}
```

Figure 15-1:
This tclet
add more
buttons to
itself when
the "Make
two more
buttons"
button is
clicked.

Figure 15-2:
Add more
buttons by
clicking the
first button.

The first thing this button does when someone clicks on it is check whether the variable done is set to Yes. If it is, the variable output is set to be " ". The main action of this button is appending the text 3 onto the end of the string output. Check out Chapter 9 if you need a refresher course on the append command.

The commands that involve the variable done (the second line and second-to-last line in the preceding example) deal with setting flags so that the window of the calculator gets erased correctly. These commands are in this button so that the display gets updated each time the value of the output variable changes, and the screen shows what was typed.

You find more on setting flags in the documentation of the tclet calc1.tcl. The update idletasks command also appears in more detail on the same documentation.

You may notice that most buttons in the examples on the CD ROM have the names of procedures as their commands. I did this for a number of reasons. First, most of the interesting things to do with Tcl/Tk require more than one step, and it often improves the clarity of your code to write a whole button on a single line, like this.

```
button .three -text "3" -command {click 3}
```

By looking at just this first line, you can tell that the button does the procedure click using the value 3. Most likely, if this were code you had written, you'd easily remember that the procedure click clears the window if necessary, and appends its input to the output string. Actually, you shouldn't even rely on your memory to be able to interpret your code. If you write a line like the preceding one, you should probably write a comment to explain what the button for. That comment may look something like this.

```
# Button 3, when clicked proc "click" appends \
```

```
"3" to output and updates
```

If you didn't document your code (tsk-tsk) and don't happen to remember what click does, you can always look at the code for the procedure itself, which is given here:

```
# when a number or operator is clicked, do this proc
proc click {val} {
    # use the following global variables
  global222Gutput done
    # if the user forgot to clear the window, clear it
    # anyway
    if {$done == YES} {
       clear
    }
    # stick the clicked character onto the end of output
    append output $val
    # change the display to reflect new state
    update
    # set flag that we're not ready to clear yet
    #(enter has not been pressed)
       set done "NO"
}
```

Embedded in this procedure is another procedure, again with a relatively self-explanatory name, called clear. If the comment before the line that calls the procedure clear isn't enough (and you don't remember if you wrote the procedure clear to replace the output string with a single space) you can check out that code also. It looks like this:

```
# when it's time to show a new expression
proc clear {} {
    # use the following global variables
    global output
    # change output to nothing
    set output " "
```

```
    # update the display
    update idletasks
}
```

On the other hand, you may have written the whole thing as a single command for the button, on multiple lines, like this:

```
button .three -text "3" -command {
    # if the user forgot to clear the window, \
    clear it anyway
    if {$done == "YES"} {
    # change output to nothing
      set output ""
      # update the display
      update idletasks
    }
    # stick the clicked character onto the end of output
    append output 3
    # update the display
    update idletasks
    # set flag that we're not ready \
    to clear yet (enter has not \
been pressed)
    set done "NO"
}
```

A single command has the advantage of putting everything in the same place, but has the disadvantage of being more confusing to figure out what's going on, especially if it's not properly commented.

The final reason to use procedures is sheer laziness. The number one rule of lazy programming is: *If you can reuse code, do it.* Never write anything twice if you can write it once and use it twice (or more). For example, if you write a procedure like the click procedure above, you can call it from more than one button, as I show in the following example.

```
button .zero -text "0" -command {click 0}
button .one -text "1" -command {click 1}
button .two -text "2" -command {click 2}
button .three -text "3" -command {click 3}
button .four %text "4" -command {click 4}
button .five -text "5" -command {click 5}
button .six -text "6" -command {click 6}
button .seven -text "7" -command {click 7}
button .eight -text "8" -command {click 8}
button .nine -text "9" -command {click 9}
```

If you were to write out each of these without using procedures, you'd have to write dozens of lines of code more; the code would be harder to understand; and it would probably even look sloppy. So, use procedures whenever you can. You can save yourself time by writing the code now, and you will spend less time cursing yourself six months from now when you have to expand it.

Making Choices

Standard buttons are useful for executing a command or series of commands. In practice, most button-clicking results in changing variables, one way or another. For example, the click procedure in the last section changes the value of the variable output (though that's not all it does). However, sometimes that's all you want to do — change the value of a variable. The checkbutton and radiobutton widgets are useful in this case. More importantly, checkbuttons give you the ability to group multiple buttons in a manner that makes it obvious that they belong together and affect the same parameters of the tclet. Radiobuttons are even more specialized — they present a choice between different values for a single parameter.

Checkbuttons

Unlike regular buttons, checkbuttons don't execute a Tcl/Tk command. Instead, checkbuttons set the values of certain variables, which you can than use as the argument of a command. Checkbuttons are different from regular buttons primarily in that, once clicked, checkbuttons stay clicked. So instead of executing a command that happens and is then over, checkbuttons are more useful for setting parameters (text styles, widget characteristics, and so on) that stay in effect as long as the checkbutton stays checked.

A checkbutton sets a global variable, which the -variable feature names. The variable is set to 1 if it is checked, or 0 if it is unchecked. For example, here's a neat but useless little program called checkbutton test.tcl. All the program does is make a checkbutton called .b, whose variable is called test, and a label, called .l which also displays the variable test. If you try it out and click the button, the display looks like Figure 15-3.

```
checkbutton .b -text "test" -variable test
label .l -textvariable test
pack .b .l -padx 5 -pady 2
```

Figure 15-3:
Click the
"test"
checkbutton
to set the
variable
test.

The variable that a checkbutton sets is accessible throughout your tclet. You can have a checkbutton control how you set anything, from display parameters (like foreground and background colors) to how you calculate things. All you have to do is build in an if statement that responds one way if the variable is 0, and another way if the variable is 1. For example, the following tclet has a button that makes a frame appear. Depending on the status of the checkbutton .size, the frame that appears is big or small.

Radiobuttons

A radiobutton is so named because it acts like those buttons on your car radio that tune the radio to a preset station just by pressing a button. When you push a radiobutton, it automatically *unselects* the previously selected button.

Radiobuttons are very handy for presenting mutually exclusive choices, such as "Do you want to see the page in color, or in black and white?" By using a radiobutton in this case, you prevent smart-aleck users from selecting both color and monochrome in their never-ending quest to find bugs on your page.

A simple radiobutton is made with the following code (found on the CD-ROM as monitor_color1.tcl).

```
message .msg -text "What kind of monitor do you have?" \
-width 300
frame .rb
radiobutton .rb.color -text "Color" -variable monitor \
-value color
radiobutton .rb.bnw -text "Monochrome" -variable monitor \
-value bnw
pack .rb.color .rb.bnw -in .rb -padx 2 -pady 2 -side left
pack .msg .rb -side top -padx 2 -pady 2
```

The preceding is a pretty trivial example; the variable monitor is established but unused. However, this example illustrates that both radiobuttons here make use of the same variable, monitor.

Radiobuttons also include the -value feature, which is simply the string assigned to the variable named in the -variable feature. In this example, if the button .rb.color is clicked, the variable monitor is assigned the value color. Similarly, if the button .rb.bnw is clicked, the variable monitor is assigned the value bnw. Because these are radiobuttons that refer to the same variable, clicking on one button automatically causes the other to unclick.

Unlike checkbuttons, the variables for radiobuttons contain strings, not just 0 or 1. Still, the principle is the same. After creating this choice, somewhere later in the tclet there will probably be a *decision* statement (perhaps something like this):

```
if {$monitor == "color"} {
    # do some cool color tricks
} else {
    # can't do cool color tricks
    message .no-color  -text "Sorry, no color tricks \
    available for your monochrome  monitor."
}
```

Chapter 16

Label, Message, and Text Widgets

· ·

In This Chapter

▶ Creating label widgets

▶ Creating message widgets

▶ Creating text widgets

▶ Handling text-widget selections

▶ Handling text-widget tags

· ·

In this chapter, I run throught the three basic widgets that you can use to present type:

✔ Label widgets

✔ Message widgets

✔ Text widgets

Labels and messages are simple ways to present information to the user; text widgets are the basic means to allow users to enter and edit large blocks of text.

Label Widgets

A label widget is the simplest way to plop some type onto the screen. You can use label widgets for whatever you like, but most often, you'll use them to label interface components in the tclet — hence the name *label*. Figure 16-1 shows a typical use of labels in the very-nearly-real world.

(I love the Adam West "Batman" television series like few things in this world and have always loved the fact that every prop on the sets — both in the Batcave and the villains' lairs — was neatly labeled. Figure 16-1 is my little homage to Batman.)

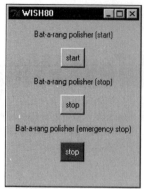

Figure 16-1:
Labels
usually
identify
other
interface
elements.

Labels are created with the basic label command, like so:

```
label .l -text "Bat-a-Rang Polisher (start)"
```

You can also use the -textvariable option with a label so that the label displays the contents of the specified variable, rather than a fixed text message. Suppose that you want to create a little type-tester tclet that allows the user to see how a particular phrase appears after it's rendered in different fonts and sizes. You can use the -textvariable option to put the user's test string into each of a series of labels, as follows:

```
#create the labels, and assign each a unique font option
label .l1 -textvariable test_string \
-font "*-Stone Sans-*-*-*-12-*-*-*-*-*-*"
label .l2 -textvariable test_string -font \
"*-Stone Sans Semibold-*-*-*-12-*-*-*-*-*-*"
label .l3 -textvariable test_string -font \
"*-Stone Sans Bold -*-*-*-12-*-*-*-*-*-*"
label .l4 -textvariable test_string -font \
"*-Stone Serif-*-*-*-12-*-*-*-*-*-*"
label .l5 -textvariable test_string -font \
"*-Stone Serif Semibold-*-*-*-12-*-*-*-*-*-*"
label .l6 -textvariable test_string -font \
"*-Stone Serif Bold-*-*-*-12-*-*-*-*-*-*"

# pack the labels
for {set ctr 1} {$ctr <= 6} {incr ctr} {
    pack .l$ctr -pady 5
}

# create an entry box, using the same text variable as the
# labels above
entry .e -textvariable test_string
pack .e -pady 5 -padx 5
```

Now, after the user enters a test string in the entry box, each label displays the string according to its specific option settings. As soon as the -textvariable is updated (whenever the user changes the contents of the entry box, for example), the label widgets automatically update their displays to reflect the new value. Figure 16-2 shows how the string-tester widget works with the word *hamburger*.

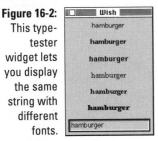

Figure 16-2:
This type-tester widget lets you display the same string with different fonts.

You can use variations on the preceding basic code to test different point sizes, colors, or other label-widget options. Configure each label with its own options, but give all the widgets the same -textvariable.

Basic label options

Labels can take any of the basic options that Chapter 14 discusses, such as

- ✔ Color of foreground and background
- ✔ Size (both width and height)
- ✔ Font
- ✔ Border (thickness and relief)

As with most widgets, you can also specify a picture to display in a label widget. Often, specifying an image is the easiest way to add a decorative element to your tclet, such as a logo or special border.

Special label options and commands

Like frame widgets, labels are so darn simple that there aren't really any special label options or commands. Sorry. A label is designed to sit there and display its text (or image).

Things to remember about labels

There are a few special characteristics to think about when you work with label widgets:

✔ **Label widgets don't add any line breaks to text.** No matter how much text you give a text widget, the widget uses the same line breaks from the text. If you don't break up text with carriage returns, the label widget leaves the message exactly as it is and displays the text message in one long (or very long, or very, very long) line. Suppose that you want to use a text string like the following:

```
set joyce_string {Stately, plump Buck Mulligan came from
    the stairhead, bearing a bowl of lather on which
    a mirror and a razor lay crossed. A yellow
    dressinggown, ungirded, was sustained gently
    behind him on the mild morning air.}

# put the sting into a label widget and pack the label
label .joyce -text $joyce_string
pack .joyce
```

I didn't add any of the line breaks in the preceding text — it's the normal automatic wrap like a word processor. (If the text looks familiar, it's because I took it from the first page of James Joyce's *Ulysses*.)

If you pack this string in a label, the entire string appears as one line in the label. Figure 16-3 shows the joyce string displayed in a label without any special treatment. Even though I've stretched out the window as far as it can go, the text still doesn't quite fit.

Figure 16-3:
A long text
string, as
displayed by
a label
widget.

However, if you add the line breaks by hand with the good old Return (or enter) key, the label displays the text as entered, line breaks and all. In the following text, I added the symbol <cr> to show the places where I inserted breaks manually. (The breaks aren't really part of the string, and I didn't really enter them — I just pressed the Return key to break the line.)

```
set joyce_string_2 {Stately, plump Buck Mulligan <cr>
came from the stairhead, bearing a bowl of lather <cr>
on which a mirror and a razor lay crossed. <cr>
A yellow dressinggown, ungirded, was sustained <cr>
gently behind him on the mild morning air.}

# put the sting into a label widget and pack the label
label .joyce2 -text $joyce_string_2
pack .joyce2
```

Figure 16-4 shows the result. As you can see, the lines in the label are broken exactly the same way as the lines of code are broken.

Figure 16-4:
The same text string displayed with a label, with line breaks added by hand.

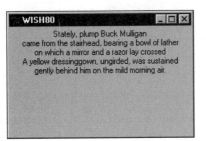

▶ **Text in label widgets is centered by default.** Usually, the text of a label widget is displayed in one line. The widget is just big enough to hold the widget's text message, so you may not notice that the text is centered in the widget's area. Well, it is.

If you make the widget larger than the text by supplying a width option, or if you create more than one line of text (as shown in Figure 16-4) you'll see that each line of text is centered.

This default is sensible — normally, a label widget is just a few words or less.

If you use more than one line of text, however, you may want to set up the label so that the text is flush left. It's easy to change the text alignment. Just use the standard widget option justify. To set the text in the .joyce label flush left, for example, simply use the following:

```
.joyce configure -justify left
```

▶ **Text in label widgets is bold and sans serif by default.** You can set the text of a label widget however you want, of course, but by default, the text displayed by a label widget is in a bold sans-serif font. If the user is running Windows, the font probably is Avenir. If the user's system is a Mac, the font probably is Geneva. By default, the text in a label widgets is also a point size larger than the default point size for message widgets.

Message Widgets

Message widgets are pretty much like label widgets. The important difference? Message widgets automatically break their text strings into several lines. If you put the original `joyce_string` text in a message widget, the widget thoughtfully supplies the line breaks, as follows:

```
set joyce_string {Stately, plump Buck Mulligan came from
                the stairhead, bearing a bowl of lather on which
                a mirror and a razor lay crossed. A yellow
                dressinggown, ungirded, was sustained gently
                behind him on the mild morning air.}
message .james -text joyce_string
pack .james
```

The content of `joyce_string` is really one long unbroken line of text. The resulting message widget (shown in Figure 16-5) breaks the text into separate lines. By default, the text is broken so that the widget is about one-and-a-half times as wide as it is high.

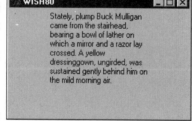

Figure 16-5:
The same text string, displayed in a message widget.

Special message options and commands

There's really only one special message option, but it's essential to making your message widgets behave. This option is called `aspect`, and it controls the relative proportions of the widget's height.

The value of the `option` command is a number, and it's easiest (at least for me) to think of the number as being the width of the message widget, reckoned as a percentage of the widget's height. A value of 50, for example, means that the widget is half as wide as it is tall, whereas a value of 200 means that the widget is twice as wide as it is tall.

The default value of `-aspect` is 150. Figure 16-5, in the preceding section, uses this value. If you want to play around with widget options, you can use the `configure` command to test different option values. The following code, for example, yields the tall and skinny widget shown in Figure 16-6:

```
.james configure -aspect 25
```

This code yields the short wide widget shown in Figure 16-7:

```
.james configure -aspect 500
```

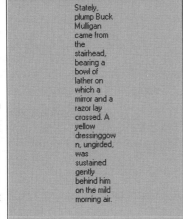

Figure 16-6:
The same
message
widget,
with an
aspect
of 25.

Figure 16-7:
The same
message
widget,
with
an aspect
of 500.

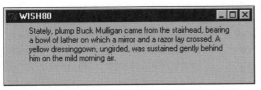

A fancy aspect-finder

If you don't like the trial-and-error approach to choosing aspect values, or if you're just feeling a little adventurous, you can write a routine to change the aspect of your widgets interactively. I don't recommend putting this kind of routine into your final code; it's just to help you find the perfect aspect setting without typing different aspect values by hand.

Here's the basic idea: You set up a binding for your message widget. Whenever the mouse moves around inside the widget, the bind command figures out the aspect of the mouse's position with respect to the top-left corner of the widget and resets the message's aspect to match the mouse's aspect.

The only thing that's a little funny in this little tclet is the use of the int() and double() commands. If you simply divide two integers, such as 105 by 100, the interpreter rounds the result down to an integer — in this case, down to 1. You want a little more precision than that, so use double() to change the coordinates to floating-point numbers to get 1.05 instead of 1. Unfortunately, aspect accepts only

integers, so you need to convert the calculated aspect back to an integer with int() so as to feed it to the configure command.

Instead of specifying a particular widget name, I used widget_name as a placeholder in the code. Be sure to use the real widget's name when you enter the code.

Finally, notice that I used the puts command to display the -aspect value of the message widget, because this routine is designed to be used to test widgets in Wish. If, for some reason, you choose to adapt this approach to a Web-page tclet, be sure to remove the puts command. Here's the code that creates the actual aspect ratio readout:

```
bind widget_name <Motion> {
        set my_aspect \
        [expr int((double(%x)/
(double(%y)) *100)]
        widget_name configure
aspect $my_aspect
        puts "aspect equals
$my_aspect"
        }
```

Things to remember about messages

There are a few special features of messages that you should think about when you're working with message widgets:

✔ **By default, the text of a message widget is always broken.** A message widget always breaks the text of the message so that the widget has the specified (or default) -aspect value. Even if the message widget's text is only a few words long, the message widget tries to break the text.

If you really want the text of your message to be in one line, you can tweak the configuration of the message widget in two ways:

• Set the -width value of the message widget so that it's wide enough to hold the entire text in one line.

- Set the `aspect` value to a large number (the longer the text, the larger the number) so that all the text fits in one line.

The easiest solution, of course, is to use a label widget instead of a message widget.

✔ **By default, the text of a message widget is flush left.** As you can see in Figures 16-5, 16-6, and 16-7, each line of text in a message widget is lined up on the left side. This setting is the default. Setting the text so that it's centered or flush right is easy. Just use the `-justify` option with the value `center` or `right` to change the text's alignment.

You can change your basic message widget like so:

```
.james configure -justify right
```

This code produces the result shown in Figure 16-8. As you can see, all the lines of text are lined up on the right.

Figure 16-8:
You can set the text in a message widget to flush-right alignment.

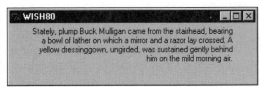

Likewise, the command

```
.james configure -justify center
```

causes each line of text to be centered, as shown in Figure 16-9.

Figure 16-9:
You can center each line of text in a message widget.

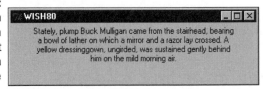

✔ **The font of a message widget is bold sans serif by default.** Like label widgets, message widgets use bold sans-serif fonts by default. (The size of message-widget type is a little smaller than label-widget type, but otherwise, the type is the same.) You can change the message widget's font as you like with the `font` option.

Text Widgets

Text widgets are the third major kind of text-wrangling widgets, and they're quite a bit different from (and quite a bit more complicated than) either message widgets or label widgets. For starters, text widgets

✔ Can be edited directly by the user

✔ Can contain selections (just like a word processor's selection features)

✔ Can contain text with different fonts, sizes, and colors within the same widget

✔ Can contain other widgets embedded in the text of the widget

In fact, you can specify every single letter of every string of text in a text widget and treat each letter as a separate unit with its own properties — even its own bindings!

You create text widgets with the `text` command, like so:

```
text .t
pack .t
```

Figure 16-10 shows this basic text widget.

Notice a couple of factors right away:

✔ By default, text widgets are fairly big — 80 characters wide by 24 characters tall (in other words, about the same size as a typical word processor window).

✔ Text widgets ordinarily use the sunken `relief` option, but you can specify any relief option you want.

Default behavior of text widgets

Even a basic text widget without any options acts quite a bit like a simple word processor, as the shown by the following default behaviors:

✔ **The user can enter text.** You can type whatever you want in a text widget as soon as the widget is born.

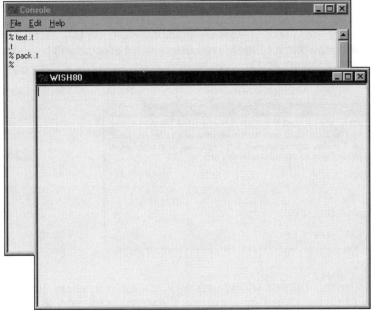

Figure 16-10:
An empty
text widget.

- ✔ **The user can select text.** You can use the mouse to select text, and you'll find that the selection process works the way that you expect (double-clicking a word selects the entire word, Shift+clicking adds to the current selection, and so on). If you've *ever* used a text editor under Windows 95 or the MacOS, the way that selection works in a text widget is completely familiar.

- ✔ **The user can edit text.** Editing tools work the same way that they do in standard text editors, too. You can delete text with the Delete and Backspace keys, and replace any selected text simply by typing replacement text.

  Note: The standard editing keyboard shortcuts Ctrl-Z (Windows) and ⌘+Z (Mac) to undo the preceding edit aren't built into the text widget.

- ✔ **The user can navigate.** The basic navigation keys (such as the arrow keys, Home, Page Up, and Page Down) all work the way that you expect them to.

Special text options

You can control the appearance of text in a text widget with standard widget options such as `-font`, `-foreground` and `-background`. In addition to these basic commands, you can use several special options to specify the appearance of type in a text widget. *These commands are unique to the text widget* — you can't use them in label or message widgets.

I'll add a little sample text to the widget, so that you can see how the options affect the display of text. I'll use the same text from *Ulysses* that I used for the label and message examples earlier in this chapter, simply pasting the text into the widget from a word processor. The widget with text looks like Figure 16-11.

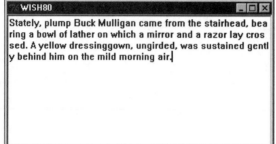

Figure 16-11: You can type text into a text widget, just as you'd enter text into a word processor.

Notice that the text widget isn't very interested in where the words begin and end; the widget simply breaks the words in the middle at the end of each line. Also, the space between the lines (the *leading*) is like single-line spacing in a word processor.

First, let's fix the line breaks in the preceding image. They really drive me nuts as they are. To change the way that the wrap works, simply use the -wrap option. Right now, -wrap is set to its default value, char. To change the wrap to word-processor style line breaks, set the -wrap option to word, as follows:

```
.t configure -wrap word
```

Figure 16-12 shows the result, which is more like I want. Each line in the image ends at the end of a word, not in the middle of each word.

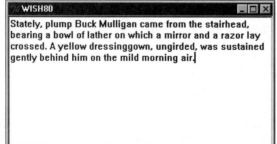

Figure 16-12: Use the -wrap option to control the way that a text widget handles line breaks.

TIP

(By the way, one more possible value for `wrap` — none — causes the entire text to appear in one line.)

Next, look at the line spacing. Three related options affect the line spacing in a text widget:

spacing1	Increase blank space above a paragraph
spacing2	Add height to the lines inside a paragraph
spacing3	Increase blank space below a paragraph

By *paragraph*, I mean a paragraph in the sense that a word processor does: a bunch of text that *isn't* broken with the Return (or Enter) key. No matter how long or short the text is — one character, or 500 lines of text without any manual returns — it's still one character as far as the spacing tags are concerned.

The space added is normally reckoned in pixels. After a little cutting and pasting to create three separate paragraphs, add space like so:

```
.t configure \
    -spacing1 10 \
    -spacing2 3 \
    -spacing3 10
```

Figure 16-13 shows the revised version of the text widget. The new version shows a bit more space between lines, thanks to the 3 pixels that you added with spacing2. Between the paragraphs, there's 20 points of new space — 10 points are contributed by the spacing1 option, and 10 points are added by spacing3. The first paragraph is only 10 points from the top of the widget, because only spacing1 is adding space here.

Figure 16-13:
Use spacing,
spacing2,
and
spacing3
to control
the amount
of space
between
lines and
between
paragraphs.

WISH80

Stately, plump Buck Mulligan came from the stairhead, bearing a bowl of lather on which a mirror and a razor lay crossed. A yellow dressinggown, ungirded, was sustained gently behind him on the mild morning air.

Stately, plump Buck Mulligan came from the stairhead, bearing a bowl of lather on which a mirror and a razor lay crossed. A yellow dressinggown, ungirded, was sustained gently behind him on the mild morning air.

Stately, plump Buck Mulligan came from the stairhead, bearing a bowl of lather on which a mirror and a razor lay crossed. A yellow dressinggown, ungirded, was sustained gently behind him on the mild morning air.

Character positions in a text widget

You can insert, delete, and otherwise manipulate text with Tcl/Tk commands. Before we discuss specific commands, however, you should understand how to specify positions and groups of characters within the text.

First, create a simple tclet that contains a text widget and a label widget that displays information about what's going on inside the text widget. Put the readout on top so that it's easier to see, but it doesn't really matter how you choose to lay out the tclet.

```
label .readout -textvariable readout
text .t
pack .readout .t
```

Now put some text in the text widget.

The simplest way to do this is to open the text file `yeats.txt` on the *Tcl/Tk For Dummies* CD-ROM and paste it into a text box that you've created. Alternatively, you can simply type the text (from W. B. Yeats' *The Second Coming*) into the text widget by hand:

```
Turning and turning in the widening gyre
The falcon cannot hear the falconeer;
Things fall apart; the centre cannot hold;
Mere anarchy is loosed upon the world,
The blood-dimmed tide is loosed, and everywhere
The ceremony of innocence is drowned;
The best lack all conviction, while the worst
Are full of passionate intensity.
```

The basic tclet with text should look like Figure 16-14. Notice that the text is in Roman (not bold) serif type — probably Courier, but this font may vary, depending on the fonts that you have installed on your system.

You can specify characters in a text widget in a few basic ways. Specifying may be confusing because the categories seem to overlap a little. After you get the hang of the system, you'll find that it very easy to specify any group of characters, using categories like the following:

✔ The first word of the first line

✔ The first 25 characters

✔ The current selection

✔ The character to the left of the cursor

✔ All the characters between the cursor and the end of the text

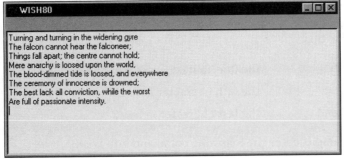

Figure 16-14:
A text
box that
contains the
example text
from the
Yeats poem.

Specifying a group of characters gives you absolute power over them. You can delete them, replace them, change their appearance, or anything else you can dream up.

With that little warning out of the way, here are the systems for specifying positions within the text:

- **Indexes.** An index is the most basic form of specifying the "addresses" of characters in text widgets. For example, the index 1.23 specifies the twenty-third character in line 1 of the text. The index @10,20 specifies the character closest to the point that's 10 pixels from the left edge of the text widget and 20 points from the top of the widget.

- **Marks.** *Marks* are just names for positions in the text. I think of marks as special variables that store locations, not numbers or letters. Tcl/Tk has a few ready-made marks , such as `insert`, which is the position of the text-insertion cursor, and `current`, which is the position closest to the arrow cursor.

- **Tags.** A *tag* is a name for a group of characters. You can name all characters in the first line of the text `first-line stuff` or the first 25 characters `first_25`. Tcl/Tk has some ready-made tags built in, such as `sel`, which is the name of the current selection.

Indexes

An index doesn't really store anything the way that a mark or a tag does. Indexes are just a way to tell Tcl/Tk where you want to perform an action. If you look up text-widget commands in the online reference material, you see commands like the following:

```
.widget_name get index1 ?index2?
```

The `get` command retrieves the characters that are between the two positions specified by `index1` and `index2`. You can specify indexes in several ways. The following sections describe the basic index styles in detail.

Line and character

You can use the line number and the character in the line separated with a dot, like this:

1.0	the 0th (first) character in line 1
2.5	the fifth character in line 2
3.end	the last character in line 3

For example, enter the following command into Wish:

```
set readout [.t get 1.0 2.0]
```

The interpreter grabs all the characters between 1.0 (the first character of the first line) and 2.0 (the first character of the second line), and puts the entire string in the .readout widget's textvariable. You can see the result in Figure 16-15. The first line of the poem is displayed at the top of the tclet window.

Figure 16-15:
The code
set
readout
[.t get
1.0 2.0]
displays the
first line
of text
widget text
at the top
of the tclet.

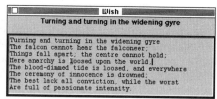

Coordinates

You can also specify indices in terms of positional coordinates. Use the index format

```
@x-coordinate,y-coordinate
```

You use this index format just like you use the preceding line-and-character format. You can track the cursor's movement with this little bind command:

```
bind .t <Motion> {set readout [.t get @%x,%y]}
```

Inside the body of a `bind` command, `%x` stands for the current x coordinate of the mouse position, and `%y` stands for the current y coordinate of the mouse. So the index `@%x,%y` specifies the character closest to the current mouse position.

After you enter the preceding command into Wish and drag the mouse over the text widget, the readout widget shows the character under the mouse — one character at a time (see Figure 16-16).

Figure 16-16:
This tclet
displays the
character
under the
mouse
pointer in
the display
at the top
of the tclet.

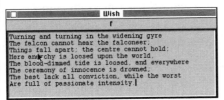

Marks

A mark is simply a name for a position within text — *not* necessarily a single character or a group of characters, just a position between characters. Create your own marks by giving an index a name, or use the ready-made marks (`insert` and `current`) that are built into Tcl/Tk.

Think of an index as being a value that can store the position of the cursor. The cursor is never "inside" a character, even if a character is selected; it's always between characters or else at the beginning or end of a line.

Marks are kinda like variables, and the commands that store positions in marks are much like the commands that store data in variables. The basic command for creating a mark is `set`, which looks like this:

```
.widget_name mark set mark_name index
```

In the preceding example, `widget_name` is the name of the particular text widget where you're placing the mark, and `index` is the position that you want to mark. In the following example, you create a mark at the beginning of the second line of the text widget `.t`:

```
.t mark set my_mark 2.0
```

Now you can refer to position 2.0 as `my_mark` in any command that accept a position as an argument. The following example returns all the characters between the insertion point and the mark.

```
.t get insert my_mark
```

Likewise, the following code sets the value of the ready-made mark `insert` to the value of `my_mark`. Consequently, the insertion point moves to `my_mark`'s position:

```
.t mark set insert my_mark
```

To see a list of all the marks in a widget, use this command:

```
widget_name mark names
```

If you're feeling destructive, you can delete marks with the `unset` command, which goes like this:

```
widget_name mark unset mark_name
```

For example, to delete the mark `my_mark` from the widget `.t`, you use this command:

```
.t mark unset my_mark
```

Tags

Tags define a group of characters. Basically, a tag is just a string of characters, which is defined by a first index position and a final index position. A tag can consist of anything from one character (or even no characters) to all the text in the widget. You can make many uses of tagged text:

- Apply style attributes (such as font, color, and size changes) to the tagged text.
- Create bindings to the tag, which work exactly like widget bindings.

To see tags in action, let's use the ready-made tag `sel`, which holds any text that's currently selected. Configuring a tag is much like configuring ordinary widgets. The command is very nearly the same:

```
.widget-name tag configure tag-name -option1 value1 \
-option2 value2
```

As you can see in Figure 16-17, the selected text is marked in the regular Tcl/Tk text-widget way — the selection is in raised relief, but the color of the text and the selection's background are exactly the same as the rest of the text.

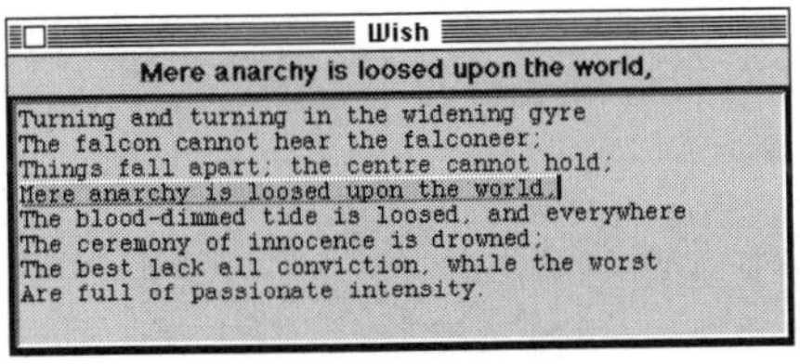

Figure 16-17:
Selected
text is in
raised relief.

Suppose that you want the selection to look more like a standard MacOS/ Windows selection, with a black background and white text. The configuration command looks like this:

```
.t tag configure sel -background black -foreground white \
-relief flat
```

This isn't too hard to figure out. The basic options-and-values part of the tag configuration command is exactly the same that you'd find in a command such as the plain old configuration command, as follows:

```
-background black -foreground white -relief flat
```

The preceding command affects only the text inside the tag — all the other text in the widget uses the widget's settings, not the tags.

Enter the preceding code into Wish, and look at the revised appearance of the selection. As you see in Figure 16-18, the selection now has the standard Mac/Windows look.

Creating a binding between tags and events works just like creating the widget bindings discussed in Chapter 15. Just like the tag configure command, the tag bind command looks pretty much like a regular bind command:

```
widget-name tag bind tag-name <event> command-body
```

You can create the following little binding to causes the selection to cycle through a series of colors after the mouse enters the selection:

```
.t tag bind sel <Motion> {
    foreach color {red orange yellow green blue violet} {
        .t tag configure sel -background $color
        after 500
        update
    }
}
```

Figure 16-18:
You can
configure the
text widget
to resemble
a standard
Mac/
Windows
look and feel.

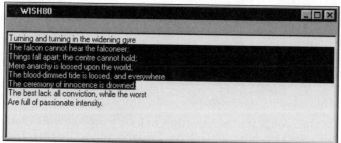

You don't need to limit yourself to the `sel` tag that's built into Tcl/Tk, of course. You can create your own tags. All you need is a pair of indices to define the boundaries of the tag. The formula for defining marks is this:

```
widget-name tag add new-tag-name index1 index2
```

Suppose that you want to create a tag that consists of the third and fourth line of the text. Build the command like this:

```
.t tag add my_tag 3.0 4.end
```

When formats get friendly

You can mix and match index formats with reckless abandon. All the following commands are perfectly legal:

`.t get 1.0 current` — The characters between the start of the first line and the current mouse position

`.t get sel.last insert` — The characters between the end of the selection and the insertion-point cursor

`.t get @0,0 current` — The characters between the top-left corner of the tclet and the current mouse position

Chapter 17

Canvases (Or Painting with Pixels)

In This Chapter

▶ Creating a canvas widget

▶ Adding stuff to a canvas widget

▶ Naming canvas items with tags

▶ Moving around canvas items

▶ Setting up bindings for canvases

Canvas widgets are named after the canvases that artists use for painting. You can create all sorts of graphical elements — like polygons, circles, lines and curves — using canvas widgets, and put these parts together to build your own artistic masterpiece. Okay . . . let's paint.

Creating the Canvas

Just like frame widgets, canvas widgets start out as plain old squares of blank-screen real estate in the middle of a tclet. Canvas widgets are basically . . . well, canvases that you can draw or paint on. You can also add pictures and text to canvases, and (as you can't with real-world canvases), you can easily move the paint around *after* you put it down on a canvas widget.

Creating the canvas is simple. Just use the basic `canvas` command, like this:

```
canvas .c
```

A default canvas is about 28 pixels high by 400 pixels wide. The default canvas is the same utility gray as the default tclet background, and it doesn't have any kind of border relief or any other special features. You can alter these basic options with the regular commands, as follows:

```
.c configure -width 200 height 200 background white \
borderwidth 3 -relief ridge
```

Note: One thing about canvas widgets is a little funny, standard-options-wise: Canvas widgets don't use the standard -foreground option. Rather, you specify the color of each object that you draw in the canvas when you draw the object. (You probably don't want to paint with just one color anyway.)

Adding Stuff to the Canvas

An empty canvas widget is fairly pointless — just a frame with unrealized potential. To make a canvas widget interesting, you draw in it.

There really isn't a name for the stuff that you draw inside a canvas widget. In some place, the Tcl/Tk documentation calls things like individual instances of rectangles and lines *items*; elsewhere, it calls them *elements* or avoids the issue altogether. I'll try to avoid the issue, too, or call this stuff *stuff* or, if I'm talking about a specific glob of paint, I'll use item.

You add all the basic stuff to canvases with different variations on the create command. To add a rectangle to a canvas widget called .c, for example, you use the command

```
.c create rectangle 25 25 150 150 -fill red -outline blue
```

To add some text, you use a command like this:

```
.c create text 25 175 -text "hello, Mercury" -anchor w
```

When you try these commands in Wish (try them now, if you haven't already), you'll notice that each command that draws something in a canvas returns a number. The Wish session looks something like this:

```
% .c create rectangle 25 25 150 150 -fill red -outline blue
1
% .c create text 25 175 -text "hello, Mercury" -anchor w
2
```

The numbers are like serial numbers for the stuff that gets drawn, so that you can manipulate the item later. (You can see the canvas widget in Figure 17-1, with each item within the widget labeled with its serial number.) The serial numbers make it easy to specify individual items in a canvas later.

If you want to remove the rectangle from the canvas *without* removing the text, you use a command like this:

```
.c delete 1
```

.c create rectangle...

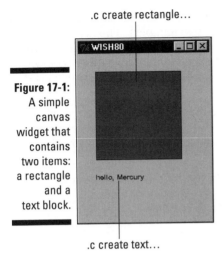

Figure 17-1:
A simple
canvas
widget that
contains
two items:
a rectangle
and a
text block.

hello, Mercury

.c create text...

To individually reconfigure stuff, you use a command like this:

```
.c itemconfigure 2 -fill black
```

You'll probably want to keep track of which item has what serial number when you're drawing in a canvas widget. Don't draw the stuff in the canvas directly with a command like this:

```
.c create rectangle 50 50 100 100
```

Rather, get the serial number and put it into a variable, like this:

```
set my_rectangle [.c create rectangle 50 50 100 100]
or even into an array
set rectangles([.c create rectangle 50 50 100 100]) \
"rectangle information here"
```

An easy way to clear away all the widgets in a canvas is to use .canvas-widget-name delete all. This command is especially useful during the design stages, when you're deciding what you want the tclet to look like.

The coordinate system

Whenever you paint anything in a canvas, you must specify its position. You have three basic rules to follow when you specify coordinates (remember these rules, and telling the interpreter where to put stuff is easy):

✔ **Coordinates are pairs of horizontal and vertical measurements.** When you specify a position, you always use two numbers. The first number — the *x-coordinate* — measures the distance between the left edge of the canvas widget and the new item. The second number — the *y-coordinate* — measures the distance from the top edge of the canvas widget to the new item.

✔ **Coordinates are measured from the top-left corner of the canvas widget.** X-coordinates get bigger as you move farther to the right of the widget; y-coordinates get bigger as you move down toward the bottom of the widget.

✔ **Coordinates are measured in pixels.** No matter what system you use to specify the `-height` and `-width` of the canvas widget, all measurements *within* the widget are in pixels. Sorry, bubba.

Rectangles and ovals

The two most basic shapes — rectangles and ovals — are created in pretty much the same way. The trick is to specify the two corners of the shape. Ovals don't have corners, of course — you must imagine where the corners would appear. Figure 17-2 shows how reckoning the "corners" of ovals pans out in the real world.

Figure 17-2:
Creating
rectangles
and ovals
is a simple
matter
of figuring
out the
coordinates
of the
corners
of the item.

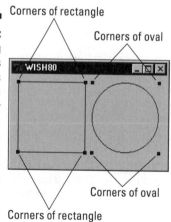

Corners of rectangle

Corners of oval

Corners of oval

Corners of rectangle

If the coordinates of the top-left corner of the shape are x1, y1 and the coordinates of the bottom-left corner are x2, y2, the command to build a rectangle is

```
canvas-wdget-name create rectangle x1 y1 x2 y2
```

Using the same coordinates, the command to create a circle is

```
canvas-wdget-name create oval x1 y1 x2 y2
```

Note: You don't need to specify the top-left corner first and the bottom-right corner second — as long as you enter two points, you can use them to create a shape.

To specify the color of a rectangle or oval, you can use the -fill and -outline command when you draw the shape. To create a black-and-white circle, for example, you use a command like this:

```
.c create oval 20 20 100 100 -outline black -fill white
```

You can also specify how thick the outline should be. Unfortunately, this option has the confusing name -width. *The- -width option affects only the thickness of the outline,* not *the dimensions of the rectangle or oval.* To draw a rectangle with a seriously black border, use a command like this:

```
.c create rectangle 50 50 150 150 -outline black -width 15
```

Arcs

Arcs are the same things that they were in your high-school geometry classes — portions of a circle. You can specify any portion of a circle from $1°$ to $360°$ and position the arc however you like.

The most basic arc command creates a $90°$ arc that starts at the middle of the right side of the circle from which the arc is taken. Following is the basic command, which looks much like the command that you use to build a circle:

```
canvas-widget-name create arc x1 x2 y1 y2
```

The coordinates in this example specify the circle from which the arc is taken — not the ends of the arc itself. To see how arc positioning works, use the following command to draw a basic circle:

```
.c create oval 10 10 110 110
```

Now create an arc widget with the same coordinates but with a thick outline, so that you can clearly see where the arc begins and ends. Use this command:

```
.c create arc 10 10 110 110 -width 5
```

You can see in Figure 17-3 that the arc is right on top of the circle that uses the same coordinates.

Figure 17-3:
Arcs are
positioned
in the same
place as an
oval with
the same
coordinate.

You can specify an arc of any size that you like. The option that controls the size of the arc is `-extent`, and it takes a value measured in degrees. Rather than create a new arc, reconfigure this one to a new size with the `itemconfigure` command. If you want the arc to show a half-circle rather than a quarter-circle, use this command:

```
.c create arc 10 10 110 110 -fill red -width 5 -extent 180
```

Figure 17-4 shows the new arc. I've filled the arc in to make it easy to see.

Figure 17-4:
You can
use the
`-extent`
option to
control the
length (in
degrees)
of the arc.

Note: The value of `extent 180` is in the preceding example, because there are 360 degrees in a circle, and we wanted to draw half a circle — basic stuff if you remember any basic geometry. If you don't, find a geometry-savvy friend; there's no *Geometry For Dummies* . . . yet.

You can position the arc anywhere in the circle by using the `-start` option, which essentially rotates the arc around the circle's center so that the arc starts in a new place. To create another semicircle to match the first, you use this command:

```
.c create arc 10 10 110 110 -fill blue -width 5 \
-extent 180 -start 180
```

Polygons

A polygon, at least so far as canvas widgets are concerned, is a collection of connected points. A polygon can contain as few as three points or as many as you care to add. Polygons don't need to be regular, and it's perfectly okay if the lines of a polygon cross one another.

The basic `polygon` command looks like this:

```
.canvas-widget-name create polygon x1 y1 x2 y2 x3 y3 . . .
          more points . . .\
    last-x last-y
```

The lumpy-looking polygon shown in Figure 17-5 was created with this command:

```
.c create polygon 87 113 52 171 108 219 198 218 238 142 \
173 58
```

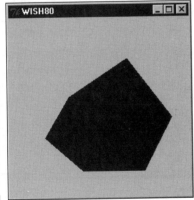

Figure 17-5:
You can use the canvas widget to draw polygons.

Creating a little tclet that can help you draw polygons in Wish is fairly simple, so you can work out your polygon by pointing and clicking, rather than figuring out where you want your points to go. Here's the game plan:

1. **Use a `bind` command to put down little squares when the mouse is clicked.**

2. **Store the positions of the mouse clicks in a list called `point_list`.**

3. **Use another `bind` command to build the polygon from the list when the mouse is double-clicked.**

When Tclets write Tcl

So far, I've managed to shield you from the `eval` command. You don't need `eval` often for simple tasks, but sometimes — as in the polygon-drawing tclet shown in Listing 18-1 — you can't do without it.

The basic principle is easy: The `eval` command simply causes the Tcl/Tk interpreter to evaluate a Tcl command. The basic form is like this:

```
eval list-of-words-that-happens-
    to-be-a-Tcl/Tk-command
```

The command

```
eval beep
```

is the same as

```
beep
```

and

```
eval "label .l -text "Hello,
    World""
```

is the same as

```
label .l -text "Hello, World"
```

Basically, `eval` is used to get around thorny substitution problems. When you want to create a command while the tclet is running, but you can't quite do it within the interpreter's single substitution pass, use the `eval` command.

I used `eval` in the polygon-drawing program, in this line:

```
eval ".c create polygon
    $point_list"
```

If the interpreter simply saw the command

```
.c create polygon $point_list
```

it would decide that the `create` command doesn't have enough arguments. The interpreter doesn't treat the list in `$point_list` as separate words but as one big grouped word. When you use `eval`, the coordinates are substituted into the command; then the command is evaluated.

Again, using `eval` is a little out of the ordinary. You may never need to use the `eval` command at all, especially if you stick to using little Web tclets.

I'll use one special command, called `eval`, that you haven't seen yet. If you're interested, `eval` is explained in the sidebar "When Tclets write Tcl." The `eval` command is a little complicated, so you can certainly blow off the explanation if you like and simply use the little tclet to plan your polygons.

Lines

Lines, in their simplest form, connect two points. If you like, you can get quite a bit more complicated than that:

✔ You can make curved lines.

✔ You can make jaggy lightning-shaped lines.

✔ You can add arrowheads to lines.

✔ You can add different ends and connecting joints to lines.

Naturally, you can make the same adjustments to the line's thickness and color as you can to a rectangle or circle's outline and color.

The basic command for building a line, which follows, is pretty much like the command for building a polygon:

```
canvas-widget-name create line x1 y1 x2 y2 . . . more
                  points . . . last_x last_y
```

You can specify as many points as you like. The Tcl/Tk interpreter simply draws a line that connects all the dots. The line can cross itself, spiral outward, or whatever. Really, the only differences between a line and a polygon (at this point, anyway) are that the line isn't filled and that the interpreter doesn't draw a final segment to connect the last point to the first point. Figure 17-6 shows a line created with the following command:

```
.c create line 56 54 67 48 66 60 49 63 43 46 62 34 81 47 \
79 71 51 81 25 56 39 22 81 13 105 51 105 50 -width 5
```

Figure 17-6:
You can use
the canvas
widget to
draw lines,
like this
funky one.

The simplest way to dress up your line is to customize the way that the ends and the joints in the line work. Look at the big fat line in Figure 17-7. As you can see, the ends of the lines are capped with pointy ends, and the joint that connects the lines is squared off, as though the corner had been clipped off with a pair of scissors. (The same thing happens with a thinner line, but it's easier to see the effect when the line is nice and thick.)

Figure 17-7:
You can customize the way that the ends of lines and joins between lines look.

Because this section describes several ways to change the line, store the line's serial number in a variable so that you can reconfigure the line, not draw a new line for every variation. Call the variable my_line. Here's the code that draws the line on the canvas:

```
set my_line [.c create line 18 22 47 77 82 22 -width 10]
```

To change the configuration of a drawing item that's already in the canvas, you can use the itemconfigure command. No doubt you've come to appreciate Tcl/Tk's predictability by now, and you've probably guessed that itemconfigure looks like this:

```
canvas-widget-name itemconfigure item-serial-number \
option1 value1 option2 value2 . . . more options . . .
             last_option last_value
```

So to change the new line so that it's red instead of black, you use this command:

```
.c itemconfigure $my_line -outline red
```

Remember that you stored the line's serial number in my_line when you created the line. If you know the line's number (say, 1), you can just cite it instead, like this:

```
.c itemconfigure 1 -outline red
```

Ends and joints

Now you can examine some options. You can draw the end of a line in three ways. The choice of styles is controlled by the -capstyle option, which takes the following values:

butt (huh-huh)   The default; the line ends squarely, right on top of the end point

projecting   The end of the line tapers off slightly past the end point

round   The line is rounded at the end

To change the example line so that it has rounded ends, use this command:

```
.c itemconfigure $my_line -capstyle round
```

The way that lines behave at corners is controlled by the -joinstyle option, which takes the following values:

bevel   The default; the points of corners are rounded off

mitre   The points of corners stay pointy

round   The corners are rounded to form a smooth joint between lines

To change the example line so that it has rounded corners, use this command:

```
.c itemconfigure $my_line -joinstyle round
```

If you're a regular user of Adobe Illustrator, you're probably familiar with these decisions about lines; they're in the Paint Style palette.

The latest version of Wish *and* the plug-in for the Mac don't actually change the lines. Look for a bug fix in future versions of the software.

Arrowheads

To add an arrowhead, simply use the -arrow option, which can take four values:

none   The default; the line has no arrowheads

first   The arrowhead is attached to the first point specified in the line-building command

last   The arrowhead is attached to the last point specified in the line-building command

both   The arrowhead is attached to both ends of the line

Just for laughs, attach arrowheads to each end of the sample line, as follows:

```
.c itemconfigure my_line -arrow both
```

Figure 17-8 shows the arrowed version of the sample line.

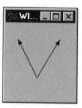

Figure 17-8:
A line with
arrowheads.

If the default arrowheads don't suit you, you can alter the shapes of arrow-heads as you like. The basic option is called -arrowshape, and it takes as a value a list of three numbers:

1. The distance between the tip of the arrow and the end of the line

2. The length of the "blades" of the arrow (on the outside edge)

3. The distance between the back points of the arrow and the line

Look at the diagram in Figure 17-9 to see what each value represents in the arrow.

First value

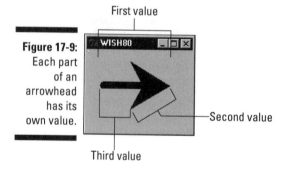

Figure 17-9:
Each part
of an
arrowhead
has its
own value.

Second value

Third value

To use these arguments, just group them with double quotes or curly braces, like this:

```
.c itemconfigure $my_line -arrowshape {4 6 3}
```

or

```
.c itemconfigure $my_line -arrowshape "4 6 3"
```

Curved lines

Lines can be curved, too. When a line is curved, you must specify at least three control points in the command that creates the line. The line starts at the first point specified in the command and ends at the last point, but it doesn't pass through the intermediate points. Rather, the intermediate points act like tiny magnets that pull the middle of the line from its straight course between the starting point and end point. The farther the middle points are from where the straight line would be, the more the points bend the line.

Try building a curved line from the V-shaped line that you already have. To make the line bend, use the -smooth option (which takes a true or false value):

```
.c itemconfigure $my_line -smooth true
```

Text

Adding text to a canvas widget isn't too different from adding a text label to a tclet. The same options apply, pretty much, and text behaves in a predictable way.

The basic command goes like this:

```
canvas-widget-name create text x1 y1
```

x1 and y2 are the coordinates within the widget where the text goes. You've probably noticed that the command has no space for you to actually specify the text to be placed. You'll almost always use the create text command with the -text option, like so:

```
canvas-widget-name create text x1 y1-text your-text-mes-
                sage-here
```

In the real world, a typical text-creating command looks like this:

```
set my_text [.c create text 300 100 \
-text "...this never happened to Pablo Picasso"]
```

Figure 17-10 shows how this text appears in the canvas widget.

Figure 17-10:
You can use
a canvas
widget to
paint text
messages.

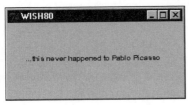

Writing a curve-drawing tclet

To really get a feel for curves, you can tweak the polygon-drawing tclet that you created earlier in this chapter, so that it draws curved lines instead of polygons. Just find the line near the end of the tclet that reads

```
eval ".c create polygon
   $point_list"
```

and replace it with

```
eval ".c create line $point_list
   -smooth true"
```

When you double-click, the tclet draws a wondrously wavy line rather than a plain old polygon.

The text is drawn at the specified point. By default, the center of the text is at the specified location; in the preceding example, the *e* in *happened* appears at the point (300,100). If you like, you can put any of the corners of the text at the coordinates by using the -anchor option.

The -anchor option in a canvas widget is exactly like the -anchor option in a pack command: It takes as its value any of the basic compass points (n for north, e for east, and so on). To put the top-left edge of the text at (300,100), use the nw (for northwest) anchor, like so:

```
.c itemconfigure $my_text -anchor nw
```

Ordinarily, the text in a text widget is in one line, just like a label widget. If you put a line break into the text, the line breaks are carried over onto the canvas widget. Text like

```
.c create text 100 100 {One line of text
        Followed by another}
```

appears as two lines in the canvas, because a line break already appears after the word *text*. Alternatively, you can force line breaks by using the -width option, which controls the length of each line of the text, as though the text in the canvas were a message widget. Add this text (which contains no line breaks) to a canvas widget:

```
set sterne {Well, you may take my word, that nine parts in
        ten of a man's sense or his nonsense, his successes
        and miscarriages in this world depend on the motion
        and activity [of animal spirits], and the different
        tracks and trains you put them into; so that when
```

(continued)

(continued)

```
                they are once set a-going, whether right or wrong,
                'tis not a halfpenny matter—away they go cluttering
                like hey-go-mad; and by treading the same steps
                over and over again, they presently make a road
                of it.}
set my_text [.c create text 10 10 -text $sterne -anchor nw]
```

When you add this text, it simply keeps going and going, just like unbroken text in a label widget (or like *Tristam Shandy,* the incredibly bizarre book from which the quote was lifted). To break the text into readable rows, use the -width option, like so:

```
.c itemconfigure $my_text -width 200
```

Figure 17-11 shows how the -width command breaks the text.

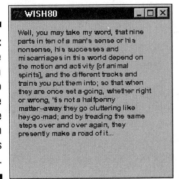

Figure 17-11: You can use the -width option to control the appearance of text on a canvas widget.

Other kinds of widgets

Finally, you can add other widgets — any kind, really, including frames, text widgets, and even other canvas widgets — inside a canvas widget. Sometimes, of course, this widget-within-a-canvas-widget capability seems to be plain stupid. Why add a label widget when you can just add text? The option is available, however, and you can use it whenever you can see a clever solution to a problem.

When you add a widget to a canvas, it retains all its ordinary widget behavior. Buttons still execute their commands, scales still slide around, and so on. If you add a frame that contains other widgets, all the other widgets come along when you paint the frame in the canvas.

If you've already packed a widget somewhere in the tclet and then you paint the widget into a canvas, the widget disappears from its preceding position. The rule (which isn't too hard to remember) is that a widget can appear in only one place at any given time.

The general format for adding widgets to canvases is (drum roll, please) create window. Here's how it looks:

```
canvas-widget-name create window x1 y1
```

Yes, you're right — there's no way to specify the actual widget in the basic command. (The create window command is just like create text and create image — and that's just what I love about Tcl/Tk.) Typical commands look like this:

```
canvas-widget-name create window x1 y1 -window widget-name-
                   with-dots-and-all
```

Create a few buttons and add them to your test canvas .c, as follows:

```
button .red -text red -command \
{.c configure -background red}
button .green -text green -command \
{.c configure -background green}
button .blue -text blue -command \
{.c configure -background blue}
.c create window 10 10 -anchor nw -window .red
.c create window 10 50 -anchor nw -window .green
.c create window 10 90 -anchor nw -window .blue
```

As you can see in Figure 17-12, the figures are added to the canvas.

Figure 17-12:
You can
draw any
kind of Tk
widget onto
a canvas.

If you enter the code in Wish and play with the buttons, you'll see that they behave like plain old Tk buttons. In fact, the whole shebang looks pretty much like a tclet, doesn't it? A few tiny differences exist, however:

✔ The buttons aren't quite as snug as they would be if you had packed or gridded them.

✔ The relative positions of the buttons don't change when you resize the Wish window.

✔ You can easily overlap buttons by accident (or paint them so that parts or all of the buttons appear off-screen) when you render them by painting them in a canvas.

Binding Stuff

You don't need to create bindings that affect an entire canvas widget; you can create binding to individual items (polygons, text, and so on) within the canvas widget. Creating a binding for a canvas item is exactly like creating a binding for an entire widget. (Chapter 13 contains the complete low-down on bindings.)

The syntax for item binding, which follows, is a variation on the basic `bind` command:

```
.canvas-widget-name bind tag-or-item-serial-number event
           body
```

You can substitute any event you like for `event`, using the same syntax and format that you use in a regular `bind` command. To bind to mouse motion, for example, you use `<Motion>`, and to bind to mouse movement that takes place when the Shift key is held down, you bind to `<Shift-Motion>`.

As with an ordinary `bind` command, the body of the command consists of one or more legal Tcl/Tk commands, grouped into one word with curly braces.

That's it. Here's a real-world example of a command that creates a binding between one canvas item and a mouse click:

```
.c create text 10 10 -anchor nw -text "Hello, M31" \
-tag blink
.c bind blink <1> {
    #blink three times
    for {set ctr 0} {$ctr < 3} {incr ctr} {
        #change the type to white
        .c itemconfigure blink -fill white
        after 300 ;# pause for a third of a second or so
        update; #redraw the screen
        .c itemconfigure blink -fill black
        after 300; redraw; # pause and redraw again.
    }
}
```

If you have any other canvas items in the canvas, you'll notice that those items are unaffected by the mouse click — only the items that you tagged with `blink` actually respond to user input.

Moving Stuff

Moving around an item that has been added to a canvas is easy. (Try doing that with paint sometime!) The basic command is called `move`, and it looks like this:

```
canvas-widget-name move tag-or-serial-number x-distance y-
                  distance
```

Simple, isn't it? As you've probably guessed, x1 and y1 are measurements of distance. The item (or items) are repositioned on the canvas x pixels to the right (or left, if x is negative) and y pixels below (or above, if y is negative).

Suppose that you draw a rectangle at 10,10, like so:

```
set my_rect [.c create rectangle 10 10 30 30]
```

Later, you want to move the rectangle down to 100,100. You use the `move` command, like so:

```
.c move $my_rect 90 90
```

Setting up a key binding so that you can nudge items around with the arrow keys is simple. First, enter some rectangle-drawing code:

```
bind .c <Shift-1> {
    .c create rectangle [expr %x - 10] \
                [expr %y - 10] \
                [expr %x + 10] \
                [expr %y + 10] \
                -fill black
}
```

After you enter this code, you can create a bunch of rectangles to play with. Then set up a little routine so that you can select one rectangle. I've set this example up so that only one item can be tagged `selected` at any time, although you can easily reuse the selection routine from your tag experiment, if you like. Here's the code that allows you to select individual rectangles:

```
.c bind all <1> {

    # turn the previous selection back to black
    .c itemconfigure all -fill black

    # clear the selected tag from all of the items on the
    # canvas
    .c dtag all selected

    # add the selected tag to the item under the cursor
    .c addtag selected withtag current

    #turn the currently selected item blue
    .c itemconfigure selected -fill lightblue
}
```

Now all you need to do is set up bindings between the arrow keys and a set of move commands. I've set this example up so that the selected item jumps five pixels with every tap of the keys, but you can customize the distance that the arrow keys move the squares however you like by changing the arguments in the bind command. Here's the code that sets up the bindings:

```
focus .c
bind .c <Up> {.c move selected 0 -5}
bind .c <Down> {.c move selected 0 5}
bind .c <Left> {.c move selected -5 0}
bind .c <Right> {.c move selected 5 0}
```

Don't forget the focus command, which tells the canvas to "listen" for keyboard input. (Otherwise, the canvas widget just ignores the keystrokes.)

Using Other Commands

Canvases are complicated things, and I haven't covered every possible command that you can use to manipulate a canvas — just enough to get you into trouble for now. The stuff that this chapter covers should be adequate for most of the things that you'll need to do with canvases, but you should be aware of a few basic categories in case you decide that you need to do something fancy. When you get to that point, refer to the canvas documentation for the particulars of canvas-wrangling commands. Here are the general categories to look for in the documentation:

✓ **Layers.** Every single thing that you put down in a canvas widget is in its own layer — if you put one item on top of another, the top item conceals the bottom one. (Using layers is a lot like using an illustration or page-layout program, if you're used to using such things.)

✔ **Coordinates.** You can find (and even change) the coordinates of any tag.

✔ **Editing text.** An entire galaxy of commands is available for editing the text of text items in a canvas. Basically, you can add or delete any characters, indexing the text with an indexing system similar to the one that you use for canvas widgets.

✔ **PostScript output.** Astonishingly, a canvas widget can crack out a pure, high-quality PostScript description of its contents. The current implementation of the plug-in doesn't support the postscript command, but it's nice to know that the command's around (if you know what PostScript is and how to use it, anyway).

✔ **Scaling.** You can take any part of a canvas and shrink it or blow it up as you like. Similarly, you can move parts of a canvas to other parts of the canvas.

The canvas documentation contains so much material that you may want to print the entire thing — it's way too long to read on-screen, and it's the straight-up, from-the-source documentation that you'll want to read most often. Just open the canvas.html file with your Web browser and then print it.

Chapter 18

Making Web Connections

In This Chapter
▶ Connecting to Web pages
▶ Checking the progress of Web transactions
▶ Downloading information to Web pages
▶ Sending information to Web servers

*B*efore you start cookin' up Web-based tclets in earnest, have a quick look at the way that Web transactions take place. Making Web connections isn't strictly a widget thing, but it's not pure Tcl, either. Web transactions rely on a special extension to Tcl called the http package. This software is built into the Tcl/Tk plug-in and the latest versions of Wish.

What Is HTTP?

The basic idea is that Tcl/Tk provides some basic tools that do the most important things that Web browsers do: make Hypertext Transport Protocol (HTTP) connections. Using one simple Tcl command, http_get, you can download the HTML source code of any page on the Web. Tcl/Tk doesn't have many fancy built-in tools for rendering the source code as a Web page (that's what your browser's for anyway, right?). But you can find plenty of interesting and useful information in a Web page's source code.

Some tools out on the Net make it relatively easy to turn HTML code into simple pages. It's way beyond the scope of this book to lead you through writing your own Web browser (and that's really what we're talking about), but it's not so crazy as it sounds. It's a heck of a lot easier to write a simple browser in Tcl/Tk than it is in something like C. Check http://www.tctk.com for more information about HTML-wrangling packages that you can use.

Basically, HTTP is a system for passing information back and forth over the Internet; more specifically, it's a way for browsers to request files (usually, HTML or image files) from an HTTP server. In other words, the `http_get` command simply requests that a server somewhere on the Net send a file to the computer that's running the tclet. (You may want to think of `http_get` as being the "Hey! Can I get a file over here?!" command.)

Because a great deal can go wrong with a Web transaction, and because Web servers usually are interested in establishing a relationship with the software that requests the file, a Web server always sends some extra information along with the file. Your tclet downloads this information, and you can do whatever you like with whatever data your tclet downloads: search a page for keywords, display an image, present a list of the page anchors, or whatever.

Things to Remember about the Web

I'd like to review a few Web basics before I show you how to pull a file down from the Web with Tcl/Tk. Presumably, you've spent some time surfing around on the Web, and you know a few things about it. (If you haven't, and you're reading this book, you're probably one of my grandparents.) You may be familiar with many of the basic ideas in this section, and you can skip whatever you want to.

Connections can fail

When you use a command like `http_get`, you're not really asking Tcl/Tk to make a connection to another machine on the network — you're asking the Tcl/Tk interpreter to ask the computer's operating system (Windows 95, the MacOS, or whatever) to make the connection. Tcl/Tk is very cool, but it can't do everything; specifically, it doesn't make Net connections by itself.

This uncertainty means, then, that Tcl/Tk is at the mercy of the host computer's operating system and at the mercy of the network. If a problem occurs with either of these players, the Tcl/Tk interpreter can't do anything special to solve the problem.

Understand and remember the basic principle: *Anything that can screw up a Web browser session also screws up a Tcl/Tk Web transaction.*

Suppose that a user accesses the Web through a modem. If the user turns off the modem during a session, if the service provider hangs up on the modem, or (as is the case with one of my machines) the modem simply hangs up by itself when it's in a bad mood, the user won't be able to access any more pages.

A zillion things like this can go wrong before the request ever reaches the server to which the request is addressed. Here's a partial roster of the grand parade of connection headaches that I've had in just the past few years:

✔ The user has networking software improperly installed.

✔ The user doesn't have networking software installed.

✔ The user's modem isn't turned on.

✔ The user (or her officemate) kicked a cable and disconnected the computer from the modem or the network.

✔ The user's local network collapsed.

✔ The service provider's machine is down.

✔ All the service provider's dial-up lines are busy.

✔ The service provider's connection to the Internet is down.

✔ The service provider's Domain Name Server (DNS, essentially an Internet phone book) software is not running or is otherwise malfunctioning.

All these problems (and many more besides) cause a Tcl/Tk network request (or a Web browser) to fail. (Unfortunately, different problems create different error messages on-screen, so these problems can be hard to diagnose.)

Servers can fail

Even if you can make a network request without any problems, there's no guarantee that the server at the other end of the line will successfully handle the request. In fact, Web servers routinely fumble, for a variety of reasons:

✔ The server isn't running when the request comes.

✔ The server is handling the maximum number of requests that it can manage, and it refuses the new request.

✔ The server doesn't accept requests from the requester's address.

✔ The server crashes in the middle of processing the request.

✔ The server takes too long to process the request and decides to cancel the job.

✔ The server sends the request to a helper program (called a CGI, which stands for Common Gateway Inteface) that can't handle the request for reasons of its own.

Weird little glitches like these happen all the time. If you're using a Web browser like Netscape Navigator, the browser eventually gets tired of waiting, cancels the request, and presents an error message like the one shown in Figure 18-1. Really, all that this message means is that something's wrong with the server.

Again, these kinds of problems also afflict your Tcl/Tk programs that make requests of the server. Your Tcl/Tk application can't do anything to fix someone else's server that's acting up (or even your own server). Unfortunately, your tclet won't automatically cancel the request when it's tired of waiting — you'll need to handle this situation yourself.

This kind of problem doesn't always show up when the request first hits the server. Sometimes, just when everything seems to be okay — the request arrives at the server, and the server responds — everything falls apart. A Web page or image file simply stalls in the middle of loading, or something bizarre happens during the loading process. Any number of things, including the network problems detailed in the preceding section, can cause this stalling. And a stalled page is nearly as useless as a page that never came in the first place.

Figure 18-1:
An error message that indicates that the sever hasn't responded to the browser's request.

Security is an issue

Remember, remember, remember: The safety features that are built into the plug-in are there to protect *only* the computer that is running the tclet. The user is protected from malicious tclets that may try to erase the user's files or peek at things like system password files. None of the information that passed between the tclet and a Web server, however, is protected from the prying eyes of bad guys who may access the information as it's transferred over the Internet. If you send information to a server via `http_get`, that information is unprotected.

Is this situation a significant problem? *It is* if your tclet sends a user's credit card number and the unprotected information is intercepted. This situation doesn't occur often (at least, it's uncommon now, in 1997), but it's certainly possible — even easy — to grab information as it passes between a browser or tclet and a server.

Web browsers like Netscape Navigator and Microsoft Internet Explorer use encryption to protect sensitive information, such as credit card numbers, that is transferred to servers via the Internet. Browsers use a high-end, theoretically unbreakable system for encoding information. This system, called public-key encryption, isn't built into Tcl/Tk.

Waking up the Web Genie

Before you start to use web-based commands with Tcl, you'll need to notify the interpreter, so that it can load the necessary commands. If you simply start out with the `http_get` command (or one of its cousins) the interpreter will claim that it has never heard of `http_get`, and has no idea what you want it to do.

Although the basic web commands come bundled with Tcl 8.0 and Version 2.0 of the Tcl Plug-in, these commands are not automatically loaded when the interpreter starts up. Rather, they are part of a *package* — a set of commands that can be loaded when they are required. (Waiting until the last minute to load the command saves time and memory.)

Notifying the interpreter that you want to use web commands is simple. Just issue the command:

```
package http
```

and Tcl will load the necessary commands. The interpreter will let you know that it has successfully found and loaded the requested package by returning the version number of the package. The Wish session will look like this:

```
% package require http
1.0
```

(If you're using a newer version of the http package, you'll see a different version number — that's just fine.)

Connecting to a Web Page

Okay . . . now that *that* stuff's out of the way, let's hook up to a Web page. As I hinted in the introduction to the chapter, the basic command for making a connection is `http_get`. The `http_get` command does quite a bit behind the scenes.

Understanding the basic game plan

The following is a rundown of what the interpreter does when it makes a HTTP request. (Don't worry about the particulars of the options now — just try to get a feel for what the big steps are.)

1. The interpreter sends a request for the file specified in the command's `url` argument.

2. If the `-request` option has been specified, the value of the request is sent to the server as data.

3. The interpreter creates a new Tcl array to store the requested document and extra information from the Web server.

4. The server returns the name of the array as the result of the `http_get` command.

5. If the `-progress` option has been specified, the interpreter automatically calls the procedure specified as the `-procedure` value. This procedure usually gives the user an update on how much of the file has been downloaded.

6. If the `-command` option is specified, when the entire Web document has been downloaded, the interpreter calls the procedure specified in the -command option. (This way, you won't accidentally start processing the page in the middle of a download.)

None of the steps above are too tricky, but as you can see, there's a lot going on. The following sections describe the process step by step.

Sending the request

The basic form of `http_get` is simply

```
http_get url
```

`url` (which stands for Universal Resource Locator) is pretty much the same as a regular old URL that you'd type into your browser or create an HTML link to in your Web page. A few restrictions, however, are special to Tcl/Tk:

✔ Most browsers support URLs that can handle different protocols. You can use Navigator to link to URLs that point to Gopher pages (such as `gopher://gopher.umn.edu`), newsgroups (`news:rec.music.bluenote`), or mailing addresses (`mailto:captain_kirk@enterprise.com`). The only protocol that `http_get` supports is ("Jeopardy!" music, please) HTTP, as in `http://www.sunlabs.com`. This protocol is used to move Web pages around.

✔ At this writing, `http_get` supports only URLs that include the name of the file to be downloaded. This level of exactness is probably is a little different from what you're used to seeing. The URL `http://www.sunlabs.com/research/tcl/plugin`, for example, isn't quite right, because it doesn't include a file name, and you need to include everything. In this case, you'd use `http://www.sunlabs.com/research/tcl/plugin/index.htm`.

Just in case you hadn't noticed, URLs are always one Tcl/Tk word, without any spaces or tabs between the characters that make up the word. Still, it's a good idea to wrap up the URL in curly braces, just in case the URL contains something like $ (The interpreter would try to do a substitution, right?) So a properly formed basic command looks like this:

```
http_get {http://www.orbis-tertius.com/tcl/welcome.html}
```

The Status Array

When the interpreter executes an `http_get` command, it returns j- array that contains information about the Web page and about the transaction that's taking place between the interpreter and the Web server that serves up the requested page. If you use Wish, you'll see something like this:

```
% http_get {http://anyserver.com/home.html}
http#1
```

Successive `http_get` commands yield new arrays — `http#2`, `http#3`, and so on. Actually, the thing that the command returns isn't the name of the array; it's a bread-crumb trail that leads to the array. If you enter something like

```
puts $http#1(status)
```

to get to a field called `status` inside the array, you'll get a nasty error message. Without fretting too much about what's going on under the hood, let me tell you the easy way to deal with this problem: Use the `upvar` command to get hold of the real array. If you want to call the array `my_page`, use this command:

```
upvar #0 http#1 my_page
```

Don't worry about how this code works; just steal it. After you use upvar, you can use the command

```
puts $my_page(status)
```

to read the status field of the array.

"So," you are no doubt wondering, "what are the fields in this magical array?" Good question. Table 18-1 summarizes the contents of the array, called the *state* array.

Table 18-1	Inside the http_get State Array
Name of Field	*Content of Field*
body	This field contains the content of the requested file. If the page is a Web page, this content probably is just a bunch of HTML code. If the document is a text file, the content is the text of the file.
currentsize	This field contains a number that represents the size of the stuff that has already been transferred from the server to the machine running the tclet. The size is measured in plain old bytes. Naturally, the number increases as the file is down-loaded.
error	If this field is empty (actually, undefined), everything is fine; the file was transferred without problems. If the transfer was aborted, this field contains an error message from your system software.
http	This field contains a numerical HTTP reply code. A standard set of replies is part of the HTTP specification. If you know what "HTTP reply code" means, you know how to use the code. If you don't, you probably don't need to worry about what it means.
meta	This field contains information that the Web server provides about the file that has been requested. This information may (or may not) include things like the MIME type of the file and its size. The contents of the field (if any) depend on how the server is configured; the HTTP specification allows the server to provide a wide range of possible meta values.
status	The status field can contain any of three possible values: ok (the value to hope for, which means that nothing went wrong), error (which means that something went wrong), and reset (which means that the tclet reset the transaction).
totalsize	This field contains a number that indicates the size of the file. (For the record, this value is extracted from the Content-Length information in the meta field.)

Name of Field	Content of Field
type	This field contains information about the MIME type of the requested file. The MIME specification is simply a system for labeling files — Web pages are labeled text/html, for example, and .GIF pictures are labeled image/gif. The idea is to let the web browser (or in this case, the tclet) know what it has downloaded.
url	A spare copy of the requested URL.

The -progress *option*

I don't know about you, but I've spent far too many precious hours of my remaining youth watching pages download. As you know, Web transactions don't take place instantly — and if you (or a tclet's user) are connected to the Net over a modem, you know that Web transactions can take forever.

Because a command like http_get can't do all its work at once, Tcl/Tk provides a mechanism for allowing processing to go on in the background. While Web files are downloading, a tclet can go ahead and do other things, just as you may try to get some actual work done in a word processor while you're waiting for a gargantuan file to download in your Web browser.

You don't want to completely lose track of the download that's going on in the background, however. Fortunately, the http_get command takes care of managing the download for you by executing designated procedures at strategic points in the download's life cycle. This procedure (called, descriptively enough, a *callback*) is specified with the -progress command. The procedure executes whenever the tclet finishes transferring a block of data from the server.

Here's how -callback works: First, you create a procedure to be executed when the tclet is finished. The interpreter calls the procedure automatically at the appropriate points, with the following arguments:

Parameter arguments	Description
token	The name of the state array that holds the information about the current request
total	The total number of bytes (according to the Web server, anyway)
current	The number of pbytes that have finished downloading at the time that the procedure is called

You can call your procedures whatever you like, of course. Your procedure can call these parameters `state`, `final`, and `fraction` or `larry`, `curly`, and `moe`, if you want. The important thing to understand is that the interpreter passes these parameters when it calls the procedure. Your procedure must include these parameters in its arguments section, even if the procedure doesn't actually use the arguments for anything. In other words, your procedure should look like this:

```
proc progress_handler {token total current} {
    # do something fun
}
```

If you want to use any of the information that's in the `state` variable, you need to grab it with the `upvar` command, like so:

```
proc progress_handler {token total current} {
    upvar #0 $token state_array
    #do something important
}
```

To get really specific, suppose that you want to create a display that uses a scale widget to show the progress of the file's download. First, wake up the web genie and set up the scale outside the `progress_handler` procedure (because you don't want to repeat these steps and create a brand-new scale every time that `progress_handler` is called):

```
package require http
scale .progress_bar -width 10 -length 250 -orient h \
-variable progress
set progress 0
pack .progress_bar -pady 10
```

Now create a procedure that displays the download's progress. The procedure, which uses the `current` and `total` parameters to reconfigure the slider, is simple:

```
proc progress_handler {token total current} {

    # reference the value variable in the scale variable
    global progress

    # update the slider widget to reflect the total size of
    # the file
    .progress_bar configure -to $total

    # update the file download progress
    set progress $current
}
```

Just to make things super-flexible, throw in an entry widget so that you can enter any URL you like, rather than code a specific address to fetch. Set up a binding so that the tclet fetches the URL after it's been entered in the entry box, as follows:

```
label .l -text "URL to fetch:" -anchor w
pack .l
entry .url -textvariable url -width 33
pack .url

bind .url <Return> {

    # check to make sure that the URL is in a more-or-less
    # correct form before sending the URL along to the
    # server
    if [regexp {^http://[^ ]+\.[^ ]+/[^ ]} $url] {
        http_get $url -progress progress_handler
    } else {
        set url "Please enter a valid URL here"
    } ; #end if
} ; #end bind
```

The resulting tclet should look more or less like Figure 18-2.

When you enter an URL in the entry box and press Return (on a Mac keyboard) or Enter (on a PC keyboard), the tclet either

✔ Loads the requested URL, moving the scale's slider as the file loads

✔ Asks you for a new URL

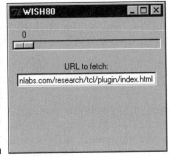

Figure 18-2:
This tclet downloads web pages, displaying its progress with a scale widget.

TECHNICAL STUFF

Idiot-proofing your tclet

Wondering about that regular expression? We'll break it down into parts:

`^http`: Matches the string `http:` *only* if it's at the beginning of the string

`[^ ]+` Matches one or more characters — anything that's not a space

`\.` Matches a dot, (as in a period)

`[^ ]+` Matches one or more characters — anything that's not a space

`/` Matches a plain old slash character

`[^ ]+` Matches one or more characters — anything that's not a space

In other words, the regular expression means "the string `http:`, followed by a bunch of characters that contain at least one dot and one slash between characters." This formula isn't universal for all URLs, but it's a fairly good match for the URLs that `http_get` accepts.

The -command *option*

The interpreter also watches out for the final completion of the `http_get` download, and when the download finishes, the interpreter executes the `callback` command specified in `http_get`'s `-command` option. Like the `-progress` callback procedure, the `-command` callback is executed automatically. `-command` is a little bit simpler than `-callback`, however; because its only parameter is `token` (the name of the state array).

Your final callback should look something like this:

```
proc final_callback {token} {

    upvar #0 $token state_array

    # do something crazy

}
```

Now write a little procedure to tack onto your progress-bar tclet. In this simple example, you just grab the body of the Web page and display it in a text widget. (You won't do anything really fancy with it — just stick it in the text box.) Here's the code that creates a text window to display your HTML:

```
#create a text widget and attach a scrollbar
frame .f
text .f.contents -width 40 -height 20 \
```

```
-yscrollcommand {.f.s set}
scrollbar .f.s -command {.f.contents yview}
grid .f.contents -column 1 -row 1
grid .f.s -column 2 -row 1 -sticky ns
pack .f -pady 10

proc final_callback {token} {

    #gain access to the state array
    upvar #0 $token state_array


    #put the body of the page into the text widget
    if [string match $state_array(status) ok] {
        .f.contents insert 1.0 $state_array(body)
    } else {
        .f.contents insert \
        1.0 "Sorry — something weird happened."
    }
}
```

Don't forget to go back and tweak the `http_get` command in the entry
binding, like so:

```
http_get $url -progress progress_handler \
-command final_callback
```

The final tclet should look like Figure 18-3. When the tclet finishes downloading an URL, it displays the source code for the Web page (or whatever else
the URL contains) in the tclet's text window. (Think of this tclet as Netscape
Navigator Ultra-light.)

Sending Information Back to a Server

Sometimes, you want your tclet to send information back to a server.
Whenever you fill out a Web-page form like the one shown in Figure 18-4,
your Web browser sends the form's data to a server to be processed. A
regular Web-page form like the one shown in the figure relies on the form-
handling functionality that's built into your Web browser. Navigator or
Internet Explorer, for example, takes care of packing up the information and
sending it off when you click the submit button.

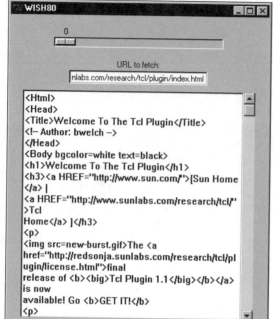

You can send information over the Net in two ways:

> ✔ GET. The form's information is attached to the URL that is to receive the information, like this:
>
> ```
> url?information
> ```
>
> ✔ POST. The form is packed up in a separate bundle and sent to the URL.

In any case, the server on the receiving end must be equipped to handle the data. Before you write a tclet that sends data to a server, be sure to contact the site's Webmaster and make sure that you're sending the right kind of data in the right format. If you're the Webmaster of the site, and you're not quite sure, look at your server software's documentation.

No matter whether the receiving server uses GET or POST, you need to format your data in the proper data-transferring style. If you've ever taken a good look at the URL of an InfoSeek search-result page, you probably noticed that the URL is in this form:

```
http://www.infoseek.com/Titles?qt=%22Elvis+Presley%22
```

This URL is an example of sending data by GET. The stuff after the ? is the data from the form, encoded so that special characters (spaces, quotes, and so on) are replaced with special character stings. Form data is always submitted in pairs; every chunk of data has a name and a value. In the preceding example, the data's name is qt, and its value is (before encoding) "Elvis Presley".

You don't need to know the specifics of this encoding system; the Tcl/Tk http package provides a handy utility called http_formatQuery, that takes care of encoding things for you. The general format of the command is

```
http_formatQuery name1 value1 . . . more values . . . last-
            name last-value
```

To encode qt and "Elvis Presley", you use this command:

```
http_formatQuery qt {"Elvis Presley"}
```

The interpreter returns this:

```
qt=%22Elvis+Presley%22
```

Note: I wrapped up Elvis Presley in curly braces because I wanted the quotes to be encoded, too. Without the curlies, the interpreter assumes that the double quotes are just there for Tcl-grouping purposes.

If you want to send this kind of data by POST, you can attach it to a URL and submit the modified URL with http_get in the usual way, like this:

```
# store the base URL in a variable
set my_url {http://any-old-site.com/cgi-bin/wrangler}

# add a question mark and the data to the end of the URL
append my_url ?[ http_formatQuery qt {"Elvis Presley"}]

# submit the modified URL
http_get $my_url
```

To send the data by POST (to send it in a separate package, for example), you use the http_get with the -query option. The value of -query is the data to be sent, such as this:

```
http_get -query [ http_formatQuery qt {"Elvis Presley"}]
```

Don't worry if get_httP is a little fuzzy right now — you'll see this kind of command in action in the next few chapters.

Chapter 19

Tcling the Browser

*T*he tclets in this chapter are different from the others because these interact with browsers, such as Netscape Navigator or Microsoft Internet Explorer. A browser doesn't interact with tclets that aren't running in a Web page, and thus can't possibly interact with the tclets.

Having your tclets interact with the browser offers two main advantages:

✔ Browsers offer lots of useful information. With Version 2.0 of the Tcl/Tk Plug-in, you can now get at some of that information.

✔ Browsers read and display HTML code. Controlling the browser means you can manipulate the code of a page from within a tclet.

Getting information from the browser and getting the browser to do your bidding are not entirely different processes, but I separate them in this chapter to simplify the learning process.

Controlling the Browser

One of the advantages of using Tcl/Tk for writing applets is that you can rapidly develop a complex graphic user interface without having to mess around with complex code. However, many of the tasks you may want to do within the context of a Web page will certainly involve controlling the appearance of graphics or text specified in HTML. By allowing tclets to affect pages written in HTML (via controlling the browser), the clever folks at Sun have given us the best of both worlds. You can now use the easy interactivity of Tcl/Tk while still manipulating, displaying, and interpreting HTML code.

Creating a frame-based HTML document

Enough praise — here are some examples! If you've ever done anything serious (or frivolous but fun) with HTML, you've probably dealt with frames. (If you haven't, don't worry, they're pretty simple and I explain something about 'em as you go along.) Using the Tcl/Tk Plug-in Version 2.0 and higher you can control what gets displayed in any browser frame.

Beware — Tcl/Tk frame widgets and HTML frames are both called frames, and they do similar things. Try not to confuse them. A Tcl/Tk frame widget has to exist within a top-level widget, whereas an HTML frame has to exist within a top-level page. The Tcl/Tk frame widget and the HTML frame both display information, but here's the crucial difference: You must create and fill an HTML frame within the HTML code of a page, using HTML, while you create and fill a Tcl/Tk frame widget within the code of a tclet, obviously using the Tcl/Tk language. Furthermore, HTML frames display HTML information, and so they interpret any text written to them as HTML code. You use Tcl/Tk frames mostly for layout within a tclet.

Of course, the normal way to put HTML information into HTML frames is by saving HTML code, text and images in files. For example, a page with three different frames may display three different files, one in each frame. These files may be called (somewhat unimaginatively) *upper.html, middle.html,* and *bottom.html.* Then, in the source code for the main page, you specify the names of those files as the source for each frame, as in the following HTML code:

```
<frameset rows="30%,*,10%">
    <frame src = "upper.html">
    <frame src = "middle.html">
    <frame src = "bottom.html">
</frameset>
```

This code just specifies that there are frames in the page, gives their dimensions, and names the files that are to be displayed in them. The first line specifies that the frames lie as rows within the page (one above the next), and determines what fraction of the page each frame occupies. (If the first line appears as `<frameset cols="30%,*,10%">` then users assume the frames lie along the page vertically, one to the right of the next.)

The rest of the first line specifies that the first frame occupies 30 percent of the browser window width, whatever that width is, the third frame occupies 10 percent of the browser window, and the middle frame occupies the rest of the page. (An asterisk specifies the middle frame. The asterisk acts somewhat like the Tcl/Tk wildcard, in that it doesn't have a specific value, but instead must be interpreted from context.) The next three lines just name the source files for the HTML code to be displayed in the same order as the dimensions are specified in the *frameset* line.

So, if it's so easy to just put HTML right into frames using just HTML, why bother doing this with a tclet?

The answer is simple. Flexibility. What if you want to give your online visitors the chance to flip through photos from your photo album, one after the other, in the same frame? If you have 20 different pictures of your new puppy and you think everyone on the Web really deserves the chance to see all of them, you have to write 20 different pages, each one containing the source code to call a different picture. For example, on the first page, which shows the first picture, you may have the following code.

```
<frameset rows="30%,*,10%">
   <frame src = "upper.html">
   <frame src = "firstpic.html">
   <frame src = "bottom.html">
</frameset>
```

Then, in the second page, you'd have very similar code, except the name of the middle frame is different.

```
<frameset rows="30%,*,10%">
   <frame src = "upper.html">
   <frame src = "secondpic.html">
   <frame src = "bottom.html">
</frameset>
```

And so on. Of course there are slicker ways of doing this, and your local HTML guru can probably tell you a dozen ways of making this process more efficient. You can even write 20 links into the upper frame so that people can summon the pictures in any order just by clicking on the links. But, the principle remains the same. You, the Web page author, have to decide what each frame displays, and then you have to write it down in the code of the page or the link.

But what if you want the visitor to be able to decide what to display in the frame? Remember, tclets are *interactive*. With a tclet, you can ask cyber-visitors to type in the URL of their favorite Web pages; and your tclet can call up their URLs and display them. In the following extended example, you create a page that does exactly that, with a twist (after all, any browser calls up a page and displays it — that's what browsers do). The advantage of using the Tcl/Tk Plug-in to fetch URLs is that you can manipulate the HTML code that's displayed.

This tclet allows the user to call up any URL and display it in one frame next to another frame that simultaneously displays the source code of the URL on display. The page this tclet resides in has the following HTML code:

```
<frameset rows="30%,*,10%">
  <frame src = "upper.html">
  <frameset cols="50%,*">
    <frame src = "blank.html" NAME="lookhere">
    <frame src = "blank.html" NAME="sourcespot">
  </frameset>
  <frame src = "bottom.html" NAME="sourcespot">
</frameset>
<noframe>
    Your browser does not appear to support frames, and
        therefore also probably not the Tcl/Tk Plugin
        (v. 2.0 or higher). As a result this page is
        likely to be uninteresting to you. Please take a
        look at the <a href="http://
        sunscript.sun.com">Tcl/Tk homepage</a> to see
        what you're missing.
</noframe>
```

The code for this page simply sets up four frames — one across the top that takes 30 percent of the vertical dimension, one across the bottom that takes 10 percent of the vertical span of the page, and two in the middle that take up the rest of the height of the page. Each of these frames is also initially assigned a URL to display, although the contents of some of these frames are processed by the tclet. When you're done, the page should look something like Figure 19-1.

Writing the HTML to contain the tclet

After you have the main page set up, you need to decide where to put the tclet. The tclet can be in any of the files displayed in any of the frames of the main page. For this example, I embed this tclet in the top frame, which contains the HTML file called *top.html*. This tclet, which I call *sourcer.tcl,* is embedded in the file top.html just like any other tclet. Here's the important part of the source code for `top.html`.

```
<body>
<center>
<h2>
<b>Another page reserved for Tcl/Tk Plugin 2.0 users!</b>
<embed src="source.tcl" width=450 height=35>
</h2>
<font size=+1>
This tclet displays a URL and its source code in side-by-
            side frames.
</font>
</center>
</body>
```

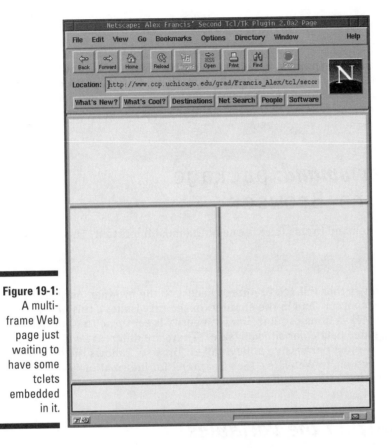

This HTML code displays a title for the page, places the tclet in the center of the next line, and adds a caption to explain briefly what the tclet does. The resulting frame looks like Figure 19-2 (shown in its natural habitat, a multiframe Web page).

Figure 19-2:
A close-up
of the top
frame of a
multiframe
Web page
with the tclet
sourcer.tcl
embedded
inside.

Another page reserved for Tcl/Tk Plugin 2.0a2 users!		
URL:	Show URL	Clear
This tclet displays a URL and its source code in side–by–side frames.		
Click here for the next one.		

So, now that the HTML pages are all set up to accommodate the tclet, take a look at the tclet itself.

This tclet is on the CD-ROM that comes with this book, under the name `sourcer.tcl`. You can load it directly from there, or type in the code in this chapter yourself. You may want to write your own pages, however, so make sure you note the references to names of frames so you can customize them yourself.

Tclet command: `package require Browser`

The first command in this tclet is one of the most important. The command

```
package require Browser
```

tells the Plug-in that this tclet requires access to the browser. As you find later in this chapter (and in the chapter on security issues), this notification is not as trivial as it may sound. Tcl/Tk security is set up so that the browser user designates particular sites as "safe." There are different levels of security; the most permissive policy, called "Browser" allows the browser to make connections to Web sites. (See Chapter 1 for information about configuring the Tcl/Tk plugin's security settings.)

Initializing the variables

The next two lines just set some variables to default values.

```
set page ""
set DEFAULT_PAGE \
{http://www.orbis-tertius.com/tcl/index.html}
set flag write
```

The variable `page` holds a Web page address, and the variable `flag` just marks whether you're writing code to a page or clearing the page before displaying new code. To make the structure of this tclet a little clearer, I present it out of order here. However, you can see the source code for the complete tclet at the end of this section.

Creating the tclet's widgets

The tclet itself consists of two buttons (one to summon a URL and display it next to its source code, and one to clear the display frames), an entrybox widget for the user to enter a URL, and a label to tell users what the entrybox is for.

```
button .show -text "Show URL" -command showit -bd 2
button .clear -text "Clear" -command clearit -bd 2
```

The two commands for these buttons are procedures that appear earlier in the tclet, but I discuss them later in this section. The procedure showit calls the procedure showsource, which is the heart of the tclet. The procedure clearit just clears the display frames, but does this in a way that highlights the difference between writing and displaying HTML code. You find out more about all these procedures later in this chapter.

```
entry .enter -width 30 -relief sunken -bd 2 \
-textvariable page
label .label -text "URL: "
```

After you create these widgets, gridding them is a simple matter. Put them all in a line for simplicity's sake.

```
grid .label -row 1 -column 1 -padx 1
grid .enter -row 1 -column 2 -padx 5
grid .show -row 1 -column 3 -padx 5
grid .clear -row 1 -column 4 -padx 5
```

Setting up the bindings

Next, set up some bindings. The first four of these bindings use a command that is unique to the Plug-in.

```
bind .show <Enter> {browser_displayStatus \
"Click here to view a URL and its source"}
bind .show <Leave> {browser_displayStatus ""}
bind .clear <Enter> {browser_displayStatus \
"Click here to clear the frames"}
bind .clear <Leave> {browser_displayStatus ""}
```

The first two lines bind commands to the button .show, and the second two bind the same kind of commands to the button .clear. If you're not familiar with the syntax of the bind command, take a look at Chapter 13. What's new in all of these lines is the command

```
browser_displayStatus
```

The preceding command simply tells the browser to display a string in the Status space of the browser's main display. (In both Netscape Navigator and Microsoft Internet Explorer, the Status space is in the lower-left corner.) The two lines

```
bind .show <Leave> {browser_displayStatus ""}
bind .clear <Leave> {browser_displayStatus ""}
```

are just there to clear the status bar when the user moves the mouse off each button. The last binding,

```
bind .enter <Key-Return> {showit}
```

is also pretty standard, and simply enables users to press the enter key rather than click on the .show button. Again, since people are used to entering text in a window and then just pressing the enter key to make something happen with that text, you may as well oblige them and make your tclet work that way as well.

Creating the showit *procedure*

The procedure showit (which is called when the user clicks the .show button or presses the Return key while the entrybox is active) has the following form.

```
proc showit {} {
    global page DEFAULT_PAGE
    if {$page == ""} {
        set page $DEFAULT_PAGE
    }
    browser_getURL $page showsource
}
```

This procedure really has only one important command, the last line. I explain why shortly. The first line is necessary so that the procedure has access to the contents of the variables DEFAULT_PAGE and page. As you'll recall, I set up *page* (which stores the URL of the page to retrieve) and *DEFAULT_PAGE* (which stores the name of the page to retrieve if the user hasn't entered a URL) when I initialized the variables.

The if command block in the preceding code just assigns the default URL to the variable page if page does not yet have a value. You can do some more complicated, regular-expression checking in this line to make sure that the string (if any) that the user enters is a well-formed URL. This is left as an exercise for the reader.

The last line of the procedure is the only really interesting one, so look at it in more detail.

```
browser_getURL $page showsource
```

This line consists of the command `browser_getURL` followed by two arguments. You probably see a pattern here — any command that requires interaction with the browser starts with the string `browser_` and then has a normal-looking command name from which you can probably guess what the command does. In this case, the command "gets" a URL that an address specifies. The address (starting either with `http://` or `ftp://`) is the first argument to the `browser_getURL` command. In this case, that address is whatever string is contained within the variable `page`.

Saying that the command "gets" the URL does not tell the whole story, however. "Getting" the URL means calling up the Web site that the address specifies and getting all of the HTML code at that address. Thus, the command

```
set junk [browser_getURL $page]
```

should result in having a very long string being stored in the variable `junk`. (The string consists of all the text that makes up the page being "gotten.") However, this is not exactly the case. If this tclet is executed within the Plug-in, the command `browser_getURL` (and most other `browser_` style commands) requires a second argument after the address of the called URL. This second argument is the name of a command or procedure. Specifically, it's the name of the command or procedure that `browser_getURL` should feed the retrieved web page to when the page is completely downloaded. In this example, we'll process the downloaded web page with the procedure `showsource`, so we'll use `showsource` as the second argument to `browser_getURL`:

```
browser_getURL $page showsource
```

Writing the `showsource` *procedure*

One of the major advantages of using Tcl/Tk for writing applets is that you can use regular expressions. (See Appendix A for the skinny on regular expression syntax.) In the following example, the Tcl/Tk commands for manipulating text — including via regular expression substitution (`regsub`) — are very important. The procedure `showsource` starts as follows.

```
proc showsource {url status data} {
```

The first line of the procedure declares that this procedure expects to be called with three arguments. However, the command in which `showsource` is called looks like this:

```
browser_getURL $page showsource
```

On the surface, this line looks like it calls the procedure `showsource` with no arguments at all. However, that's another strange thing about many of the `browser_` commands. When you use a `browser_` command with the name of a procedure as an argument, the browser command calls the procedure with two or three arguments. In the case of `browser_getURL`, the callback is called with three arguments.

The first argument is the address of the URL that was retrieved (such as `http://sunscript.sun/com/`), which the tclet stores in the variable `url`. The second argument is a string that gives the status of the result. (If the command is successful, this string is the word `data`.) The procedure will store the result in the variable called `status`. The third argument is a very long string that is the actual text of the URL which was gotten. The procedure will store this argument in the variable `data`.

```
global page flag
```

This line just declares which global variables are used in the procedure.

```
browser_openFrame lookhere
```

This line uses another browser-specific command. This command opens the named frame for writing. Remember that in the "Creating a frame-based HTML document" section, earlier in this chapter, you set up the Web page in which this tclet is embedded and you gave names to the frames. The command `browser_openFrame` takes one argument — the name of a frame to which you want to write data.

When you open a frame, be careful to close it as soon as possible afterward. The current version of the Plug-in (2.0a2) is likely to crash the browser abruptly and without warning if a user tries to move to a new page while a frame is open for writing. Future versions of the Plug-in may likely solve this problem, but it's still just a generally good idea to close data channels when you don't need them.

The next command is also new, but still simple.

```
browser_displayURL lookhere $page
```

The command `browser_displayURL` takes two arguments:

- ✔ The name of a frame to be written to.
- ✔ The name of the URL to be written to that frame.

As you may guess from the name, `browser_displayURL` doesn't just write a string to the named frame. Instead, the command interprets the string that is its second argument as HTML code. Thus, if that string contains an HTML tag, like `<P>`, the tag will be treated as an `<HTML>` tag, rather than as text to be displayed.

If the string to be displayed contains the substring `<a src="http://www.ccp.uchicago.edu/grad/Francis_Alex/me.jpg">` then a picture of my intrepid colleague, Alex Francis, appears in the frame. The command `browser_displayURL` acts exactly as if you had used HTML code to put the URL whose address is the second argument into the frame whose name is the first argument to the command.

After displaying the page in the frame, you need to close the frame.

```
browser_closeFrame lookhere
```

The next part of the procedure seems somewhat complex, but it's easier than it looks.. The idea is that you can use this same procedure (`showsource`) to either display a URL and its source code, or to clear the two frames in which URL and source code have been displayed, depending on how the variable `flag` is set. If `flag` is equal to `"write"` then you are currently writing data and source code to the frames. If `flag` is equal to `"erase"` then you're clearing the frames. I discuss the difference as you go through the next section.

```
if {$flag == "write"} {
    regsub -all {<} $data {\&lt;} tmp
regsub -all {>} $tmp {\&gt;} tmp2
```

These lines of code take the humongous string stored in the variable `data` and change some things about it. The string that `data` contains is well-formed HTML source code, so just displaying the string or writing it to a frame with the `browser_writeFrame` command causes the formatted page, (complete with hot links and pictures), to appear in the frame. This is not, however, what you want to happen. You can get that same effect much more easily by using the `browser_displayURL` command with a Web page address as its argument. In this case, you need to turn the HTML code into something that will be displayed as simple text by the HTML interpreter.

These first two lines of our substitution just replace every `<` symbol with the string `&lt;` (the HTML code for displaying a `<` symbol) and every `>` with the string `&gt;` (the HTML code for displaying a `>` symbol). Strings such as `<p>`, which normally are interpreted as (and appear on the screen as) a HTML paragraph tag, are transformed into the string `&lt;p&gt`. The `&lt;p&gt`string will *appear* as `<p>` on the screen. Because of the way the `regsub` command works in Tcl/Tk (see Appendix A) this substitution has to be done in a series of steps.

The last three lines of the substitution are designed to insert two HTML tags at the beginning and end of the string from which you have just carefully removed all HTML tags.

```
set source {<pre>}
append source $tmp2
append source {</pre>}
```

The first line just puts the string <pre> into a variable named source. The next one sticks your long string (without any HTML tags in it) into the variable source right after the <pre> part, and then the last line places the string </pre> into the variable source at the end. The effect is to bracket the long string with <pre> and </pre>. If you are familiar with HTML, using the codes <pre> and </pre> is the way to get a browser to display text exactly as typed. In effect, the preceding lines just set up the code of a URL so that when the browser displays the code, it will be as if you are looking at the content of the file using your favorite text editor.

The next step is to write the source code to the appropriate frame. As before, this involves opening the frame in which the code appears.

```
browser_openFrame sourcespot
```

Just to make sure that users knows what they're looking at in the source frame you can write some information to that frame before writing the actual code.

```
browser_writeFrame sourcespot $url
```

Now you're ready to put the actual source code into the frame and close the frame.

```
    browser_writeFrame sourcespot $source
    browser_closeFrame sourcespot
}
```

Okay, most of what I've discussed so far within the showsource routine is carried out only if the variable flag is set to the value "write", as it should be when you display a URL and its source. However, after displaying one URL and its source, it's important to clear the frames so they can be written to again. (Otherwise, the source frame gets kind of cluttered.) Clearing the display frame (which I call *lookhere*) is simple — just use the browser_displayFrame command to display a blank URL. But if you use the procedure showsource to display the blank page, what shows up in the source frame is the *source code* of the blank page, not a blank page itself.

This is not necessarily a bad idea — perhaps someone may want to see how you make your blank page look so clean and shiny. But this means that, although you can use the same code to display both content and blank pages in the display frame, you can't use the same code to both display source code and clear the source code frame.

The first four lines of the showsource do double-duty, displaying both contentful and blank pages equally well. The entire subsequent part of the procedure (starting with the following line)

```
if {$flag == "write"} {
```

manages to display the source of the page. If you're not displaying source code but instead clearing the source display frame, then you have set the variable flag to "erase" rather than "write". The rest of this procedure deals with this situation.

```
if {$flag == "erase"} {
    browser_openFrame sourcespot
    browser_displayURL sourcespot $page
    browser_closeFrame sourcespot
    set flag write
    set page ""
}
```

The first three lines of this preceding routine just display the same page as is being displayed in the other frame. Because you're erasing (you know that because the variable flag is set to "erase"), you can assume that the variable page has been set to the address of the blank page. After a page has been cleared, it is safe to write to it again; therefore, you can reset flag to "write" and page to an empty string, just as they were when the tclet started.

Writing the clearit *procedure*

The last step is create the procedure called clearit. clearit sets up the tclet's variables so that when it calls the showit procedure the frames clear correctly.

```
proc clearit {} {
    global page flag BLANK_PAGE
    set page $BLANK_PAGE
    set flag erase
    browser_getURL $page showsource
}
```

The first line of the preceding code declares the global variables that this procedure uses. The next two lines of code set these variables to the appropriate values for erasing in the `showsource` procedure. The final line gets the URL named by the variable `page` and sends the resulting source on to the procedure `showsource` in exactly the same manner as you used in the `showit` procedure. When you put the tclet all together and you call up a cool home page, the results look something like the Figure 19-3.

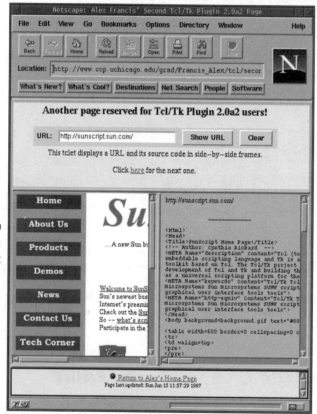

Figure 19-3: The tclet "sourcer.tcl" doing its stuff, displaying Web page side-by-side with its source code.

Talking to the Browser

One of the main things you can do with your tclet is get some information from the browser. In addition to interpreting HTML code, the browser also keeps track of a lot of information about the user. (See the sidebar called Tcl/Tk and Browser Security in this chapter for more on how and why information about users is protected.) However, your average tclet can still access some pretty useful information from the browser. The easiest way of getting information from the browser is by using JavaScript commands.

JavaScript is a little language that the designers of Netscape Navigator built into the browser to expand the functionality of the browser beyond what can normally be done with HTML code. For the most part, Microsoft Explorer also implements JavaScript commands. Still, JavaScript is simple, easy to use, and as long as you're mostly writing Tcl/Tk code you won't need to worry about much more than a few elementary commands anyway.

Because JavaScript is a scripting language in its own right, you may expect that you'd have to learn a bunch of syntax and stuff just to make it work. Actually, for the purposes of writing tclets, you can pretty much treat the commands in this chapter as strange Tcl/Tk commands. If you want to get fancy, there are plenty of books out there on JavaScript, but for the moment that's way beyond what any of you really need at the moment.

Getting browser information (navinfo.tcl)

Recently there's been a lot of fuss in the news about security and privacy issues on the Internet. You may be somewhat surprised to learn that every time you access a Web site, the authors of that site can get all kinds of information about you without asking permission, including

- ✔ Machine name (for example, cochlea.spc.uchicago.edu)
- ✔ IP address
- ✔ Hardware
- ✔ Operating system

The irony about this is, many users may not even be aware that they're displaying this kind of information to the world. Some inexperienced users may not even know some of the information that total strangers can find out easily. The following tclet uses a combination of Tcl/Tk and JavaScript to allow users of your site to find out some of the information about themselves that's available for other people to find out.

Again, here I talk about the procedures in a conceptual order, not in the order that they appear in the tclet. I provide the final code for the tclet navinfo.Tcl/Tk at the end of this chapter. The first thing to note about this tclet, shown in Figure 19-4, is that it's a bit more structured than the other tclets in this chapter.

The tclet consists primarily of a text window and two main control buttons, *Get Info* and *Clear,* which carry out the main tasks of showing the selected information and clearing the text window.

```
button .show -text "Get Info" -command checkit -bd 2
button .clear -text "Clear" -command clearit -bd 2
text .info -relief sunken -bg white -bd 2 -width 40 \
-height 5
```

Figure 19-4:
The tclet
navinfo.
Tcl/Tk
before any
information
has been
requested.

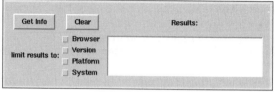

There are two frames, the second a daughter of the first, that make formatting easier. The names of the frames reflect that there will be one frame for
the combination of checkbuttons and their labels (.ch) and one within that
frame that will be on the right (.ch.r) for formatting the buttons themselves.

```
frame .ch
frame .ch.r
```

You also need some labels, just to make sure everything is clear. Notice that
one label is in the toplevel . and the other is in .ch — the first daughter frame.

```
label .ch.kinds -text "limit results to:"
label .results -text "Results:"
```

In order to allow the user to select they type of information they want to
see, you have four checkbuttons. Note that these checkbuttons are in the
lowest-level daughter frame, .ch.r.

```
checkbutton .ch.r.browser -text "Browser" \
-variable browser -anchor w
checkbutton .ch.r.platform -text "Platform" \
-variable platform -anchor w
checkbutton .ch.r.version -text "Version" \
-variable version -anchor w
checkbutton .ch.r.system -text "System" \
-variable system -anchor w
```

Next, you construct the bindings so that moving the mouse over the main
buttons displays some information in the status window.

```
bind .show <Enter> \
{browser_displayStatus "Click here for browser info"}
bind .clear <Enter> \
```

```
{browser_displayStatus "Click here to clear results"}
# and erase those messages when the mouse leaves
bind .show <Leave> {browser_displayStatus ""}
bind .clear <Leave> {browser_displayStatus ""}

grid .show -row 1 -column 1 -padx 5 -pady 5
grid .clear -row 1 -column 2 -padx 5 -pady 5
grid .results -row 1 -column 3 -columnspan 2 -padx 5 \
-pady 5
grid .ch -row 2 -column 1 -columnspan 2 -padx 5
grid .info -row 2 -column 3 -columnspan 2 -padx 5
```

However, rather than gridding the widgets that go inside the frame .ch, you pack them instead. This way, you can pack in all the checkbuttons at once, and makes it unnecessary to go to great lengths to grid them in columns. The packer aligns the columns automatically.

```
pack .ch.kinds .ch.r -side left
pack .ch.r.browser .ch.r.version .ch.r.platform \
.ch.r.system -side top -anchor w
```

Now that the tclet exists, at least conceptually, take a look at the procedures that make it do something. The two main procedures are checkit, which gets and displays the requested information, and clearit which clears the text window after a display.

```
proc checkit {} {
    global browser platform version system
```

There are four global variables which, if you remember from when you created the checkbuttons, are the checkbutton variables. They have a value of 1 if the checkbutton is checked, and a value of 0 if the checkbutton is not checked. These variables keep track of whether the user wants to find out any of the four kinds of information available. For example, if you want to know what your browser is reported as, you click on the *Browser* checkbutton, in which case the value of the variable browser is 1. If that is the only button you checked, then the other three variables (platform, version, system) are all 0.

The first thing to do is to clear the text window, just in case there is already information in it. You find out more about the clearit procedure after the checkit procedure.

```
clearit
```

After clearing the text window, you do a series of `if` statements to find out whether the user has clicked any of the checkbuttons. All of these `if` statements have the same form. If the value of the variable is 1 (the checkbutton has been clicked) then call the appropriate JavaScript command, and send its results to a procedure.

```
if $browser {
    browser_callJavascript {navigator.appName} br
}
if $platform {
    browser_callJavascript {navigator.appVersion} pl
}
if $version {
    browser_callJavascript {navigator.appVersion} vr
}
if $system {
    browser_callJavascript {navigator.appVersion} sy
}
```

You use only two different JavaScript commands here — `navigator appName` and `navigator appVersion`. However, `navigator appVersion` returns a lot more information than you want, so you use the string-handling ability of Tcl/Tk to break up its output in different ways, depending on the type of information to be extracted. As with other uses of browser commands, `browser_callJavascript` requires a callback. (A callback is a Tcl/Tk procedure or command that takes as input the output of the JavaScript command.) Each of the callback procedures used here has a two-letter name that relates to the kind of information it returns. For example, the procedure `sy` deals with information about the *system*, and `vr` deals with *version* information. Before going into more detail about these procedures, examine the last command in the `checkit` procedure.

```
    display
}
```

The preceding line of code is just a call to yet another procedure (called `display`) that displays the information collected via all the other procedures called by the `checkit` procedure. So, now examine the four procedures that set up browser, system, version, and platform information for display. Remember that, like other browser commands, `browser_call-Javascript` calls its callback with three arguments (if it's successful). Therefore, you need to declare each of these procedures with three arguments, even though only the last argument is the only one that interests us.

The first of the four procedures, `br`, is very simple and just sets the global variable `browserString` to the output of the JavaScript command, which called it in the first place.

```
proc br {url status result} {
   global browserString
   set browserString $result
}
```

The next three procedures all use the output of the JavaScript command `navigator appVersion`, which is a long string containing a lot of information. However, using Tcl/Tk, you can parse this string to extract only certain parts of it that correspond to different kinds of information about the browser. The whole string looks something like this (depending on the browser, and so on):

```
3.01 (X11; I; Linux 2.0.30 i586)
```

and you want to be able to extract information from this string so that you can display it in a sensible manner.

```
proc vr {url status result} {
   global versionString
   set versionString [lindex [split $result (] 0]
}
```

The procedure `vr` gets the Version information, which is the very first string (3.01). You can get this easily by just splitting the line at the first "(" and getting the first element (index 0) of the resulting list. Getting the platform information is a bit more complex, though the principle is the same.

```
proc pl {url status result} {
   global platformString
   set platformString \
   [lindex [split [lindex [split $result (] 1] \;] 0]
}
```

In the preceding case, you want to get the first entry in the part of the string that is between brackets. So you split the result string at the first (as before, but this time continue processing the second element (index 1) of the resulting list. That string is, for example,

```
X11; I; Linux 2.0.30 i586)
```

So to pull out the platform from this string you split it again, this time at the ; marks, and take the first element (index 0) of *that* list. To get the system part of this string you want to get the *last* element (index 1) which is

```
Linux 2.0.30 i586)
```

with a leading space and a final parenthesis, both of which you must eliminate in order to make the display line up right. Extract the space and parenthesis by saving the string, gotten by splitting and indexing as before, into a temporary variable, tmp, and then using the regsub command to substitute an empty string for all leading spaces and all parentheses.

```
proc sy {url status result} {
    global systemString
    set tmp [lindex [split [lindex [split \
    [lindex [split $result (] 1] \;] 2] )] 0]
    regsub -all {(^ )|\)} $tmp {} systemString
}
```

Now that you have the right information in each of your variables, it's time to display that information in an understandable manner in the text window.

```
proc display {} {
    global browserString platformString versionString \
    systemString
    set displayString [format "Browser: \
    \t%s\nVersion:\t%s\nPlatform:\t%s\nSystem: \t%s\n" \
    $browserString $versionString $platformString \
    $systemString]
    info insert end $displayString
}
```

This procedure simply takes all of the variables that you've collected and puts them into a formatted string (called displayString) with labels and everything already built in. Be careful to make sure that each variable that gets put into this string always has a value, either a default one which is set at the beginning of the tclet, or a value that one of the procedures assigns called from checkit. Some lines like this

```
    set browserString "<unknown>"
    set platformString "<unknown>"
    set versionString "<unknown>"
    set systemString "<unknown>"
```

at the very beginning of the tclet assure that every variable has a value, but they're not really necessary in this particular tclet. The first thing that happens in the checkit procedure is to call the clearit procedure, so you can put these lines in the clearit procedure (where they have to be anyway, in order to clear all the variables in preparation for getting new information). So, finally, take a look at the clearit procedure.

```
proc clearit {} {
    global browserString versionString platformString \
    systemString displayString
.info delete 1.0 end
```

The first thing to do is clear the display window. Doing so doesn't change the values of any variables, but it does make the screen a nice blank color.

```
set browserString "<unknown>"
set platformString "<unknown>"
set versionString "<unknown>"
set systemString "<unknown>"
```

These next four lines do set all the variables to their default values. Finally, the procedure sets the display string to the empty string just in case. This step is not really necessary, since `displayString` is reset every time the tclet calls the `display` procedure; but while you're zeroing everything else, you may as well make a clean sweep of it. (If, instead of using the `set` command in the `display` procedure you use the `append` command, then this step is absolutely necessary.)

```
set displayString ""
}
```

After you get this tclet up and running, give it a shot. Depending on your browser, platform, system, and version, your results may differ a bit from what appears in Figure 19-5, but overall the tclet should look pretty similar.

Writing alerts

Calling JavaScript commands from within a tclet is useful for more things than just getting information from the browser. Because JavaScript is built right into the browser, doing standard browser-type things via JavaScript commands is easier than trying to build Tcl/Tk routines that mimic browser behavior from scratch. A good example of this is the method for producing warning messages. If you need to warn users that they're about to do something drastic (like subscribe themselves to 10,000-member mailing lists) you can use Tcl/Tk to create a message window that pops up at the mouse location and provides the warning. But doing so is a lot of work. You must

✔ Create the message widget

✔ Decide what the right dimensions of the alert should be

✔ Decide where and how to grid the alert

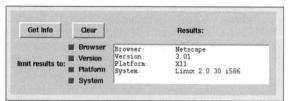

and so on. On the other hand, JavaScript has a built-in method for making three different kinds of warning messages. The following tclet consists of three buttons, each of which displays a different kind of alert when clicked.

alarm.tcl

```
#!/pkg/tk/bin/wish
# a trivial tclet with three buttons demonstrating the ease
# of using JavaScript alert windows of various types.
# Alex Francis
# tell the plugin this tclet accesses the browser
# capabilities
package require Browser
# a procedure that does nothing, because currently
# browser_getJavascript requires a callback (unless the
# tclet is executing in an external process and that can't
# be guaranteed yet), but there's nothing that needs to be
# done in the callback.
proc callback {url status info} {}
# the procedure to call the alert method, with some text.
proc alert {} {
    browser_callJavaScript \
    {top.alert("\nIt says *DON'T* Click!")} callback
}
# the procedure to call the confirm method, with some text.
```

```
proc confirm {} {
    browser_callJavaScript \
    {top.confirm("\nDo you always do\nwhat you're told?")} \
    callback
}
# the procedure to call the prompt method, with some text.
proc prompt {} {
    browser_callJavaScript {top.prompt("\
    Alright, what's your name?","Miscreant")} callback
}
# create the button that calls the alert method
button .alert -text "Don't Click Here!" -bg red -fg black \
-activebackground pink -command alert
# create the button that calls the confirm method
button .confirm -text "Click Here!" -bg green -fg black \
-activebackground lightGreen -command confirm
# create the button that calls the prompt method
button .prompt -text "Not Here!" -bg blue -fg black \
-activebackground lightBlue -command prompt
# display everything as simply as possible
pack .alert .confirm .prompt -side top -fill x
```

This tclet has one really strange thing. First, note that there is a procedure called `callback` that doesn't do anything at all. You need this with current versions of the Tcl/Tk Plug-in because the command `browser_call-JavaScript` must have two arguments, and the second argument must be a callback. It doesn't matter that the JavaScript commands that are being called do not return any value (they just make displays). However, since they don't return a value, you don't have to do anything with it, you just need an existing procedure to use as a callback.

The three JavaScript commands that are used here are similar:

```
top.alert("\nIt says *DON'T* Click!")
top.confirm("\nDo you always do\nwhat you're told?")
top.prompt("\nAlright, what's your name?","Miscreant")
```

The first part of each of these lines (before the first parenthesis) tells the browser to carry out the appropriate command (*alert, confirm* and *prompt*, respectively) within the top-level browser window. The parts in the parentheses provide the arguments to these three commands. For example, the `alert` and `confirm` commands each take a single argument — the string that is displayed in the alert or confirmation box. This string is displayed within quotes, and, as in Tcl, here you use backslash notation to indicate carriage returns (\n) and tabs (\t).

The prompt command takes two arguments, a text string that's displayed (the first string in quotes), and a default value for the entry box that's part of the prompt screen. The prompt command creates a response window with an entry space in which the user can type an answer. This answer passes to the callback procedure, and you can use it for some kind of processing within the tclet, although I have decided not to do anything with it in this case. The three different notification methods appear in Figures 19-6 through 19-8.

Figure 19-6:
The simplest kind of message — the alert.

Figure 19-7:
A confirmation message asks for feedback from the user.

Figure 19-8:
A prompt message asks for more detailed information from the user, and even gives a default suggestion.

Chapter 20

Building a Better Guestbook

In This Chapter

▶ Understanding guestbook basics

▶ Providing a better layout

▶ Offering standard keyboard binding

▶ Filtering out unwanted words

▶ Checking for HTML

▶ Finishing the guestbook

*W*hile you've been out on the Web, you've probably seen guestbooks — special forms that allow visitors to a Web site to leave a message that can be read by other visitors. When you build your guestbook as a tclet, it's smarter (and prettier) than an Hypertext Markup Language (HTML)-based guestbook.

What Is a Guestbook?

A guestbook really consists of three parts:

✔ **Front end**. The *front end* is the form that the user sees and fills out. Traditionally, a front end is built with HTML `<form>` tags. Figure 20-1 shows a typical guestbook front end, which basically is a big box for the user to type in and a button for sending the entry to the server.

✔ **Log.** The *log* is a Web page that displays the entries that readers submitted to the guestbook. Figure 20-2 shows a typical log page that contains a series of messages, separated by rules.

✔ **CGI.** A Common Gateway Interface, or *CGI* is a special program or script that helps the server process the guestbook entry. In the case of a guestbook, the CGI simply takes the information from a submitted form and adds it to the end of the log. Some CGIs may filter the information to make sure that the submission has nothing that's objectionable.

The part that you'll be rebuilding in tclet form is the guestbook's front end. You'll make it smarter, so that it looks for problems before the entry is submitted to the CGI. You can certainly write CGIs in Tcl, but

✔ The process is a little complicated and system-specific.

✔ It's not very much fun.

✔ A zillion freely available guestbook scripts are out on the Net already.

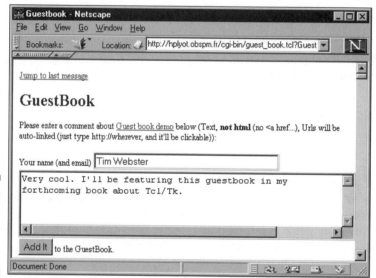

Figure 20-1:
A guest-book
created
with HTML.

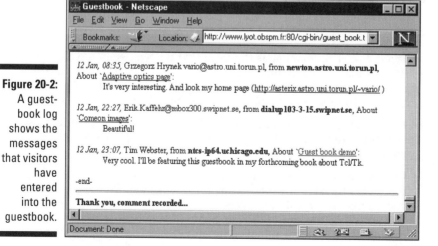

Figure 20-2:
A guest-book log
shows the
messages
that visitors
have
entered
into the
guestbook.

Why Use Tcl/Tk to Build a Guestbook?

Building a guestbook in Tcl/Tk is almost as easy as writing one in HTML, and using a tclet has plenty of advantages:

- **Improved layout.** HTML doesn't offer a great deal of control of the layout of form elements. You can't change the type in a HTML button, for example; neither can you change its color or do anything too fun with it. Furthermore, lining up form elements in a grid is a real pain — even with fancy page editors such as NetObjects Fusion and Claris Homepage. Creating a neat, organized layout with the grid tag is easy.

- **Economy.** When a CGI processes a guestbook entry, the CGI uses the server machine's computing power to do its processing. Form-processing is trivial enough for a form or two, but when a server gets dozens of simultaneous hits, it needs all the horsepower that it can muster. Doing preprocessing in a tclet means that the client computer, not the server, is doing the work. Running a tclet isn't a strain on the client, and it makes the server run faster — in short, everybody's happy.

- **Error checking.** You can make sure that the user filled out all the necessary fields before submitting the guestbook entry to the CGI. Catching errors before the form is submitted saves the server the trouble of sending out an error message, saves the CGI the trouble of figuring out that there's a problem, and saves the user some connection time.

- **Checking for HTML.** If you put raw entries in your log page, guestbook signers can add HTML to the log. A malicious user can't do anything too terribly harmful with HTML, but he or she can add a universe of unpleasantness (pictures of Barney, self-playing sound files that contain Barry Manilow hits, QuickTime, Regis & Kathie Lee clips) without your consent. Using a well-crafted regular expression, your tclet can search for HTML and ask the user to remove it. (Some CGIs perform such checks as part of their normal processing.)

- **Checking for objectionable text.** You may also want to check for objectionable text (such as obscenities) and ask the user to change them before the text is added to the guestbook. (This checking is a little too processor-intensive for most CGI applications and, therefore, is almost never built into CGIs.)

Before You Begin

You need to know a few things before you start coding your guestbook. Your Webmaster (or your guestbook CGI's documentation) should be able to provide all the information that you need, which is

- The address of the guestbook CGI
- The names that the CGI uses for its fields

For this example, I'll use a guestbook CGI written by Laurent Demailly, a longtime Tcl/Tk enthusiast and one of the first developers of the Tcl plug-in. Demailly's plug-in is written in Tcl (of course) and should work on any UNIX-based server that has a Tcl interpreter.

Every CGI is different. If you're using a CGI program other than Demailly's Tcl CGI, you'll need to adapt your tclet to use the field names that your CGI is expecting. In almost every case, adapting your tclet is a simple matter of tweaking a few names and perhaps creating a few more entry widgets.

Demailly's Tcl-based CGI expects to get four chunks of data. The first three items are things that the user enters in the guestbook front end:

name	The user's name and e-mail address
cmt	The user's comments (the guestbook entry)
subj	The subject line for the guestbook entry

The CGI uses the last chunk of data for bookkeeping purposes:

url	The address of the guestbook log

Your basic strategy for packaging the guestbook data for the server is fairly simple:

1. Create some widgets to get input from the user.

2. When the user clicks the submit button:

   - Make sure that the name field has been filled out.

   - Scan the entry for HTML code and, if any is found, ask the user to remove it.

   - Scan the entry for objectionable material and, if any is found, ask the user to remove it.

   - Send the final text to the server.

Providing a Better Layout

First, you need to create the basic layout. Which kinds of widgets do you need for a guestbook? A guestbook has a few obvious parts:

- ✔ An entry widget for the user's name
- ✔ A label widget to identify the user-name widget
- ✔ An entry widget for the subject line
- ✔ A label widget to identify the subject-line widget
- ✔ A text widget for the guestbook entry
- ✔ A message widget to give feedback to the reader about the content of the entry widget
- ✔ A button widget for sending the entry to the server

You can organize these elements to your taste. Remember, I'm a designer by day (okay, I'm a design-software expert), and I've been trained to line *everything* up with *something*. My notion of a good-looking layout looks something like Figure 20-3. (I've left the colors at their default values, but in a real-world Web site, I'd probably whip up a palette for the tclet that matches the rest of the page.)

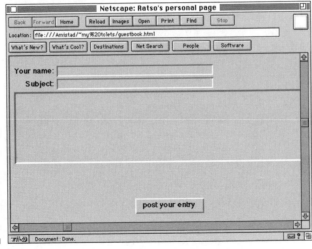

Figure 20-3:
A basic guestbook front end created with Tcl.

Listing 20-1 shows the code that I used to create the widgets in the layout. As you can see, the code is straightforward widget-making.

Listing 20-1	guestbook.tck

```
# An entry widget for the user's name
entry .user_name -width 40 -textvariable user_name

# A label widget to identify the entry widget
label .name_label -text "Your name:"

# An entry widget for the subject line
entry .subject -width 40 -textvariable subject

# A label widget to identify the entry widget
label .subject_label -text "Subject:"

# A text widget for the guestbook entry
text .comment -width 80 -height 10 -relief sunken \
-borderwidth 3

# A button widget, to send the entry to the server
button .submit -text "post your entry" -command submit

# A message widget, to give feedback to the reader about
# the contents of the entry widget
message .readout -width 40 -aspect 400 -foreground red \
-textvariable readout
set readout "\n\n\n"
```

Notice that I've given the entry widgets and the message widget textvariables, because I'm sure that I'll want to take a look at the information in the textbox later. You can name the widgets and their variables anything you like, of course, but I've chosen to use the same names for the widgets and the variables that they contain, so that it's easy to remember which variables go with which widgets.

Also notice that I've set the message label's to the string \n\n\n. This is just backslash substitution — \n stands for "line break", and \n\n\n simply makes the message widget three lines tall to begin with. This way, if we put some sort of warning message in the widget later, the widget won't change heights and cause other widgets to move to accommodate the new size.

I know that the **submit** button will eventually send the
          guestbook data to the server, so I've specified
          a command, called submit, to be executed when
          the button is clicked. I'll write the submit
          procedure in a few pages.

Now, I'll grid all the widgets. It's quite simple:

```
grid .name_label       -row 0 -column 0 -sticky e
grid .user_name        -row 0 -column 1
grid .subject_label    -row 1 -column 0 -sticky e
grid .subject          -row 1 -column 1
grid .comment          -row 2 -columnspan 3
grid .readout          -row 3 -columnspan 3
grid .submit           -row 4 -columnspan 3
```

Checking All Entries for Completeness

You want to make sure that the reader entered some value in the name
field — assuming, of course, that you don't want to allow anonymous
postings to your guestbook.

Let's put this check in its own procedure. Breaking this part out into a
separate section allows you to solve one problem at a time and to change
the way that the entire tclet works later. I'll call the procedure check_name.

All that you want this procedure to do is to make sure that something —
anything — is entered in the name field. There's no way to make sure that
the reader types his own name rather than **The Great Gazoo** or whatever,
but at least you can make sure that there's something in the field.

How can you tell whether there's something in the field? Just look at the
length of the string that's stored in the textvariable user_name. If
user_name is zero characters long, the field is empty. If user_name contains
a nonzero number of characters, you know that the user typed something in
the field.

Your procedure returns a value so that the submit procedure knows the
outcome of the test. If the field is okay and ready to be submitted, the
procedure returns a value of 1, and if the field needs work, the procedure
returns a value of 0. This way, if you can use the results of your procedure as
the test if an if command. Here's the basic outline for code that submits the
form if everything's cool, and alerts the user if something's wrong:

```
if [check_name] {
   # the value's ok — go ahead with the submission
} else {
   # something's wrong — hold on a second!
}
```

Ready? The procedure's simple:

```
proc check_name {} {

   global user_name

   # if the string length is zero, return the value 0
   if [string length $user_name] {
      return 1
   } else {
      return 0
   }
}
```

As you may have guessed, you could skip this procedure and just use the [string length] test later, but putting this code in its own section makes it easy to modify the test later. To change the test to make sure that the user entered at least 5 characters in the entry box, for example, you can change the if statement test to this:

```
if [expr [string length $my_string] > 4] {
```

To make sure that the reader entered at least two words (a first and last name, for example), you can use a regular expression, like so:

```
if [regex {[^ ]+ +.+} $my_string] {
```

Checking for HTML

Now you check for HTML code in the document. Basically, you search through the text by using a regular expression, and if you find something that looks like an HTML tag, assume that it *is* an HTML tag. To show the reader which text you're concerned about, mark the suspect text in red.

The problem, really, is to come up with a regular expression that recognizes HTML tags and ignores everything else. It's impossible (or at least incredibly tedious) to build a regular expression that can recognize every possible HTML tag, but there's a fairly good way to zero in on problems:

- Every HTML tag is enclosed in pointy brackets, as in `<a href = "so and so">`.
- All tags that link to other things (images, sounds, Java applets, ActiveX components, and so on) contain the keyword `SRC`.

Tags that contain the `SRC` keyword are the tags that you're worried about. You can search for `SRC` between pointy brackets to find the trouble tags. A regular expr_¯sion to find such a beastie looks like this:

`<`	Matches the opening pointy bracket
`[^>]U`	Matches any non-closing-bracket characters between the bracket and `SRC`
`SRC`	Matches the string `SRC`
`[^>]*`	Matches any characters between `"SRC"` and the closing bracket
`>`	Matches the closing bracket

Put 'em together, and what do they spell?

```
<[^>]*SRC[^>]*>
```

(By incredible coincidence, this is the first name of the Borg Queen in *Star Trek: First Contact!*) Now all you need to do is search for this regular expression in the text widget and, if you find a match, turn it red. Here's the basic procedure:

```
proc check_html {} {

    # search for an HTML tag.
    # if a tag is found, return zero. Otherwise, return 1
    if [regexp -nocase {<[^>]*SRC[^>]*>} \
    [.comment get 1.0 end]] {
        return 0
    } else {
        return 1
    }
}
```

You can modify this procedure as you want. As it stands, the procedure ignores hypertext links to other pages. Such links seem to be harmless enough, but if you want to disallow them, you can rewrite the regular expression to look for HREF (as well as SRC) between pointy brackets, like so:

```
if [regexp -nocase {<[^>]*(HREF|SRC)[^>]*>} \
[.comment get 1.0 end]] {
```

Filtering out Unwanted Words

Now, if you like, you can make a pass through the text to look for words that you'd just as soon leave off your Web page. It's up to you to decide whether you want to do this filtering, which, to some people, may sound like censorship. Personally, I think that anyone who wants to wax scatalogical or use racial epithets can confine such material to usenet and to his own Web page — but your guestbook is your own, and you can set whatever rules you like.

You can take two approaches when you recognize a problem word:

- Ask the user to remove the word.
- Discreetly replace the word with a placeholder, such as
  —, [expletive deleted], or (my preference) $#&@! .

In my capacity as a former social worker, I am inclined to simply make the replacement.

Rather than use the regexp command to perform this scan, use the regsub to search for problem words and replace them with placeholders.

First, you need to compile a list of problem words. Rather than demonstrate this procedure by using actual obscenities, we'll suppose that you want to filter out the names of colors; red, green, blue, and the like are forbidden to appear in the pages of your guestbook. Assemble the list in regular-expression format and, for ease of handling, store it in a variable, like so:

```
set bad_words \
{ red |orange|yellow|green|blue|indigo|violet}
```

If one of your words might be used as part of a larger, legitimate word (*red* might be part of *redo* or *kindred,* for example), be sure to put spaces before and after the word to make sure that the regsub command doesn't try to sanitize words that are okay. As you can see, I added spaces around red in the preceding regular expression.

Now all you need to do is make the substitution run through the text. The `regsub` command puts its results in a new variable, and you use this sanitized text to replace the text in the widget. Because you won't ask the user to change anything, you don't need to set up a return value for the procedure. Here's the code, which is simple:

```
proc check_words {} {

    # words that we don't want to appear in the guestbook
    set bad_words \
    { red |orange|yellow|green|blue|indigo|violet}
    # a character string to replace the bad words.
    # quoted with curlies to prevent substitution.
    set replacement {$#@!}

    # if any bad words are found, replace with new string
    # and store the sanitized text in the variable
    # sanitized_text
    if [regsub -nocase -all $bad_words \
    [.comment get 1.0 end] $replacement sanitized_text] {
        .comment delete 1.0 end
        .comment insert 1.0 $sanitized_text
    }
}
```

Figure 20-4 shows a guestbook entry that contains the suspect words *orange* and *green*. After you run the `check_words` procedure, the entry looks like Figure 20-5. (It's a lot more fun than Figure 20-4, anyway, isn't it?)

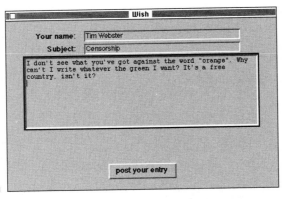

Figure 20-4: A guestbook entry with the forbidden words orange and green.

Figure 20-5:
The
guestbook
tclet
removes
the
objectionable
words and
replaces
them
with the
placeholder
$#@!

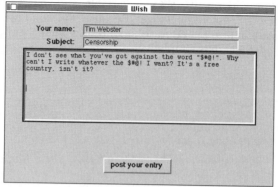

Bundling the Data

Just to make things simpler later, put all the instructions that pack up data for the server into one procedure, so that you can send the data with one elegant command. All you need to do is put together the names that the CGI is expecting with the information from your text widgets and encode the entire thing in HTML-friendly format by using http_formatQuery.

Note: If you're using a CGI other than Laurent's Tcl guestbook, you need to replace the value names in the following code with the value names that your CGI uses. Also, be sure to use the URL of your own CGI instead of the placeholder in the code. Here's the procedure that compiles the data for the server:

```
proc pack_entry {} {

    # use the text_variables that hold the name and subject
    # information
    global user_name subject

    # store the name of the guestbook log page
    # >>>  Be sure to use your own page's URL !!  <<<<
    set log_url {http:/ your-server-here/log-page-pathname}

    # encode the data, and return it as the result of the
    # procedure
    return [http_formatQuery \
        name $user_name \
        cmt [.comment get 1.0 end] \
        subject $subject \
        url $log_url]
}
```

Finishing the Guestbook

Now all that remains is to write the submit procedure that's called when the user clicks the .submit button widget. Here's what submit needs to do:

1. Call check_words to filter out unwanted words.

2. Call check_html to make sure that the entry contains no HTML, and call check_names to make sure that the name entry is filled out. If both of these things are okay, submit should send the guestbook data to the guestbook CGI.

3. If the form contains HTML, ask the user to remove it.

4. If the name entry is blank, ask the user to fill it out.

That procedure is simple enough, isn't it? Now do it (see Listing 20-2).

Listing 20-2   The submission procedure from guestbook.tcl

```
proc submit {} {

    #access the message widget's textvariable
    global readout

    # store the name of the guestbook CGI that will handle
# the data
    # >>>>>>  Be sure to use your own CGI's URL !!  <<<<<<<
    set cgi_url {http://your-server-here/cgi-pathname}

    # create a message to show when the entry has been
    # submitted
    set success_warning \
    (Your guestbook entry has been submitted. Thanks.

    }

    # create a warning message to show when the name field
    # is empty
    set name_warning \
    {Please enter your name in the field above.
    We'd like to know who you are. This guestbook entry
    can't be submitted until a name has been entered.
    Thanks!}
```

(continued)

(continued)

```
#create a warning to show when html is found in
# guestbook entry
set html_warning \
{Sorry — no HTML links to multimedia are allowed
in the guestbook. This guestbook entry can't be
submitted until all such links are removed.}

#check name field and look for HTML.
#If clean, send to server
if {[check_name] && [check_html]} {

    #replace obscenities with a replacement string
    check_words

    http_get $cgi_url -query [pack_entry]

    set readout $success_warning

} else {
    #if the name field is empty, as the user for input
    if ![check_name] {
        set readout $empty_name
    } else {
        # if the guestbook entry contains HTML,
# ask reader to remove
        if ![check_html] {
            set readout $html_warning

        } ;# end html check

    } ;# end name field check

} ;# end the name field/html combined check
}
```

Part V
The Part of Tens

The 5th Wave   By Rich Tennant

"I don't know how it happened, but there's an applet in the toaster and some guy in Norway keeps burning my toast."

In this part . . .

Ah, the famous Part of Tens.

Every ...*For Dummies* book has one. In fact, a set of clay tablets recently unearthed in Syria is believed to be *Sumerian For Dummies*. It concludes with a Part of Tens section.

Turn the page to see how Tcl/Tk compares with its more famous sibling, Java.

Chapter 21

Almost Ten Differences Between Java and Tcl/Tk

● ●

*W*hat's the relationship between Java and Tcl/Tk? There are some technical differences, but these crucial differences stand out.

The Java Virtual Machine

Java is a funny kind of language. A Java program *is* an application, and the Java program runs on a special platform — the Java virtual machine. Sometimes, a Java machine is an actual Java-specific machine (like a Java chip built into a network computer), and sometimes the Java virtual machine is a *simulation* of a computer that runs on another computer. When you look at Java applet inside a web page, you're really looking at the output of this Java-machine simulation running on your own machine. When you look at a tclet in a web page, you're looking at the output of Tcl/Tk running on your own machine — there's no virtual middleman.

Tcl/Tk programs are executed by an interpreter (documented at length in the rest of *Tcl/Tk For Dummies*; the Tcl genie reads the program line-by-line, and executes each step in turn. Tcl/Tk interpreters (such as the interpreter in Wish, or the interpreter built into the plug-in) are software applications that run under a particular operating system, like Windows 95 or Unix. A Tcl/Tk program isn't an application itself, and the program can't run by itself without an interpreter.

Compiling

Java source code is compiled into a special machine language that runs on the Java virtual machine. The Java machine can't do anything with Java source code — the source code must be translated into machine-readable gobbledy-gook before the Java virtual machine does anything. If you want to change the value of a variable in a Java applet, you need to change the source code, recompile the source code into a Java applet, and rerun the applet. Compiling takes a lot of time, so tweaking little details (like the appearance of buttons) takes a lot of time when you're writing Java code.

When the interpreter runs a Tcl/Tk script, the script runs line by line. Want to change the value of a variable to see what happens? Type the change into Wish. Want to define a new procedure? Type the definition into Wish. The changes to your tclet take place immediately. Furthermore, the interpreter reads and understands the same Tcl/Tk source code as you do.

Security

Like Tcl/Tk, Java provides some basic security features so that a malicious applet can't do anything to harm a user's machine. On the surface, Java's and safe-Tcl's default security models seem similar: programs just can't act in ways that harm users.

These security features are implemented in different ways, however. In the end, Java's security features rely on the fact that Java runs a virtual machine. Even if a Java application straight-up Java machine code could somehow do something crazy to gain access to areas of the computer's memory outside the memory allocated for the program (and in theory, the Java application can't), the "computer's memory" is still virtual memory on a virtual machine. A program on a simulated machine can't affect the machine that's running the simulation, any more than those little people inside *SimCity* could colonize your word processor documents.

Safe-Tcl doesn't use the virtual machine approach — it doesn't need to. A Tcl/Tk program can't gain access to such resources as specific memory locations in the computer, so there's only so much badness that a bad Tcl/Tk program can do once you remove potentially dangerous commands from the language.

Complication

Java has often been described as a much easier language to learn than C++. This is true, in the same sense that an automobile is easier to pick up than a house. Java is still pretty difficult for beginners to master. (So is the allegedly simple JavaScript, for that matter.) Java certainly is easy for C programmers to learn, and it's probably better to learn Java than C++ nowadays, but Java is not a really good language for absolute beginners. The graphics-handling libraries that Java uses are especially complicated, compared to the elegance of something like

```
button .b -text "click me"
```

Variables

Java is pretty uptight about variables, and what you store in a variable. For instance, it's no big deal to store several different kinds of data in the same Tcl variable:

```
set x 1      ;# store an integer in x
set x 1.0        ;# store a floating point number in x
set x "one" ;# store a string in x
```

This is perfectly legal Tcl. Furthermore, the interpreter doesn't care that this is the first occurrence of the variable x.

Java is quite a bit more regimented; before you use a variable, you must tell the Java compiler (a distant cousin of the Tcl genie) what kind of information a variable will store. For instance, if you want to put an integer in a variable called x, you must start by *declaring* x as a location that holds integers, like

```
int x /* tells the compiler that x stores integers */
```

Once you've declared a variable's type, the variable can only store that type of information; a command like

```
x = "one"
```

causes a compiler to generate a snide little error message because the string "one" isn't an integer.

Dynamism

Because the Tcl interpreter executes commands on a line-by-line basis, the interpreter doesn't really care when you create a new Tcl variable or command: at some level, *everything* is a new command. For instance, look at this little Tcl code:

```
set my_command "puts"
set my_message "Hello, world"
```

Now, if you give the interpreter a command like

```
$my_command $my_message
```

the interpreter swaps in the values of the variables my_command and my_message and executes the command

```
puts "Hello, world"
```

Here's the twist: the command `puts "Hello, world"` isn't really in the program. In fact, the individual parts of the command didn't exist before the interpreter ran the first two lines of code. The Tcl genie doesn't care.

The Java compiler is not so fancy-free. When the Java compiler translates source code into Java-machine gobbledy-gook, the compiler needs to know what all of the commands are up front. The running program can't create new commands for itself while running.

What does this mean? Well, it means Tcl is cooler than Java. (It's a little more complicated than that — it means that Java and Tcl belong to different language families, and serve different purposes. That's why Sun has given us two separate Internet-friendly languages.)

Objects

Java is an object-oriented language. Tcl is not.

"Object-oriented" means different things to different people. According to the folks at the Java project, object-oriented means that data (the stuff that's stored in variables) and the code that manipulates the data are stored together in buffers called objects. Rather than manipulating an object's data directly, you ask the object to change itself. This way, you don't need to know too much about the inner workings of an object to manipulate the object — you only need to know the polite way to ask.

Tcl widgets are quite a bit like Java objects. You know that a button widget must be keeping track of attributes like its size and color *somewhere,* but you don't know the details: rather than changing a variable called something like *the_color_of_button_.b1,* you ask the button to change this variable for you with the command `.b1 configure`.

The difference between Java and Tcl is that Java allows you to create your own objects. You can use the objects that are built into Tcl, but you can't create your own objects. (The Tcl-based [incr Tcl] language gives you the tools to create your own objects.)

Objects are great for software development. If the R&D boys at Sun want to change the code that implements buttons, and improve the internal workings, they can. *You* can still use the same old button commands to control the button.

Multithreading

You're probably familiar with the idea of threading, but you might not call it by that name.

Your computer's operating system (if you're using an operating system that supports Tcl) can run more than one application at one time. This isn't multithreading, it's *multiprocessing*. Multithreading is multiprocessing on the level of applications: a multithreaded application splits itself up into separate tasks that are executed simultaneously.

(Not every application is multithreaded — support for threads is a fairly new development on desktop machines.)

Threading is a great tool for applications that have several time-consuming tasks to perform and the order of the tasks is not important. For instance, web browsers are usually multithreaded: if a web page contains several images, one thread is created to transfer each image.

Writing a multithreaded program is hard. There are all kinds of complications that multithreading introduces, and bizarre, unpredictable actions can happen when you make a mistake. (I feel a little sick just thinking about it.) Dr. Ousterhout decided that multithreading is too complicated for the simple kinds of programs that Tcl is designed for, and so Tcl doesn't allow you to create separate threads in your script.

Strings

Java offers support for strings, but Java's basic, built-in string handling commands don't offer much in the way of string handling. Java was developed in the era of multimedia and fancy graphics stuff, and these are the kinds of problems that the Java folks were thinking about when they designed the language.

Tcl's roots are as a Unix utility language, and at heart, Unix is all about text and strings. Almost all of the core Unix utilities are text-based: they input and output text, and store all of their important files as texts. Because Tcl was developed in this particular ecological niche, Tcl has all of the *primo* text tools, like `regexp`, `regsub` and the whole `string` family. (Actually, the prospect of having these kinds of tools inside a web page is what got me interested in the Tcl/Tk plug-in in the first place.)

Of course, there are already Java tools available that handle strings, but there's still a huge philosophical difference between the languages. Java handles strings — Tcl is *about* strings.

Appendix A
Regular Expressions

● ●

In This Chapter

▶ What are regular expressions?

▶ Globbing

▶ "Real" regular expressions

▶ Table of wild-card characters

● ●

*R*egular expressions are a way of describing strings of characters so that a single regular expression can describe a whole set of different kinds of strings. Think of regular expressions as a recipe for an allowable string. Tcl/Tk's support for regular expressions is an excellent reason to use Tcl/Tk to build your Web page, especially if you plan to process input from online visitors.

For example, consider phone numbers. If users want to be on your mailing list, you can ask them to type in their phone numbers. Simple, right? After they enter their numbers into a tclet-based form, you can easily use regular expressions to check users' entries to make sure they haven't made an obvious typo (such as forgetting the last digit). In this example, you want to be able to accept as many reasonable entries as possible while still catching possible typos.

Here's the problem: When you write down a phone number, there are lots of correct ways to present the information. Here are just a few ways:

✔ Include the area code or not: 800 555-1212 versus 555-1212.

✔ Put the area code inside parentheses or not: (312) 555-1212 versus 312-555-1212.

✔ Separate the area code from the rest of the number with a dash, a slash, or a space: 312-555-1212 versus 312/555-1212 versus 312 555-1212.

There are really hundreds of possible correct ways to write a phone number. For a human being, it's pretty easy to figure out if a particular string of characters is a possible phone number or not — 555-1212 is; abc-123 is not. Getting a computer to do the same is a bit harder, but with regular expressions, the difficult becomes easy. In fact, you can find a tclet on the CD that comes with this book called *phone-check.tcl* that solves exactly this problem.

Globbing

Tcl/Tk has two different styles of pattern matching (kind of like two dialects of the same language). The first method is usually called *globbing* or glob-style pattern matching, since that's what it's called in Unix (a language entirely unlike English). Glob has its origins in the term *global matching*.

You use glob-style matching with the `string match` command. Basically, globbing uses so-called *wild card* characters to check through strings for matches. A wild card, like a joker in poker, is a symbol that can stand for another symbol or set of symbols, just as a joker can stand in for an ace of spades or a two of clubs (or whatever you want it to be). For example, the symbol * matches any number of any characters. So the string `"Y*"` matches any string beginning with a capital Y, such as `"Yes"`, `"Yellow"`, `"Yabba-Dabba-Doo"`, and so on. The other main wild card symbol used in globbing is the ?, which matches any single character (so `"Y?"` matches `"Ya"`, `"YA"`, `"Ys"`, and so on, but not `"Yaa"`, `"Yes"`, or, sadly, `"Yabba-Dabba-Do"`).

You can also match any member of a set of characters by putting all the characters inside square brackets. So, say you want to ask a yes-or-no question and don't care if the answer is `"Yes"`, `"yes"`, `"yeah"`, `"yup"` or whatever. You check whether the response starts with a y, or whether or not it is uppercase. The glob-style regular expression to match every string that starts with either a Y or a y is `[Yy]*`. Putting the whole thing in curly braces is a good idea, like this `{[Yy]*}` to prevent substitution. The interpreter strips off the curlies when it realizes the glob pattern.

You can also set a variable to be the regular expression that you want to match, using the `set` command. For example,

```
set x {[Yy]*}
```

makes it possible for the command

```
string match $x "Yes"
```

to be processed correctly.

Remember, Tcl/Tk uses square brackets to surround embedded commands. When in doubt, put your regular expression in curly braces, and that keeps Tcl from trying, and failing, to a command for the regular expression.

If you want to match a whole range of characters — for example the lower-case letters from a–z, or the digits from 0–9 — just put the first and last members of the series inside square brackets with a dash in between them, like this: [a-z] or [0-9]. If you want to match characters that Tcl/Tk usually uses for special purposes, such as square brackets, slashes, asterisks, parentheses, curly braces, and so on you have to use a backslash to escape the character.

This is easier than it sounds. Whenever you want to have a strange character, such as a parenthesis, in your regular expression, just type \(or \) instead of (or). If, for some reason you want to match a backslash, you have to escape it with a backslash also, like this: \\.

"Real" regular expressions

The second type of pattern-matching is simply called *regular expression matching*. It's more like the kind of thing you may have seen if you've ever used Perl or the Unix grep command. You use this kind of matching with the regexp and regsub commands. Regular expression matching is not very different from glob-style matching, except that it can recognize even subtler distinctions.

Where globbing relies only on a few wild-card characters, regular expression matching allows for the use of more than these, plus a rudimentary syntax that allows you to put wild cards together with subpatterns to create much bigger, more versatile patterns.

Wild-card characters in regular expressions act in a similar, but not identical manner as they do in globbing. The * character still matches zero or more items, and the ? still matches zero or one item. The difference is that in regular expressions, instead of matching any random character, as in glob-style pattern matching, regular expression wild-card characters match instances of the pattern preceding them. For example, Y* would match Y, YY, YYY, YYYY, and so on, as well as nothing (the empty string). When you combine this with the ability to describe more complex strings and count them as patterns, you end up with a very powerful pattern matcher.

With regular expressions you still have to put any series of more than one character in square brackets, but you can group sets of these strings together inside parentheses. For example, the regular expression ([0-9][0-9])* matches any number with an even number of digits. Look at this regular expression from the inside out:

1. [0-9] **matches any digit from 0 to 9, just like in globbing.**

2. **The string** [0-9][0-9] **matches any sequence of two digits, each from 0 to 9.**

3. **The * after** [0-9][0-9]* **matches any sequence of zero or more instances of what precedes it.**

   By putting the recipe for two digits in parentheses, you tell Tcl that that whole recipe is what is to be matched the *. (Similarly, ([0-9])? matches either a single digit, or two digits, and so on.)

You can also use some new wildcards for making true regular expressions. The . (period) matches any single character. The + character matches one or more instances of the previous pattern.

Finally, there are a couple of special characters in regular expressions.

- $ stands for the end of a string if it appears at the end of the expression, so (\.$) matches any string that ends with a period. (Remember, you have to escape the period with a backslash, otherwise the period gets treated as the wildcard character.)

- Similarly, ^ stands for the beginning of the string, so ^A matches only a string starting with A. Be careful with ^, however. When you put ^ *inside* square brackets, it signals that you want to match anything *except* the characters in the square brackets! So [^xyz] matches anything except the letters x, y, and z.

- Finally, the | symbol is super useful. It stands for "or", so ([a-z] | [A-Z]) matches any single letter, either lower- or uppercase. Because it is in parentheses, you can even add wildcards after it, such as an *. To match a string of letters, use this: ([a-z] | [A-Z])*.

Appendix B
About the CD-ROM

*L*ike Tcl/Tk, the *Tcl/Tk For Dummies* CD-ROM is a cross-platform solution, which means you can use it with both Windows 95/NT and Macintosh Computers. You don't need to do anything special to find the files for your computer's platform: Just stick the CD-ROM into the computer, and the appropriate files will appear in the CD-ROM's window. The nasty Windows/Mac files (circle one) that your computer can't read will be hidden away where you don't need to worry about them.

No matter which platform you use, the CD contains three basic parts:

✔ Wish (the application you use to develop and run Tcl/Tk scripts)

✔ Example tclets from the book (and a few that were cut for space issues)

✔ A Demoware or Shareware HTML editor

In order to work through this book and create your own Tcl/Tk scripts, you *must* install Wish. The example tclets are helpful, and they may save you some typing, but they're not strictly necessary. For your convenience, I have provided the HTML editors; they're good programs for building Web pages, but if you already have a favorite tool for working with HTML, by all means continue using your preferred software.

One essential tool for web-page tclet development is not included on the CD-ROM: the Tcl/Tk plug-in. Unfortunately, for legal and copyright reasons, we are unable to distribute the plug-in with this book. Fortunately, you can download the plug-in from Sun's scripting site at http://www.sunscript.com. See Chapter 1 for details.

Mac Users

If you're a Mac user, start by installing Wish:

1. **Double-click on the Tcl/Tk 8.0 Installer Icon.** The Installer displays a window that explains the copyright and distribution information about the Wish software.

2. **Read the Software License.**

3. **Click the Continue button.** If you don't accept the license terms (hey, it's a free country) you won't be able to install the software.

4. **Choose the appropriate Mac platform.** Next, the Installer presents a list box that allows you to specify which kind of Mac you're using. If you're using a pre-PowerPC Mac (such as an LC, Centris, or Quadra series machine), choose 68K. If you're using a PowerPC, choose the PowerPC option. If you're not sure, look at you're Mac's owner manual to see what kind of CPU your machine uses, and use Table C-1 below to pick the appropriate platform.

Table C-1	
Chip Name	*Platform*
68000	68 K
68020	
68030	
68040	
601 series	Power PC
602 series	
603 series	
604 series	

You don't need to restart your machine after you install Tcl/Tk.

You may notice that the Tcl/Tk installer creates a folder in the System:Extensions folder; this new folder is called "Tool Control Language." This folder contains much of the Tcl/Tk plumbing, and it should stay right where it is with the name as it is. None of the files in the folder are really

Mac system extensions, so you don't need to worry about anything in the folder sucking up system memory. If, however, you decide to remove Tcl/Tk from your system, go ahead and toss this folder into the Trash.

Next, Install the Web Weaver software. Web Weaver is a shareware program that's handy for building Web pages. Again, it's provided for your convenience: If you're already using something like BBEdit or Adobe PageMill or NetObjects Fusion to build your pages, don't feel obliged to change to a new tool. To install Web Weaver:

1. **Double-click on the Installer icon.** The installer presents a window that details the Web Weaver license agreement.

2. **Read the Agreement.**

3. **Click the Continue button.**

Finally, you can install the folder of example tclets by dragging the Tclets folder from the CD-ROM window to your hard drive. (If you like, you can simply leave them on the CD-ROM and open and run them right from the CD.) See Chapter 2 for information about running tclets with Wish.

Windows Users

If you're using Windows 95 or Windows NT, start by installing Wish:

1. **Double-click the Tcl80 icon.** The setup program presents a welcoming screen. (Smile at the screen, if you like.)

2. **Click the Next button.**

3. **Choose a location to install Wish.** By default, Wish is installed in the folder `C:\Programs\Tcl`. Unless you have a compelling reason to put Wish elsewhere (for instance, if you have an older version of Wish installed), use the default location.

4. **Choose your installation options.** Setup allows you to pick between the recommended typical installation, a minimal installation, and a custom installation. I recommend that you use the typical installation, which includes essential Tcl/Tk documentation and plenty of example scripts for you to examine.

5. **Wait for the Installer to finish.**

Custom Installations

If you're pressed for disk space, or, like me, you are pathologically inclined to customize every software installation, you may specify whether or not to install each of four separate components in Step 4 of the Wish installation process:

✔ The Run Time: This component is the Wish application proper. You'll need this component to work through the examples in this book.

✔ Example Scripts: These scripts provide a nice gallery of the stuff that you can do with Tcl/Tk, but they're not essential. I don't discuss them in this book.

✔ Help Files: The help files contain important Tcl/Tk language documentation. Wish will work without the help files, of course, but I strongly suggest you download this component.

✔ Headers and Libraries: This component is a set of tools for integrating Tcl/Tk with C. Such integration is an advanced topic that we won't cover in this book; you really don't need to bother with this component unless you're a programming wizard.

Once you've installed Wish, you can install the HomeSite demo, if you like. If you already have a preferred HTML-editing tool (like Microsoft FrontPage or NetObjects Fusion) feel free to continue to use your favorite editor. To install the HomeSite demo:

1. **Double-click on the hs25set icon.** The setup program presents a license agreement screen; you must accept the license terms to install the software.

2. **Read the license agreement.** Click the Next button when you're done.

3. **Select the directory where you'd like to install HomeSite.** Unless you have a previous version of HomeSite installed, the default directory should be just fine.

4. **Decide if you want to backup files that the setup program replaces.** I wish all installers offered this option. If the setup program replaces an old file with a new version of the same file, setup will make a backup of the old file, rather than simply writing over it.

5. **Choose a backup folder.** If you chose to backup replaced files in Step 4, specify which directory will contain the old files.

6. **Pick which components you'd like to install.** You'll certainly need the HomeSite application to run HomeSite; make sure this component is checked. Unless you're really, really strapped for disk space, it's a good idea to install the documentation, too.

Finally, you can transfer the example tclets for this book from the CD-ROM to your hard disk. There are two ways to make this transfer:

✔ Drag the Tclets folder from the CD-ROM drive's Explorer window to your hard disk's Explorer window. (In other words, simply copy the folder in the same way that you copy any other folder.)

✔ Run the Tcletins application, which will copy the Tclets folder to a new folder on your hard drive. By default, this folder is called C:\TCLETS; however, you can change the name to whatever you like. Tcletins bypasses the flying-paper dialog box that Windows uses when it copies files, so Tcletins moves the files to your hard disk considerably faster than a manual copy.

Some Windows 95 users have problems with their CD-ROM drives that keep them from reading long filenames off the CD. If you can't seem to open or use the contents of the Tclets folder directly from the CD with Windows Explorer or My Computer, run the tcletins program to make a copy of the folder on your hard drive.

If you prefer, you may simply leave the example tclets on the CD-ROM, and open and run them right where they are. See Chapter 2 for details on running tclets with Wish.

Index

(continued)

• *D* •

(continued)

(continued)

(continued)

Notes

Notes

IDG Books Worldwide, Inc., End-User License Agreement

READ THIS. You should carefully read these terms and conditions before opening the software packet(s) included with this book ("Book"). This is a license agreement ("Agreement") between you and IDG Books Worldwide, Inc. ("IDGB"). By opening the accompanying software packet(s), you acknowledge that you have read and accept the following terms and conditions. If you do not agree and do not want to be bound by such terms and conditions, promptly return the Book and the unopened software packet(s) to the place you obtained them for a full refund.

1. **License Grant.** IDGB grants to you (either an individual or entity) a nonexclusive license to use one copy of the enclosed software program(s) (collectively, the "Software") solely for your own personal or business purposes on a single computer (whether a standard computer or a workstation component of a multiuser network). The Software is in use on a computer when it is loaded into temporary memory (RAM) or installed into permanent memory (hard disk, CD-ROM, or other storage device). IDGB reserves all rights not expressly granted herein.

2. **Ownership.** IDGB is the owner of all right, title, and interest, including copyright, in and to the compilation of the Software recorded on the disk(s) or CD-ROM ("Software Media"). Copyright to the individual programs recorded on the Software Media is owned by the author or other authorized copyright owner of each program. Ownership of the Software and all proprietary rights relating thereto remain with IDGB and its licensers.

3. **Restrictions on Use and Transfer.**

   (a) You may only (i) make one copy of the Software for backup or archival purposes, or (ii) transfer the Software to a single hard disk, provided that you keep the original for backup or archival purposes. You may not (i) rent or lease the Software, (ii) copy or reproduce the Software through a LAN or other network system or through any computer subscriber system or bulletin-board system, or (iii) modify, adapt, or create derivative works based on the Software.

   (b) You may not reverse engineer, decompile, or disassemble the Software. You may transfer the Software and user documentation on a permanent basis, provided that the transferee agrees to accept the terms and conditions of this Agreement and you retain no copies. If the Software is an update or has been updated, any transfer must include the most recent update and all prior versions.

4. **Restrictions on Use of Individual Programs.** You must follow the individual requirements and restrictions detailed for each individual program in the "About the CD" section of this Book. These limitations are also contained in the individual license agreements recorded on the Software Media. These limitations may include a requirement that after using the program for a specified period of time, the user must pay a registration fee or discontinue use. By opening the Software packet(s), you will be agreeing to abide by the licenses and restrictions for these individual programs that are detailed in the "About the CD" section and on the Software Media. None of the material on this Software Media or listed in this Book may ever be redistributed, in original or modified form, for commercial purposes.

5. **Limited Warranty.**

   (a) IDGB warrants that the Software and Software Media are free from defects in materials and workmanship under normal use for a period of sixty (60) days from the date of purchase of this Book. If IDGB receives notification within the warranty period of defects in materials or workmanship, IDGB will replace the defective Software Media.

   (b) **IDGB AND THE AUTHOR OF THE BOOK DISCLAIM ALL OTHER WARRANTIES, EXPRESS OR IMPLIED, INCLUDING WITHOUT LIMITATION IMPLIED WARRANTIES OF MER-CHANTABILITY AND FITNESS FOR A PARTICULAR PURPOSE, WITH RESPECT TO THE SOFTWARE, THE PROGRAMS, THE SOURCE CODE CONTAINED THEREIN, AND/OR THE TECHNIQUES DESCRIBED IN THIS BOOK. IDGB DOES NOT WARRANT THAT THE FUNCTIONS CONTAINED IN THE SOFTWARE WILL MEET YOUR REQUIREMENTS OR THAT THE OPERATION OF THE SOFTWARE WILL BE ERROR FREE.**

   (c) This limited warranty gives you specific legal rights, and you may have other rights that vary from jurisdiction to jurisdiction.

6. **Remedies.**

   (a) IDGB's entire liability and your exclusive remedy for defects in materials and workmanship shall be limited to replacement of the Software Media, which may be returned to IDGB with a copy of your receipt at the following address: Software Media Fulfillment Department, Attn.: *Tcl/Tk For Dummies*, IDG Books Worldwide, Inc., 7260 Shadeland Station, Ste. 100, Indianapolis, IN 46256, or call 800-762-2974. Please allow three to four weeks for delivery. This Limited Warranty is void if failure of the Software Media has resulted from accident, abuse, or misapplication. Any replacement Software Media will be warranted for the remainder of the original warranty period or thirty (30) days, whichever is longer.

   (b) In no event shall IDGB or the author be liable for any damages whatsoever (including without limitation damages for loss of business profits, business interruption, loss of business information, or any other pecuniary loss) arising from the use of or inability to use the Book or the Software, even if IDGB has been advised of the possibility of such damages.

   (c) Because some jurisdictions do not allow the exclusion or limitation of liability for consequential or incidental damages, the above limitation or exclusion may not apply to you.

7. **U.S. Government Restricted Rights.** Use, duplication, or disclosure of the Software by the U.S. Government is subject to restrictions stated in paragraph (c)(1)(ii) of the Rights in Technical Data and Computer Software clause of DFARS 252.227-7013, and in subparagraphs (a) through (d) of the Commercial Computer–Restricted Rights clause at FAR 52.227-19, and in similar clauses in the NASA FAR supplement, when applicable.

8. **General.** This Agreement constitutes the entire understanding of the parties and revokes and supersedes all prior agreements, oral or written, between them and may not be modified or amended except in a writing signed by both parties hereto that specifically refers to this Agreement. This Agreement shall take precedence over any other documents that may be in conflict herewith. If any one or more provisions contained in this Agreement are held by any court or tribunal to be invalid, illegal, or otherwise unenforceable, each and every other provision shall remain in full force and effect.

Using the *Tcl/Tk For Dummies* CD-ROM

● ●

The *Tcl/Tk For Dummies* CD-ROM includes

- ✔ Wish, the Tcl/Tk development environment
- ✔ Sample programs (tclets) from the book
- ✔ Demonstration or shareware HTML editors.

The *Tcl/Tk For Dummies* CD-ROM is designed to support these operating systems:

- ✔ Windows 95
- ✔ Windows NT
- ✔ Macintosh

To work through this book and create your own Tcl/Tk scripts, the Wish program must be installed on your computer system.

For more information about the *Tcl/Tk For Dummies* CD-ROM, see Appendix B of this book. The *Tcl/Tk For Dummies* CD-ROM is subject to the License Agreement that is included in this book.

To access the CD-ROM contents, insert the *Tcl/Tk For Dummies* CD-ROM in your computer's CD-ROM drive and follow the instructions in Appendix B.

IDG BOOKS WORLDWIDE REGISTRATION CARD

Visit our Web site at http://www.idgbooks.com

ISBN Number: 0-7645-0152-6

Title of this book: TCL/TK For Dummies®

My overall rating of this book: ❑ Very good [1] ❑ Good [2] ❑ Satisfactory [3] ❑ Fair [4] ❑ Poor [5]

How I first heard about this book:

❑ Found in bookstore; name: [6] _____ ❑ Book review: [7] _____

❑ Advertisement: [8] _____ ❑ Catalog: [9] _____

❑ Word of mouth; heard about book from friend, co-worker, etc.: [10] ❑ Other: [11] _____

What I liked most about this book:

_____

_____

What I would change, add, delete, etc., in future editions of this book:

_____

_____

Other comments:

_____

Number of computer books I purchase in a year: ❑ 1 [12] ❑ 2-5 [13] ❑ 6-10 [14] ❑ More than 10 [15]

I would characterize my computer skills as: ❑ Beginner [16] ❑ Intermediate [17] ❑ Advanced [18] ❑ Professional [19]

I use ❑ DOS [20] ❑ Windows [21] ❑ OS/2 [22] ❑ Unix [23] ❑ Macintosh [24] ❑ Other: [25] _____

(please specify)

I would be interested in new books on the following subjects:

(please check all that apply, and use the spaces provided to identify specific software)

❑ Word processing: [26] _____ ❑ Spreadsheets: [27] _____

❑ Data bases: [28] _____ ❑ Desktop publishing: [29] _____

❑ File Utilities: [30] _____ ❑ Money management: [31] _____

❑ Networking: [32] _____ ❑ Programming languages: [33] _____

❑ Other: [34] _____

I use a PC at (please check all that apply): ❑ home [35] ❑ work [36] ❑ school [37] ❑ other: [38] _____

The disks I prefer to use are ❑ 5.25 [39] ❑ 3.5 [40] ❑ other: [41] _____

I have a CD ROM: ❑ yes [42] ❑ no [43]

I plan to buy or upgrade computer hardware this year: ❑ yes [44] ❑ no [45]

I plan to buy or upgrade computer software this year: ❑ yes [46] ❑ no [47]

Name: _____ Business title: [48] _____ Type of Business: [49] _____

Address (❑ home [50] ❑ work [51]**/Company name:** _____)

Street/Suite# _____

City [52]/State [53]/Zip code [54]: _____ Country [55] _____

❑ **I liked this book!** You may quote me by name in future
   IDG Books Worldwide promotional materials.

My daytime phone number is _____

IDG BOOKS WORLDWIDE

THE WORLD OF COMPUTER KNOWLEDGE®